MISSISSIPPI ZION

THE STRUGGLE
FOR LIBERATION IN
ATTALA COUNTY, 1865–1915

MISSISSIPPI

❊ ZION ❊

EVAN HOWARD ASHFORD

UNIVERSITY PRESS OF MISSISSIPPI / JACKSON

The University Press of Mississippi is the scholarly publishing agency of
the Mississippi Institutions of Higher Learning: Alcorn State University,
Delta State University, Jackson State University, Mississippi State University,
Mississippi University for Women, Mississippi Valley State University,
University of Mississippi, and University of Southern Mississippi.

www.upress.state.ms.us

The University Press of Mississippi is a member
of the Association of University Presses.

Publication of this book was supported in part by the UPM First Author's Fund.

First printing 2022
∞

Library of Congress Cataloging-in-Publication Data

Names: Ashford, Evan Howard, author.
Title: Mississippi Zion : the struggle for liberation in Attala County,
1865-1915 / Evan Howard Ashford.
Description: Jackson : University Press of Mississippi, [2022] | Includes
appendixes | Includes bibliographical references and index.
Identifiers: LCCN 2022006009 (print) | LCCN 2022006010 (ebook) | ISBN
9781496839725 (hardback) | ISBN 9781496839732 (trade paperback) | ISBN
9781496839749 (epub) | ISBN 9781496839756 (epub) | ISBN 9781496839763
(pdf) | ISBN 9781496839770 (pdf)
Subjects: LCSH: African Americans—History—1863–1877. | African
Americans—History—1877-1964. | Attala County (Miss.)—History.
Classification: LCC F347.A7 A84 2022 (print) | LCC F347.A7 (ebook) | DDC
976.2/64406—dc23/eng/20220208
LC record available at https://lccn.loc.gov/2022006009
LC ebook record available at https://lccn.loc.gov/2022006010

British Library Cataloging-in-Publication Data available

To my loving and dedicated parents:
Mr. Charles Henry and the late Mrs. Linda Joy Ashford

CONTENTS

ACKNOWLEDGMENTS

All acknowledgements are first and foremost given to Allah, Cherisher and Sustainer of the Worlds.

Mississippi Zion was as much a community effort as it was that of my individual work and determination. My parents have been the one constant in my life, teaching me that the pitfalls of life should never deter me from achieving my dreams. Their undying and unyielding support from the beginning made this book a reality. Through my older brothers, Charles, Derrian, Derek, and Brandon, I learned how to navigate life and to stay dedicated to my goals and dreams. Dr. John H. Bracey, to whom I will be forever indebted, played the most significant role shaping the research contained within this book and my identity as a historian. He saw the significance of Mississippi and its place in American history and pushed me to tell the state's history proudly and accurately.

I thank the Association for the Study of African American Life and History (ASALH) for providing me the opportunities to present multiple chapters of what is now *Mississippi Zion*. Through this space, I met my editor, Emily Bandy. I thank Emily for listening and believing in the concept of this book from its inception. I appreciate her dedication to the project through the revision process. To the University Press of Mississippi, I thank the editorial board for its unanimous approval for this project. I find it fitting that my first monograph center on Mississippi and be published by the state's university press. I owe a great debt to the Attala County Regional Library, where I conducted extensive genealogical research used within the pages of this book. A special thanks to Ann Breedlove who has assisted and supported my research for over ten years. It was through our conversations over our respective genealogies and Attala County itself did I see the power that history has to unite people. I also want to extend thanks to the staff at the Attala County Circuit Clerk office for their kind assistance.

When I began this project at age eleven, I began writing to family members across the country asking them questions about family and inquiring about photographs. While the majority of those letters went unanswered, there were a few special people who took the time to help me. To those family members who opened their doors, answered emails and letters, and trusted me with their family's histories and photographs, I am forever grateful for the help and continued support you gave me for the past twenty years, namely, Ahmad, Angela, Cheryl, Effie Dell, Ellie Hugh, Eva, James, Jerone, John and Winnifred, LaShawn, Marion, Peggy, Shedralyn, Sherron, Trenace, and Virginia. To the family members who passed before seeing their contributions in print, I thank you for the love and support you provided the past twenty years. Finally, to Attala's African American foremothers and forefathers, whose persevering, educating, voting, community building, and relentless struggle to create an equal and just society made it possible for me to write this book, your legacy will never be forgotten.

MISSISSIPPI ZION

INTRODUCTION

Mississippi's African American experience is more complex and complicated than most may assume beyond the standard historical narrative. W. E. B. Du Bois stated in *The Souls of Black Folk* regarding our knowledge of the [Negro] condition, "We seldom study the condition of the Negro to-day honestly and carefully. It is so much easier to assume that we know it all. Or perhaps, having already reached conclusions in our own minds, we are loth to have them disturbed by facts. And yet how little we really know of these millions."[1] When applied to Dennis J. Mitchell's *A New History of Mississippi*, which stated, "Mississippi is a place and a state of mind. The name evokes strong reactions from those who live here and from those who do not, but who think they know something about its people and their past"[2] one arrives at how historians approach the African American experience in Mississippi.

Mississippi's historical image does not depict the lives of its Black citizens in their totality. Inside the narrative of white domination and Black oppression lies a complicated struggle for control that historians overlook to push a familiar and accepted history. The story of post-emancipation and early-twentieth-century Black Mississippians is the story of liberation, not of Reconstruction, Jim Crow, and certainly not of victimhood. Liberation served as the fuel for the former slaves to make their mark and claim their rightful place as citizens. To begin ascertaining liberation's role and impact throughout Mississippi, in the post-slavery years, the state's geographical center, Attala County, is the focus of this book.

Nestled in the Mississippi Pine Region is the state's centermost county, Attala. In September 1830, the Treaty of Dancing Rabbit Creek initiated by Andrew Jackson's secretary of state, John Eaton, forced the Choctaw Nation to cede vast land in Mississippi's central and southern regions.[3] In 1833 Attala County formed from this treaty, along with Winston, Carroll, Montgomery, Holmes, Leake, Choctaw, and Madison counties. The county's earliest settlers consisted of Native Americans and whites who settled in small communities and towns throughout, including its county seat, Kosciusko.[4] If Attala sounds unfamiliar, it should because of its omission from the Mississippi historical narrative. One may think this means nothing significant happened worthy of historical inquiry or mentioning; however, this is far from the truth. Early demonstrations of Black armed resistance, the use of African American testimony to convict a white man for murder, the site of one of the largest land booms outside the Mississippi Delta, the only white-majority county to vote in favor of ratifying the 1868 constitution, and the only Central Mississippi county with two independent higher learning institutions are among a few of its notabilities.

Attala County had a white population majority, making it a white county. Most Mississippi histories focus on the state's Black-majority counties in the Mississippi Delta region or the Natchez District. While those areas are of historical importance, they telegraph a narrative of whites reacting to fears of "negro domination" to establish an impenetrable white-supremacist power structure. One may assume that African Americans living in a white county succumbed to instant white domination, as Edward C. Coleman depicted in "The Period of Reconstruction in Attala County"; however, Attala's race-neutral population differentiated it from other counties. In 1866, 12,603 residents lived in the county. The population consisted of 5,003 African Americans, including 2,331 men and 2,672 women. African Americans made up 39.7 percent of the county's population, but a population breakdown shows population equality. The population under ten years of age was 24.61 percent Black and 24.45 percent white. Within each race, the population ten to nineteen was 59.5 percent and 59.5, respectively. Those aged between thirty and seventy-nine were 35.76 percent Black and 32.36 white. Attala County's Black population was neither too small to be significant nor significant enough to be an immediate threat. The population composition allows for a more nuanced look into liberation within an area where no race numerically dominated the other.

African Americans created their post-slavery Zion in the symbolic and literal heart of the Old South, Mississippi, and the literal heart of the state, Attala County. By asserting themselves as equals to their white counterparts at the onset of emancipation, they made liberation occur alongside redemption and shaped the county's landscape for the next fifty years. *Mississippi Zion: The Struggle for Liberation in Attala County, 1865–1915* explores these two parallel and intersecting missions. African American liberation efforts complicated the social, economic, and political agenda imperative for southern white redemption, prompting the need for anti-Black apparatuses to thwart forward progress. This book asserts that the emergence of the county's twentieth-century Jim Crow society and, to a more considerable degree, of the state itself resulted from the need to curtail African American advancement in interconnected areas such as land, labor, education, politics, and progressive race relations.

Given the significant amount of scholarship written on Mississippi, the state remains a historical abyss, Attala's omission being evidence of that abyss. This void correlates to African American positionality. African Americans are written as a people who lack autonomy without federal assistance and whose actions are in response to white protagonists and antagonists. The glaring flaw in Mississippi's historiographical works is the omission of Patrick Henry Thompson's *History of Negro Baptists in Mississippi* and Patrick Henry Thompson and Isaac Crawford's *Multum in Parvo* as sources. These works provided an in-depth look into the Mississippi African American educational, business, theological, and political classes and their role in constructing the pivotal institutions that propelled Black peoples to shape Mississippi society. Scholars overlook the individuals they seek to discuss or claim to feature while perpetuating Black peoples as response agents.

The emphasis on southern white action drives the main narrative flattening an otherwise dynamic experience. Scholarship on African Americans in Mississippi has three significant fallacies: the continued focus on white Mississippians and showing the state's history through its white citizenry, the focus on the state's African American–majority counties, and segmentation of the state's history into distinct historical periods such as Reconstruction, Nadir, and Jim Crow. What occurs is that African Americans battle for positionality within their narrative. Scholars do not focus on how Black action prompted an anti-Black response. They echo a general assumption made by Carter G. Woodson. Woodson stated, "Yet in the Lower South, especially in South Carolina and Mississippi, where the rural Negroes outnumber the whites, they are kept in such a backward condition that their large numbers have not meant very much for the higher strivings in the economic world."[5] He assessed that rural African Americans lacked mobility or recreation because of their socioeconomic and political circumstances. Hortense Powdermaker's anthropological study of a Mississippi community, Cottonville, focused considerable time establishing the white mindset and attitudes towards African Americans, stating, "To understand his [the Negro's] life there must be an understanding of the Whites who form so large a part of it."[6] In reality, African Americans knew whites quite well; however, did southern whites know African Americans?

Vernon Lane Wharton's *The Negro in Mississippi 1865–1890*, first published in 1947, examined African Americans through the state's white citizens' actions seeking to restore or maintain some semblance of slavery. Wharton's discussions on labor, land, and politics focused on the ways and means poor whites and the political elite used to suppress the former slave. Wharton's work rarely showed African Americans' action to counterpoint the state's necessity to redeem its pre-emancipation society.[7] Albert Kirwan's *Revolt of the Redneck: Mississippi Politics, 1876–1925* assessed the "struggle of the redneck to gain control of the Democratic party in order to effect reforms which would improve his lot."[8] Kirwan studied the state's white population's trials and tribulations to maintain both racial dominance and race loyalty through the prism of the state's volatile yet indestructible Democratic Party. Like Wharton, Kirwan wrote African Americans as static participants in southern redemption.

Neil McMillen's *Dark Journey: Black Mississippians in the Age of Jim Crow* analyzed Mississippi from predominately African American majority counties, making over-generalizations about the African American experience. He omitted the African Americans as agents of their own progress, evidenced by his minimizing education and political advancements. McMillen did not consider African American activity independent of white control or its impact on white bodies and white politics. McMillen focused on the obstacles placed before African Americans, such as voting and education, while minimizing or ignoring African American activity. Stephen Cresswell's *Rednecks, Redeemers, and Race: Mississippi Politics after Reconstruction* echoed McMillen in how he wrote the Black experience, stating, "Few black

Mississippians offered direct challenges to the state's system of race control."[9] Given that McMillen and Cresswell released their works contemporaneously, the similar emphasis on Black invisibility and white power signaled a reluctance to delve into the African American experience. These works depict African Americans as entangled within the structures of white supremacy and Jim Crow. Current scholarship such as Dennis J. Mitchell's *A New History of Mississippi* mimics past scholarship in regarding African Americans as objects rather than subjects within the Mississippi experience. Mitchell wrote a Mississippi that fit popular historical imagination.

Scholars seeking to show a more nuanced representation of Black life in Mississippi attempted to move beyond the dominant "oppression narrative" to humanize the state's African American citizens as independent and freethinking. William Harris's *The Day of the Carpetbagger: Republican Reconstruction in Mississippi* and Michael Perman's *Road to Redemption: Southern Politics, 1869–1879* provided insight into the role African Americans played in establishing their political framework as part of Mississippi's constitution. While limited to the political sphere, Harris's work gave African Americans relevance. He addressed their impact on Mississippi's political structure; however, Harris's overall analysis indicated that African Americans became marginalized after the 1868 constitutional convention. Harris surmised that African Americans became objects of the white Democratic machine; therefore, Black progression went only as far as their white benefactors.[10] Michael Perman analyzed African Americans as a politically savvy group who fought to push pro-Black legislation within a political party that wanted Black support but not to the point that it disillusioned whites.[11] Perman captured the tension between African Americans seeking liberation and pushback from allies and enemies alike.

Recent scholarship on Mississippi moved the historiography to focus on liberation. Christopher M. Span's *From Cotton Field to Schoolhouse: African American Education in Mississippi, 1862–1875* followed a similar trajectory as Harris and Perman. He captured the Black liberating mindset, analyzing how African Americans saw education as the pathway to landowning, labor autonomy, and suffrage, and more importantly, how Black action prompted a white response. Justin Behrend's *Reconstructing Democracy: Grassroots Black Politics in the Deep South after the Civil War* examined Mississippi's Natchez District to ascertain how African American communities built the necessary political structures to gain power and influence.[12] While these works do a better job centering African Americans within their narrative, their chosen historical timeframe emphasized period, not people. Reconstruction did not define the African American experience. Life continued after the federal project ended. By ending their analysis at this arbitrary point, they omit significant African American activity during post-Reconstruction and its impact on shaping African Americans and Mississippi. The result assumes that African Americans lacked the autonomy to dictate their pathway without federal intervention, a white savior.

Mississippi Zion: The Struggle for Liberation in Attala County, 1865–1915 examines African American activity through a liberation era, which this book defines as the fifty years between 1865 and 1915. African Americans have not been free the equivalent time of their enslavement. Cramming their history within "traditional" eras cannot capture what African Americans sought upon their emancipation. Because the fight for liberation persisted since enslavement in North America began, the actions of the former slave generation need an expanded period of analysis rather than Reconstruction's 12–14-year or the Nadir's 24-year window. C. L. R. James and Herbert Aptheker studied liberation through revolt and rebellion. They addressed both the individual and collective efforts slaves made to liberate themselves by overturning the slave institution. James established a narrative of self-emancipation, which Aptheker explained consisted of freedom and liberty fueling resistance to oppression.[13] Examining African American liberation efforts over an extended period post-slavery provides space to understand how former slaves used the tools of the master to liberate themselves through the new freed person's perspective.

To emphasize the liberation era, the Reconstruction era must occupy its proper place. This book treats Reconstruction as a secondary agent that existed but did not define African Americans, thus removing it as a "historical crutch" explaining or rationalizing African American activity. Reconstruction cannot be viewed as a "golden age" because Reconstruction had more to do with the economics of reestablishing the Union and getting even with ex-Confederates than it did with ensuring that the former slave class received social, political, and economic equality with whites. Historians revisiting Reconstruction portray an idealized experience that focused on uplifting both African Americans and the notions of true republicanism. Justin Behrend used John Roy Lynch's memory of Mississippi Reconstruction to challenge misguided and racist notions of African Americans and Republicans.[14]

Regarding Lynch's purpose, Behrend stated, "He offered another memory—a counter-memory—where African Americans and white southerners worked together toward common goals.[15] Behrend followed a similar trajectory as Eric Foner. Eric Foner's *Reconstruction: America's Unfinished Revolution 1863–1877* embodied this "golden age" mentality, framing the era as one of noble obligation as America "[lived] up to the noble professions of their political creed—something few societies have ever done," resulting in "a sweeping redefinition of the nation's public life and a violent reaction that ultimately destroyed much, but by no means all, of what had been accomplished."[16] While Foner sought to show how "various groups of blacks and whites sought to use state and local government to promote their own interests and define their place in the region's new social order,"[17] Reconstruction, as an American obligation, positioned the era as America's nineteenth-century Camelot. Michael Perman summed up Reconstruction in simpler terms, describing it as the development of southern politics and not as a finite event that sought to create a new political order and move the South in a new economic direction, one where its Republican minority cared more about bringing more whites into the party.[18]

Romanticizing Reconstruction paints a distorted picture of post-slavery life for freed peoples. What were former slaves trying to reconstruct? African Americans sought to build, not reconstruct, with and without assistance. Leon Litwack's *Been in the Storm So Long: The Aftermath of Slavery* captured this building mentality. Litwack noted that "once emancipation had been acknowledged, what mattered was how many freed slaves would find separation indispensable to their new status." They did not want to relinquish any of their freedoms and refused to be obedient to whites in the areas of land, labor, and politics.[19] Freedmen's actions cannot be viewed solely as opposition, but rather as their continued mission to find true freedom in the nation they had built. That their efforts continued following Reconstruction's downfall gets overshadowed by the instant switch from Reconstruction to the white-operated politics of the Nadir and Jim Crow eras.

Because no one ever asked who gave Toussaint L'Ouverture, Nat Turner, or Harriet Tubman permission to pursue their liberation, it would be wrong to ask which benevolent white agent or mission allowed the Black masses to act as free people. They needed no permission to define themselves, family, and community because they emerged from slavery with a citizenship mindset and yearned to showcase their humanity. As Frederick Douglass stated,

"No man can be truly free whose liberty is dependent upon the thought, feeling, and action of others; and who has himself no means in his own hands for guarding, protecting, defending, and maintaining that liberty."[20] African Americans adopted the identity of republicanism and framed their liberation within the pages of the United States Constitution. In *Liberty and Union: The Civil War Era and American Constitutionalism*, Timothy Huebner assessed that African Americans participated in Black constitutionalism, which sought to transform the constitution into a document that enforced and protected African American rights.[21] Neither emancipation nor Reconstruction liberated African Americans. They removed the physical shackles of slavery and established a series of unenforced amendments. Former slaves understood that their liberation relied on their actions, and thus they undertook the arduous tasks needed to secure control of their lives.

Liberation, as an end goal, needed power and control as its fuel. While scholars discuss power and liberation as related concepts, power and liberation are difficult to maintain and sustain without control. Control lacks in the overall discussion of power and liberation because scholars write from the perspective of Black political power. This focus treats politics as a separate entity from education, landowning, mentality, and community-building, all necessary to create a Black political class. Politics serves more to demonstrate eventual racial powerlessness by contrasting the fall of Black political leadership during and after Reconstruction with the rise of southern redemption politics.[22] Associating Black peoples with powerlessness assumes that power temporarily or never existed, insulting those who possessed control of their mind, labor, and voice. African Americans held power in various aspects of their lives; otherwise, southern whites would not have expended such efforts to control Black peoples. The need to control created tensions with those who only knew Black peoples as the subordinate group. As Ransom and Sutch stated, "Emancipation proved to be a cause of friction, not because Blacks were incapable of establishing their independence, but because they asserted their independence and insisted upon institutional arrangements more to their liking than those envisioned for them by whites."[23]

Chokwe Lumumba stated, "Our problem is one of insufficient power";[24] however, insufficient control is a better assessment. African Americans did not lack power; they lacked consistent control of their power. This inconsistency stemmed from a determined and scared post-slave society reacting to undermine Black progress. Scholars fail to understand that power recognizes power; therefore, Black liberation coincided with a redemption agenda to render Black peoples powerless by preventing them from controlling their destiny. In *Slavery in White and Black: Class and Race in the Southern Slaveholders' New World Order*, Elizabeth and Eugene Genovese examined "Slavery in the Abstract." The term referred to "slavery as a normal condition of labor abstracted from race," which "encouraged assimilation of all dependent (unfree) labor to slavery or—what came to the same thing—assimilation of slavery to a pattern of social subordination in which chattel slavery served as the extreme form of dependent and unfree labor appropriate to time, place, and circumstance."[25] Slavery in the Abstract came to permeate the slave south, shaping southern culture to reflect a world where labor (or people) were either free or controlled.[26]

Charles C. Bolton's *Poor Whites of the Antebellum South: Central North Carolina and Northeast Mississippi* exemplified the Slavery in the Abstract concept. Bolton stated, "The existence of independent free blacks alongside dependent poor whites blatantly belied the notion that all whites occupied a status elevated above all blacks."[27] Eugene and Elizabeth Fox-Genovese's work established a framework to understand why one group sought control of another. Bolton's work captured poor whites' reality that Black peoples in a free society could elevate themselves beyond their societal expectations. A critical question is how did liberation look through the lens of Black peoples?

Liberation, like redemption, is a concept and an era. Rayford Logan historicized redemption as the Nadir; the South's turn to socially orchestrate society in a way that Reconstruction had done prior.[28] Leon Litwack added, "It is the story of how white Southerners defended, tolerated, and rationalized the systemic abuse and exploitation of black men and women in the name of ensuring their own supremacy."[29] Saying that white supremacy reestablished itself is too simplistic and ignores Black impact. Logan and Litwack assumed that the African American existence had no timeframe that ran parallel to southern whites. The traditional segmenting of history into historical periods does not speak entirely to the African American situation. As the ink dried on Lee's signature at Appomattox, the former slave began the pursuit of liberation, and the South began its pursuit of redemption; therefore, two eras began simultaneously.

This book focuses mainly on Attala County. The book does not serve as a comparison to other counties, nor does it use the county as broader representation. A single-subject focus provides an in-depth view of individual lives and familial and community connections that are more difficult to capture in broader studies. As Jonathan M. Bryant stated, "The study of a single community offers a consistent vantage point from which to explore these changes and their effects. This approach also emphasizes that the people of that time experienced events within the cultural, social, and economic context of their community. To ignore that context would only limit our comprehension."[30] Attala serves as a lens through which to understand how African American liberation efforts shaped their respective localities. While Attala is the central focus, the county did not exist in a vacuum. Therefore, the book spans out to show the county's relationship to its neighboring counties and the state to provide insight into broader social, economic, and political currents.

The focus on a single county, as opposed to a community, a town, a collection of counties, a state, or the broader South, is essential. It prevents taking random and unrelated examples and writing of them as representative of a group. African Americans in Attala County demonstrated that liberation rested in their willingness to pursue, acquire, and control the same tools as their white counterparts, such as education, land ownership, suffrage, and most importantly the belief that no one group controlled these power sources. As African Americans obtained possession and greater control of these sources, they threatened a white power structure seeking to control the same institutions for themselves. A single-county approach allows individuals and groups to have their respective moments without the assumption that their actions represent a previous association or movement. Exiting Slavery, not all freed people knew or instantly bonded with one another. Individual action or even collective action at times spoke to individual interest or the interests of the collective.

Mississippi Zion uses genealogy to capture and trace individuals, families, and institutions over time. A genealogical approach allows the "everyday person" to remain centered within the narrative and the liberation narrative to stay centered on the people and the collective unit. John Blassingame explained that the slave community taught the next generations what it took to survive. The family taught the principles of not only survival but also the concepts of freedom and liberation.[31] Referencing James and Caroline Byas of Attala County, Green Polonius Hamilton stated, "These devoted parents were born in the days of slavery, but they had enough of instinctive knowledge to appreciate the value of education and to try to give to each of their children every educational advantage that was in their power."[32]

Building on Blassingame's analysis, Thomas Webber linked the freedom mentality to the slave family.[33] When the two are combined, one sees the impact the slave family and community had on the actions former slaves took across the South to assert their citizenship. Within the insular world of the slave cabins, the Black family molded the mindsets of future generations.[34] Attala County's liberation genealogy included several individuals, some related, most not. Their actions primarily speak for themselves while possibly being representative of others. Specific individuals appear multiple times within this work, while others have a single appearance, representing the varying facets of liberation that individuals attempted and achieved. Tables capture the broader African American population within the county, region, and sometimes state, allowing for a broader scope to understand liberation efforts and those who fell short of their goals.

Local histories allow for a nuanced understanding of complex societal issues and structure from the perspective of the individual whom the system impacted. Unlike other local histories, *Mississippi Zion* does not segregate the Black population from the white population; instead, it shows the two groups existing within the same time and space. Norman Crockett's, *The Black Towns* discussed the necessity of autonomy and control through developing self-sustaining communities. Crockett's work showed the successful and unsuccessful liberation efforts within racial vacuums.[35] Elizabeth Rauh Bethel's *Promiseland: A Century of Life in a Negro Community* used local history. She showed how African Americans in the post-emancipation era created an economically viable, socially robust, and politically conscious community within a society that deemed them inferior to whites.[36] *Mississippi Zion* takes a similar approach to Mark Schultz's *The Rural Face of White Supremacy beyond Jim Crow*. Schultz analyzed interracial interactions in Hancock County, Georgia, examining the complexities of everyday life that transcend our typical understanding of the African American experience. As Schultz stated, "Different southern contexts gave rise to many different experiences and hence different memories of the 'true' South."[37] Schultz used local history to show how people affect systems, and that understanding people's individual and collective experiences gives a better understanding of how broader systems take shape. Referring to Jim Crow, Schultz stated, "Recognizing the continuity of black resilience and strength seems a better way to honor African Americans than does focusing solely on their dehumanization. . . . The human condition under Jim Crow is honestly told only when both traditions are taken into account."[38] *Mississippi Zion* uses local history to show how life unfolded for the people living through the time and the impact of people's actions on creating larger systems, rather than using societal structures to define a people. Attala County's history remained relatively intact, making it easier to see its evolution over time without significant gaps in historical records. Sources from the Freedmen's Bureau records, Works Progress Administration, newspapers, census, court, probate, diaries, school records, congressional testimony, court records, land, and photographic records give voice and recognition to the otherwise unknown. The records capture the individual and collective acts of liberation in the interconnected areas of labor, mentality, landowning, education, politics, interracial interactions, and family life to highlight people's lives as single agents and as part of a broader collective.

Mississippi Zion contains six chapters. The chapters are arranged chronologically by decade and chronologically within each decade. At various points within a chapter, backstory or forward projection moves the narrative for continuity purposes. The book's setup provides a view into how the liberation struggle unfolded from the people's perspective. The chapters are continuations of the previous chapters, rather than standalone chapters to trace action, impact, and change over time. The chapters' titles reflect different phases in Attala's liberation era. "Chapter 1: A New Dawn: Embarking on the Liberation Journey" examines Attala County during the Civil War era and the first years of emancipation. The chapter captures the liberation mindset of the enslaved class and how the mindset carried over into emancipation. The chapter explores the actions taken by former slaves via the Freedmen's Bureau, labor contracts, court system, and politics to assert themselves as societal equals. "Chapter 2: Pick Yo' Own Damn Cotton: Building the Foundations of Zion" examines how African Americans laid the foundations for autonomy amid the rise and fall of state Republican leadership during the final Reconstruction years. The chapter focuses on the role African Americans, such as Jackson Presley and Alfred Frazier, played in creating the various institutions and communities that included the Sam Young school and the Buffalo Community. The chapter also explains the origins of the Jim Crow mentality that coincided with the Social Equality Bill and its impact on Republican leaders, such as Jason Niles and Rasselas Boyd. "Chapter 3: Taking Flight: Moving Towards a Liberated Zion" examines how African American daily life reflected the benefits of past decade's hard work. The chapter focuses on individual households, the church, and schools to demonstrate how liberation continued its upward trajectory in the decade following the Reconstruction experiment. The chapter explores how Black women such as Ceele Johnson, Jeanette Evans, and Harriet Adams shaped the color line; how African American student enrollment and attendance outpaced white students; and the rise of prominent church leaders such as Alice Alston and Charles Buchanan. The chapter also examines individual and collective white citizens' responses to demonstrate the redemption struggle that included the murder of Jordan and Dora Teague and the racialization of the state's teaching certification system. "Chapter 4: United We Stand: Organizing in the Decade of White Supremacy" examines the spread of the Jim Crow mentality at the local and state level and the cementing of anti-Black apparatuses to halt Black progression. The chapter continues to show how landowning, community building, and education paved the way for the county's Black citizens to collectively subvert redemption efforts stemming from Mississippi's 1890 Constitutional Convention and the continued assault on Black education through equitable teacher's pay between the races. The chapter also highlights the individual tensions and collaborations between the races to bring subtle nuances to race relations in a period typically associated with racial animosity. Organizations such as the Women's General Baptist Missionary Society, the Colored Inter-State Press Association, Central Mississippi College, and the Attala County Colored Teachers' Institute and individuals such as William A. Singleton, Alice Alston, and Albert Poston are detailed to examine how individuals operated, either individually or within organizations, during the decade of attempted efforts to create a national organization for African American civil rights. "Chapter 5: There Shall Be Blood: The Price of Liberation" examines the resistance measures both whites and African Americans undertook in the twentieth century's first decade and the literal and figurative price peoples paid for their pursuit of liberation and redemption prior and during the James K. Vardaman administration. The chapter examines the height of racial tensions fueled by the federal appointment of Professors D. M. P. Hazley and William Wendell Phillips as census enumerators, the double-lynching of Jim Gaston and Monroe Hallum, and the statewide manhunt for Rufus Ousley, who killed a white man in self-defense. The chapter also focuses on voting and education, with an examination of the white primary and African American resistance through delinquent poll taxes, the rebirth of Central Mississippi College, and the creation of the Kosciusko Industrial College, which made Attala County the only county in the state's central region with two independent African American higher-education institutions. "Chapter 6: Unfinished Business: Liberation and Jim Crow" examines the continued struggle for sociopolitical control within a settling Jim Crow society and serves as a continuation of the previous chapter to discuss how liberation and redemption played out through the onset of World War I. The chapter examines continued inequity in educational spending, educational setbacks for Central Mississippi College and Kosciusko Industrial College, the alleged boycott of Black domestics, the lynching of Leander Harmon, and the rise of the Black rural bourgeois that would come to represent the county's middle class for the next fifty years anchored by individuals such as Volina Cooper, Sarah Phillips, and Lee Boston Turner.

Frederick Douglass stated, "We deem it a settled point that the destiny of the colored man is bound up with that of the white people of this country. . . . We are here, and here we are likely to be. To imagine that we shall ever be eradicated is absurd and ridiculous. We can be remodified, changed, assimilated, but never extinguished. We repeat, therefore, that we are here; and that this is our country; and the question for the philosophers and statesmen of the land ought to be, What principles should dictate the policy of the action toward us? We shall neither die out, nor be driven out; but shall go with this people, either as a testimony against them, or as an evidence in their favor throughout their generations."[39] *Mississippi Zion* captures the liberation mentality and actions that shaped the state's post–Civil War society. Analyzing the mentality frames the rise and rationale of the Jim Crow closed society, which twentieth-century Black Mississippians sought to eradicate.

John Dittmer's *Local People: The Struggle for Civil Rights in Mississippi* traced the evolution of African American organizational efforts in the decades preceding and during the Mississippi civil rights movement. Dittmer discussed how African Americans' "sick and tired" attitude related to second-class citizenship powered organizational attempts to challenge white supremacists' power structures. Dittmer examined Mississippi African American political and social activism from the activists' perspective as indicated by John Mangrum's statement, "All my life I have resented the kind of treatment I have received. Now that someone has been brave enough to step out, I will identify with them."[40] By focusing more on what African Americans did not possess rather than analyzing what they once had that needed regaining, Dittmer captured the liberation struggle that shaped the early-to-mid-twentieth-century liberation struggle through the lens of a new decade of freedom fighters.

Mississippi Zion shows a prolonged Black liberation era encompassing generational shifts. The former slave entering freedom knew the southern white better than any generation to follow. The first and second freedom generations learned what liberation meant by witnessing the formerly enslaved family seize freedom to best suit their needs, wants, and desires. Black people sought to obtain the tenants of power to secure their liberation. They accomplished this in a manner that was not covert but rather in plain view. As Dr. John H. Bracey articulated in his speech given at the 2019 Ralph Watkins Lecture Series, "Black people do not want to be white; they want to be better black people."[41] In this light, to be a better Black person meant to be a liberated Black person, as Patrick H. Thompson stated: "In my mind the Negro will never be much of anybody until he is content to be himself—until he begins to turn his eyes inward with a view to discovering his peculiar fitness for the work of the world and proceeds to develop to his utmost capacity the latent powers within himself, being governed in his development only by the specific ends in which he might with best advantaged be directed."[42] Former slaves and those born during emancipation understood that life and liberty trumped safety. The people in the pages that follow represent what Eugene Genovese described as the rebel. The rebel doubted the institutional foundation, which guided everyday life. The rebel realized he possessed the necessary skills to aid in his upward mobility.[43] Being a better Black person meant challenging and modifying the social order to reflect a society that included Black peoples as human beings entitled to the same constitutional rights as anyone else.

CHAPTER I

A NEW DAWN

EMBARKING ON THE LIBERATION JOURNEY

Forming Zion included a world where African Americans had to assert themselves as equals to their white counterparts. Despite their prior enslaved status, freedmen emerged from slavery with an outlook that countered the expected. African Americans adopted a sense of superiority over whites based on moral character rather than race.[1] The harshness of the slave institution did not create an inferiority complex in the slaves; instead, slaves understood that the institution defined their position. The hidden superiority that African Americans developed complemented that of the "the common white man." The nonslaveholding whites saw themselves as part of the ruling class as their labor and bodies retained autonomy within the slave institution, adopting a sense of privilege founded on a technicality.

White politics rooted itself in the ideology that slavery was the foundation for white liberty. In *Political Culture in the Nineteenth-Century South: Mississippi 1830–1900*, Bradley Bond stated, "In 1861, white Mississippians occupied a twilight zone in their history, willing neither to surrender their mythological past nor to reject firmly the modern world they strove to invent."[2] Kosciusko Judge Jason Niles recorded a diary entry in which he spoke of a man named Hudson who gave his thoughts on racial equality. Hudson spoke of what he feared would happen "if Lincoln's negro equality scheme prevails—of negroes being naturally inclined to be familiar and impudent—of their thieving propensities, and of there not being enough penitentiaries made to hold the convicted negro thieves if they are to be punished as whites are—of his determination to leave this region when that scheme is carried out, & going anywhere, (except to the North,) rather than stay here."[3] The privilege that whites built their identity on did not translate to slave's acceptance of this identity as slaves did not take ordinary whites seriously.[4] Control epitomized the redemption agenda, which echoed more significant debates regarding "what to do with the Negro?" This question, in varying fashion, drove local, state, and national politics. While various entities discussed this question, freedmen focused on another question: "What to do with ourselves?" As Du Bois summarized, African Americans did not adhere to white action to deny their freedoms.[5] The former slave sought to control self, and this simple notion set in motion a push for liberation that contended with the push for redemption, which sought to replicate the old social order where two classes existed, the controller and the controlled.

Attala had sizeable slave populations in the decade preceding the Civil War. In 1850, 438 slave owners owned 3,261 slaves. Throughout this period, non-Mississippi natives primarily governed Attala County. The county also lacked a dominant political party—a decade before the Civil War. Democrats held a three-person majority over the Whigs, whose northern party wing possessed antislavery sentiment.[6] The passage of the 1850 Fugitive Slave Act prompted county citizens to voice their stance regarding the slave institution. On August 17, 1850, citizens met at the courthouse in Kosciusko to ratify, approve, and confirm the Nashville Convention's resolution and address. An eleven-member committee formed consisting of S. Durham, William Dodd, Elijah Sanders, Eli Nichols, P. W. Lowe, Emanuel Friday, Barney Westbrook, William K. Johnson, Joshua Brooks, Graner Dotson, and Dr. Charles B. Galloway. The meeting also included Josiah P. Campbell, John B. Hemphill, Henry Gray, and Jason Niles. The committee drafted a resolution consisting of fourteen points. One point referred to viewing slaves as property and the right for southern states to expand slavery into territories, thus enjoying the same rights of access to those territories as Northern states.[7] Despite the county's support for the Nashville Convention, when the time came to determine Mississippi's fate regarding secession, Attala County sang a different tune. The political stance on secession conflicted with the state. On March 5, 1860, the Conservative Union Men of Attala County met at the Kosciusko courthouse. Duncan Taylor Patterson served as the committee chair. Patterson, a South Carolina native, was an early settler in the Center Community. Patterson appointed Benjamin Kern, Wylie Rimmer, and

David Knox to the resolution committee. Seven resolutions passed, with one supporting Union preservation but opposing "Southern fire-eaters" and northern "Black Republicans."[8] During the 1861 Secession Convention, Attala County sent Union delegates John Wood and Elijah Sanders to oppose the measure. John Wood, "determined to stop secession," was one of two who refused to sign the ordinance of secession.[9] While pro-Union, Attala showed no indication that it was pro-Black.

Slavery in Attala County showed a range of power dynamics and race relations. Slave owners treated slaves like products to be desired or possessed, as evidenced by William Bigby's gift of two "negroes" to his wife Malinda, or Lucy Arnold's suing her stepfather for stealing her slaves.[10] Separation kept slaves compliant, forcing them to live in constant fear. On February 19, 1859, citizens gathered at noon to bid on the slaves formerly belonging to the deceased Jane Johnston. Samuel Aston paid $1,825 for three slaves, Harriet and her two children Lydia and Dick. His sister, Elizabeth Irving, paid $5,975 for Eliza and her children Lafayette, Susan, Aaron, Mary, Jane, Ann, and Dewitt.[11] While the children remained with their mothers, the auction subjected them to the emotional trauma of possible separation. Recalling a story Jerry Roby told of slave owner Ki Roby, Jerry's son Edd Roby said he didn't 'low his slaves to read an' 'rite . . . Would whip 'em when day catched n-----s prayin' at home or anywhere else."[12] However, slaves were not content to listen to their owners and found ways to pray. One such woman, Edd said,

> prayed a heep but she allus put her head down in de pot when she went to pray so as de white folks couldn't hear her. One day dis old woman was a prayin' in de pot an' got so full o' 'ligion 'till she got her head out dat pot an' was jus' a tellin' de news. Old Missus heard her an' went to see what was de matter. Missus, she got happy an' finally Marsa heard 'em an' went to see what de trouble was. Marsa, he got full o' 'ligion too an' dey all had a big time. After dat day dey said dey never did whip 'em fo' prayin' no more.[13]

Slavery exposed the competing mentalities between slaves and whites and owners and nonowners, each feeling a sense of control over themselves and others. The slave patrols had a strong presence in the county. Beyond the boundaries of the owner's land lay the patrollers. The patrollers monitored slaves' movements. Slaves had to possess passes to leave the owners' land.

The justice of the peace appointed the patrollers and, according to William Flannagan, they "keep the slaves in their places," and if they caught a slave without a pass, the patroller, as Roby recalled, "would sho' get em an' whip em."[14] Despite the patrol's presence, slaves looked past the potential whippings and ran for freedom. In July 1863, a night patrol searched the woods for Negroes, finding what Jason Niles described as "woods full of negroes camped."[15] In January 1864, Major Lampkin Straughn Terry captured a runaway slave, claiming a cash reward.[16] The power that patrolling gave whites at times conflicted with the best interests of the slave owner when patrollers beat the slaves. William Flannigan's owner John Ashley told patrollers to "leave his slaves alone, because he ruled his own home and slaves, and . . . he would do his own punishing."[17] The "softer" side of slavery painted a picture of harmony: a slave girl and her mistress ferrying Jason Niles across the river; slaves and whites enjoying a slave wedding at David S. Comfort's residence.[18] Slavery's calmness included slaves dutifully attending to their masters as Tom Newell escorted his mistress to the schoolhouse,[19] or the friendship between Steve Jamison and his slave, Gabriel. Steve confided in Gabriel about his misgivings of being sent off to school,

> "Gabriel," Steve said, "I got to go to a man school." "How come?" drawled the colored boy. "Pa said that old professor would make a gentleman out of me," Steve said. "I sho is glad I don't have to be made no gentleman," Gabriel sighed with satisfaction and continued doodling dust with his bare toes, then inquired, "How dat man goin' to do it?" "Aw, just teach me to be polite, how to bow to ladies like Uncle Bony does, and I guess I will have to wear shoes even in the summer." "Dat sho will be bad, Reckon Doctor Bony wouldn't teach you?" "Naw! Who wants to be a doctor? I had as soon be a gentleman as a pill roller. I wish you could go with me, Gabriel." "Uh huh, I'd rather shoo flies off de table," Gabriel proclaimed. "There ain't no flies to shoo in the winter time," Steve countered. "And I don't want to be no gentleman nuther," and Steve wished at least the family could be content with one less gentleman.[20]

The slave owner possessed legal authority; however, the slave held advantages that owners could not readily control. They found ways to create independent spaces within the slave institution. Slaves wanted control of their religious activities. Slave owners used religion to condition the slave's mind to preserve the master-slave relationship, by preventing slaves from becoming enlightened.[21] The lack of slave churches within the county demonstrated this control element. Mississippi was the third state to pass anti-assembly laws.[22] Twenty years after Mississippi's first Black church organized, Fancher Hill Baptist Church, located in Northeast Attala, became the county's first organized slave church in 1856. The church arose from the Bear Creek Baptist Church, founded by Henry Fancher in September 1851.[23] Little evidence exists on Fancher Hill's history and origins; however, based on 1850 slave schedule information, only two Bear Creek Church's charter members, Henry Fancher and Isham Landrum, owned slaves, seven in total. William Flannagan recalled disobeying his master, who told him to pick cotton. William stated, "He would just keep on singing and doing as he pleased, and leave the field when he was ready."[24] Some slaves yielded more freedoms than others. Tom Newell, the great-great-grandfather of Oprah Winfrey, was born in November 1839 near Benton in Yazoo County.[25] He belonged to James "Jimmie" Newell "who reared him from the cradle." James Newell was a South Carolina native and possibly Tom's father. James hired Tom out as a logger and an iron maker in Biloxi, Mississippi.[26] James Newell died in 1859, and he left Tom to Byrd Ratliff Newell.[27] Byrd Ratliff passed shortly after his father, and William S. Newell became Tom's owner. While enslaved in Kosciusko, William hired out Tom's labor. Tom worked on the infrastructure of the then underdeveloped Kosciusko. Tom Newell laid the foundation of what became Kosciusko's town square, including its courthouse. Tom's employment earned him a yearly salary of approximately six to seven hundred dollars.[28]

The slave civilization came to an end with secession and the Civil War. On the eve of the Civil War, Attala County had 692 slave owners and 4,890 slaves. During the Civil War, 1,728 men across eighteen organized units served in combat. This number does not include the slaves who accompanied their owners, mainly in a domestic capacity. Sixteen-year-old Dock Bates served as a cook for the 15th Mississippi Infantry Company A between 1863 and 1865. John W. Sanders attested to Bates's duties stating, "I knew Dock Bates . . . as a cook for the soldiers did good and faithful service for two years or more and never deserted his post nor abonden [sic] his duty until dismissed."[29] Although slaves understood their owner's desire to maintain their slaves, slaves also witnessed others fighting for their freedom. In 1862, thirty-year-old Patrick Fondren served as a servant in Captain Henry Jamison's 20th Mississippi

Infantry Company K under his owner, William Fondren. At the Battle of Vicksburg, Union soldiers captured Patrick and William and later paroled them following Confederate surrender. Dave Kelly, serving for Berry Kelly, served in the Ballentine Calvary Regiment. During a retreat from Nashville to Murfreesboro, Dave received a gunshot wound in the leg. He remained in action until the surrender, returning home from Atlanta, Georgia.[30] Black Confederates witnessed armed resistance as a liberation option and, to a degree, likely decolonized their minds not to fear their masters.

Competing notions of control laid the foundation for how the races would interact upon slavery's abolition. Attala County emerged from the Civil War unscathed from Union destruction, while neighboring counties were not as fortunate. The county's geography and lack of significant infrastructure left it virtually unharmed. However, on February 24, 1864, Yankee soldiers came through taking mules, horses, saddles, meat, clothes, gold, and a slave named Dan from Dr. Ozias Lewis, Daniel Comfort, Benjamin Tipton, Michael Hawkins, and Joab Scarborough.[31] Local whites had more than Yankees to be concerned about. A Negro regiment killed William G. Oxford and his son while taking another prisoner in the Liverpool Community in Yazoo County.[32] Except for a few skirmishes in or near the county, including Abe Boyd, slave, being fired upon, the county experienced little wartime drama. As emancipation commenced, county whites believed that "the White man must and will control the negroes."[33] The need to control freedmen lies within county whites' psyche, setting the stage for a struggle for that control.

The Republicans held favor with the county citizens during the early years of presidential and Radical Reconstruction before the Democrats rose to local and state power, which had more to do with civil rights initiatives of the 1870s. The Republican leadership, described as "high-toned, Christian gentleman—men of honor and principle," who "represented the better element of the Republicans in the South—men who were not tempted by the 'spoils of office' and the private gain that could have been theirs had they allied themselves with the Carpet-bag and Scalawag element,"[34] included Jason Niles, Rasselas Boyd, and Elisha Carnes. Jason Niles, a Vermont native, came to Kosciusko in 1848 and, in 1851, established a law practice. As a Union sympathizer, Niles avoided combat and became Kosciusko's mayor in 1864. Following slavery, Jason Niles rose as a top political figure, heralded for providing "great service in advising the negroes as to their duty."[35] Although Niles was a former slave owner, he proved himself an ally in

Judge Jason Adams Niles

Josiah Abigail Patterson Campbell
(Collection of the Museum Division,
Mississippi Department of Archives
and History)

Reverend John Thomas (From *Multum in Parvo: An
Authenticated History of Progressive Negroes in Pleasing
and Graphic Biographical Style* by Isaiah Wadsworth
Crawford and Patrick H. Thompson, 1912)

the year preceding emancipation. In 1864, Niles defended two slaves accused of larceny.[36] African Americans forged a positive working relationship with the Niles family in the decades that followed, as Niles served as their closest source to local and state political power.

African Americans established themselves as people and citizens, inserting themselves into the everyday social structure. Edward Coleman Jr.'s recollection of Attala's Reconstruction period gave a fair assessment of social and political life among the white citizens; however, Coleman missed the mark on freedmen's daily life. Coleman assessed, "The question of controling [sic] the negro was never an issue in Attala County," further stating, "A large number were controled [sic] by their employers, upon whom the former slaves were dependent for labor and employment."[37] Freedmen controlled themselves more than Coleman sought to explore or wished to understand. Depicting African Americans as a labor-dependent class played into a narrative discussed in Ronald Davis's analysis of sharecropping in the

Natchez District. Davis concluded that the system created a Black dependent class and a white paternalist class.[38] Fixating on labor dependency overlooked the freedmen-labor spectrum, which was more independent than recognized. Although Eugene Genovese called the master-slave relationship codependent, in reality the planter class relied more on the slave. The master needed the slave more than the slave needed the master. The slave may have been the property of the master, but that property determined the master's business and personal prosperity or failure.[39] The emancipation period highlighted planter dependency and the mechanism used to prevent the working masses from becoming autonomous.

Freedmen sought to control their labor and reap the rewards of their toil. They used various options to achieve their goals. Some freedmen signed contracts, sought more significant control through a sharecropping system, and others worked independently. Freedmen knew the art of negotiation stemming from slavery; thereby, they better positioned themselves to make deals that benefited them.[40] Emancipation empowered African Americans to liberate their labor so that the original owner, the worker, controlled it. Ronald Davis stated, "Once blacks realized that freedom meant working for old masters, they began withholding their labor to pressure planters into making concessions in the working conditions and terms of labor."[41] Davis's statement is both accurate and flawed. He implied that freed people had a choice while indicating that they remained linked to former masters.

Former slaves had two advantages: quality and quantity. C. Vann Woodward explained that whites coveted Black labor because Black farmers knew how to master agriculture since most farmed in fertile soil areas. Mississippi also lacked white laborers as those returning from war remained absent from the labor force in 1865.[42] The reliance on Black labor gave freedmen negotiating power against the planter. In their article "Afro-American Families in the Transition from Slavery to Freedom," Ira Berlin, Steven Miller, and Leslie Roland explained that Black families operated as units when making deals with planters.[43] The same family unit that slave owners threatened to separate now had the power to force planters to adhere to their demands. Based on available contracts, Attala freedmen contracted for approximately fourteen hundred bushels of corn, twenty-four hundred pounds of pork, and fifty bushels of wheat. Labor contracts provide evidence that former slaves participated in negotiations. Some families had greater success than others at securing contracts.

Contracts signed between April and August 1865 varied. A. M. Davis contracted with ten freedmen: Elex, Mike, Sam, George, Sam, Frank, Henry, Green, Anderson, and Joe. They received one-sixth of the current crop to be divided equally among them, including their twenty-six dependents. In a similar contract, the former slaves of Fredric Blumenburg earned one-tenth of peas and fodder between nineteen workers and their thirty-one dependents. While such contracts showed the need for freedmen to secure labor independence, other contracts indicated business savvy. Elizabeth Woodward contracted with her former slaves Jeff and Isaac for ten bushels of corn, three bushels of wheat, and 250 pounds of pork. Billups and John Burt contracted with nine of their former slaves, collectively paying 225 bushels of corn. Henry, Jim, Alfred, Elijah, and Mary Riley contracted with James G. Riley, earning fifty bushels of corn, twenty-five bushels of wheat, and five hundred pounds of pork.[44] Other freedmen received cash compensation and negotiated work terms. Frederick Zollicoffer paid seven freedmen fifty-three dollars per month, and one freedman, Curtis, negotiated two working days per week for personal business.[45] In August 1864, the undersigned commissioners for Mississippi established buying prices for various crops. Prime shelled corn sold for two dollars and ten cents per fifty-six-pound bushel, and good clean wheat sold for five dollars per sixty-pound bushel.[46] Freedmen positioned themselves to profit from their earnings.

The former slave represented the working-class proletariat's epitome; however, they also possessed a capitalist mentality. This capitalist mindset replicated slavery economics. As Schweninger stated, "The slaves saw liquid capital not only as a means to secure freedom, but also a means to attach their paternity—and hence, their identity as persons—to something even their masters would have to respect."[47] During slavery, slaves grew and sold crops and livestock, which afforded them income that they could use to secure greater freedoms.[48] William Flanagan recalled that his owner, John Ashley, allotted his slaves parcels of land on which they grew cotton and corn, and "when it was gathered the master bought the produce, and the slaves had the money to spend as they wished."[49] Many Attala County freedmen chose not to contract their labor, a theme the echoed throughout the South in the months following emancipation.[50] The lack of contracts signaled a transition from coerced labor to a labor-selective work mentality. Ben and Cato Ayers worked for their former owner, Colonel Lansford Ayers, in a noncontracted manner in his wagon and blacksmith shop.[51] When Alsey M. Atkinson contracted with his former slaves in April 1865, one former slave, Jeanette (discussed later), did not contract her labor. She worked as an independent cook. Choice meant control, which former slaves wanted.

Control included defending self against the opposition. Physical intimidation proved essential for southern white control. Slaves found ways to protest their master's actions; however, slaves had to construct their resistance carefully. As Eric Foner assessed, "The slightest evidence of blacks holding secret meetings or arming themselves sufficed to set off waves of fear among Southern whites."[52] During the 1835 summer, Mississippi feared that alleged rebellions had reached their state. A planned July 4 attack between whites and slaves in Madison, Hinds, and Warren Counties sought to mass-slaughter white men and women. Twelve white men and several slaves died as a result. The near insurrection founded Mississippi's closed society mentality.[53] With slave owners stripped of their "master" status, the former slave now possessed a more expansive arsenal by which to defend themselves. To break whites' mental advantage, freedmen met force with force. Nell Irvin Painter assessed that demonstrating one's emancipation required the former slave to psychologically and physically challenge their oppressors.[54] On September 26, 1865, a group of freedmen recaptured their stolen cotton (five bales) and marched through town with arms until they reached the cotton mill near Leake County.[55] Freedmen were not strangers to guns, as some had had access to them during their enslavement, such as Helm Carr's slave who "fired off a gun or pistol."[56] In the emancipation era, southern whites' feelings were immaterial to Black peoples' seeking to assert their independence. The presence of freedmen, who formerly participated in the Civil War, shaped an environment where freedmen knew the value of securing and using arms. Although Confederate pension records indicated that Black service members served in a domestic capacity, as the Confederacy's hopes of victory dwindled, Black servants participated in combat, empowering them to use arms for themselves. The freedmen's willingness to engage in armed conflict showed fearlessness, which many southern whites feared and expected. A popular belief held by most whites was that upon freedom, ex-slaves would enact revenge. Freedmen never stooped to barbarism, seeking only to use arms to defend their lives and property. The society they lived in was violent, and one secured freedom through violence; therefore, one must use violence to secure and maintain their independence.[57]

The September armed march preceded the Mississippi legislature's passing the state's Black Codes in November 1865. Mississippi's conservative legislature sought "to place the freedmen in a position somewhere between that of the free Negro of slavery days and that of a citizen," though with labor restrictions and without political rights. As Dennis Mitchell explained, the legislature wanted a post-slavery slave code.[58] Using the law to weaken freedmen's action allowed whites to inflict violence without the threat of armed resistance while criminalizing Black self-defense. The state's Black Codes signified that Mississippi was not ready to accept former slaves as free people and represented the earliest battle in the liberation-versus-redemption struggle, one that former slaves fought with vigor and success.

Congress passed the 1866 Civil Rights Act granting freedmen testifying rights in court and the right to experience the "full and equal benefit of all laws and proceedings for the security of person and property, as is enjoyed by white citizens."[59] Before its passage, Mississippians remained divided over Negro testimony. The opposition opposed the measure along racial lines. The supporters supported the effort for state political purposes. In September 1865, Governor William Sharkey used his political influence to push the legislature towards accepting Negro testimony and directed "state courts to accept Negro testimony."[60] His actions helped to get a watered-down law accepting Negro testimony signed into law in November. Freedmen provided testimony in cases involving members of their race, but not in cases involving whites.[61] Although legislators relented and passed laws permitting freedmen to testify in intraracial cases, Attala County freedmen changed Mississippi politics the following year. In September 1866, a white jury convicted Sam W. Winters, a white man, of murdering Sam Winters, a freedman.[62] The jury based their decision on all-African American testimony. Samuel Wilborn Winters was Leonard and Mary Winters's son born on September 20, 1832, in Georgia. Samuel's father owned a large plantation in Attala County that held seventy slaves. By 1860, Samuel owned twenty-eight slaves. Despite the testimony's strength, a consensus developed that Winters would be acquitted; however, the jury returned a guilty verdict. Judge Josiah Abigail Patterson Campbell attested that the conviction of a white man using only Negro testimony was the first in Mississippi's history to his knowledge. Judge Campbell supported the jury's guilty verdict and refused to consider appeals. Campbell elaborated in his opinion that Negro testimony was as good as white testimony even if used against white men. The law could not diminish Negro testimony because it would devalue the justice system.[63] Campbell stated, "In the eyes of the law, of the life of a negro, and that a very moderate punishment should therefore be inflicted on you as the first victim. . . . I would extend full protection to the negro and will readily act on the testimony of negroes as of whites." Campbell elaborated, "I could account for it only by the supposition that it was not deemed possible that conviction could be had on the testimony of negroes alone; but, happily for society, this popular error has been dispelled by the virtue and manly courage of an honest jury, sworn to make a true response to the evidence according to their convictions."[64] Campbell's opinion reinforced the concept of equality before the law, stating,

> But my Sentence must signify the reprobation the law has for crime. I must guard my judgment against being carried away by the sympathies of an impressible heart. Human life, whether of the white or black, must lie guarded against the ebulitions [sic] of passion; an example must be set; society must be protected, and the law vindicated; and although you stand convicted of killing a negro, you must be punished in the same manner as if convicted of killing a white man; for the law makes no distinction in this respect, and I am but an administrator of the law.[65]

James Garner credited Campbell's progressive attitude as the driving force allowing such action to occur, which Joseph Ranney supported. Ranney attested that Campbell's efforts spearheaded acceptance of Black testimony.[66] Garner and Ranney overlooked the African American jurors, choosing to limit their actions to white permission. Slavery prevented most Black people from speaking out against their masters; now, freedmen demonstrated their ability and willingness to use their individual and collective voice to deliver justice and begin to stake their place within the judicial system. The *Daily Clarion* printed the story on the first anniversary of the freedmen armed resistance incident. In 1867, the legislature "removed all limitations on the testimony of freedmen and placed them on the same basis in the courts of the state as that of the whites."[67]

Attala's freedmen continued to define themselves as active labor negotiators. On December 22, 1866, they voiced their demands regarding labor for the upcoming year. The *Daily Clarion* printed their orders. "Freedmen are contracting for another year, but in most cases at higher rates than were paid last year. They say that the wages paid them last year, though customary, were inadequate to their necessities: that it takes more to do them now than when they were slaves, and they must have higher wages or go elsewhere to labor."[68] Demanding higher wages echoed Barrington Moore Jr.'s perspective that the South's economic identity was one driven by labor exploitation.[69] White planters thinking that the African American laborer in emancipation would be nothing more than a peasant had to deal with the reality that African Americans understood their labor's value. Black workers knew they possessed the capability to perform the type of work needed by white planters.[70] Labor knowledgeability provided Black peoples with the opportunity to construct their lives as they saw fit. With fewer African Americans working solely for whites, white labor became an alternative source. Pete Daniel described yeomen farmers' post–Civil War economic condition near freedmen as many yeomen farmers became sharecroppers.[71] As W. J. Cash explained, white laborers' inability to remain autonomous threatened their cherished labor independence that defined their frontier mentality and ruling class positionality compared to controlled Black labor.[72] Labor exposed real and imagined notions of control. In 1867, J. H. Wallace, circuit clerk, stated, "It was somewhat amusing to observe with what caution and extreme bewilderment these new citizens went about [sic] signing and acknowledging contracts with their employers before magistrates."[73] Those believing that freedmen knew little or nothing regarding contracts found that freedmen understood more than assumed. Whereas some whites saw contracts as a pathway to institute a new master/slave relationship, some freedmen saw contracts as documents of equality and equity, for which whites would abide. Wage earning gave former slaves greater freedoms, including challenging whites seeking to cheat them of their earnings. Whites seeking to withhold wages or mistreat freedmen in any fashion found themselves at odds with the freedmen themselves, who used the Freedmen's Bureau's agents, who provided recommendations, orders, or deferments.

Lieutenant Charles Henry Foster of Ohio came to Attala County to represent the Freedmen's Bureau, bringing federal soldiers. They stationed in Kosciusko, but the soldiers withdrew after "seeing that there was no danger of any trouble."[74] Foster remained, later serving on the circuit court.[75] Freedmen's Bureau agents in Louisville, located in Winston County, handled most disputes for Attala between 1867 and 1868. Cases included whites who refused to pay for services rendered and freedmen who quit mid-contract.

Charley complained that Mrs. M. A. Hayden withheld his wage. Hayden declined to pay "unless forced by an officer." Hugh Seegles, a blacksmith, sought $1,200 back wages. In these cases, the agent advised payment. When Hayden still refused to pay the $70 owed to Charley, the agent asked Hayden "to settle, to save further trouble."[76]

When a Mr. Thompson complained that Tom Toms and Jim Sims quit working for him and were "wandering about the neighborhood doing nothing," the two men were "ordered to report" back to work.[77] The agent demonstrated an inability to deliver equal justice as he enforced compliance from one group while encouraging compliance from another. Cases involving mistreatment yielded different results. George Travis and his family contracted with a Mr. Wyse; however, George and his family left Wyse's property because of ill-treatment. Wyse did not deny the allegations; however, he sought to hold the Travis family to their contract. The family found employment with another planter and had no further obligation to Wyse.[78] The agent, in this case, leaned towards compliance with employment law rather than condemning the actions of the white planter. Freedmen and women's usage of the bureau served as another avenue to use the law to demonstrate their freedom and equal status while at the same time seeing the difficulty in having the law deliver consistent and fair justice.

Former masters resorted to seizing freedmen and women's children and claiming ownership under the apprenticeship laws. Apprenticeship allowed states to take children away from families that the courts determined were unsuitable for providing children with the skills needed for common labor.[79] After emancipation Isaac, Alice, and Louisa were apprenticed. Their mother, Priscilla, either died or was rendered incapable of raising of children. In a case handled by the Attala County judiciary, Priscilla's adult son, Jackson Presley, petitioned his siblings' custody after witnessing their slave-like conditions. Jackson won charge of his minor siblings.[80] Dylan Pennington explained children's economic value to freedmen families and their desire to claim children for themselves.[81] Beyond the economic incentive, freedmen challenged apprenticeship because it opened the door for a younger generation's reenslavement. African Americans fighting for their children signaled a fight for liberation, as a family, community, or race could not push forward if a segment of their population remained in legalized slavery.

Freedmen built the necessary institutions to serve the race. The church served as the central institution within Black communities, stemming from the slave era. The church provided former slaves first-class citizenship and an avenue to decolonize the mental damage sustained during their enslavement. George Fredrickson explained that the African American church allowed freedmen to teach and preach Black Christianity. Frederickson elaborated James H. Cone's perspective that Black theology was "a theology of and for the black community, seeking to interpret the religious dimensions of the force of liberation in that community."[82] Now free to deliver services as they desired, freedmen began organizing churches. On August 26, 1866, seventy-five freedmen "gathered under a brush harbor" and formed the First Baptist Church on Rock Hill in Kosciusko. Simon Davis served as the first pastor. Jim Riley, Ike Curtis, Joe Riddle, Cal Roby, Add Edwards, Albert Kerr, Birdie Cade, and Roland Carr served as early church deacons.[83] Baptist churches Pleasant Grove and Pleasant Hill served freedmen in the county's rural areas. The type of preachers making an impact on these churches included A. C. Campbell. Campbell was born in Grenada, Mississippi, and his parents died during slavery. He received his early education in Yazoo County on Mr. Payne's plantation, where Professor Richard Louis Beal of the West Indies taught night school. In exchange for labor, Beal provided Campbell with instruction. Campbell served at Pleasant Grove and later other churches in the county, including Bunker Hill and Mount Zion.[84] Richard Louis Beal was of Trinidadian descent. He immigrated to the United States in 1868. Later cited as a "man of rare intellectual ability" and "as eloquent as Booker T. Washington,"[85] Beal represented the sort of quality educators who educated the early generation of teachers and preachers in Mississippi.

Black Republicans gave African Americans a political presence throughout the South, including Mississippi. They maintained political influence within a party with less than good intentions.[86] Before emancipation, free Blacks had reservations about the newly formed Republican Party and their ranging views on slavery; however, the Republican Party represented the better of two less-than-ideal political organizations. The Democratic Party's anti-Black politics and lack of alternative political possibilities assisted in merging African Americans and the Republican Party. The Black community collectively qualified, "We do not pledge ourselves to go further with the Republicans than the Republicans will go with us."[87] Once emancipated, freedmen organized themselves to secure their civil rights, including suffrage. In Mississippi, Black-majority counties established Republican journals and newspapers, disseminating them across the state. Freedmen became part of the new voting electorate. General Edward Otho Cresap Ord carried out the goals of military Reconstruction, which were "to protect all persons in their rights of persons and property, to suppress insurrection, disorder, and violence, and to punish, or cause to be punished all disturbers of the public peace and criminals."[88] Officials charged with overseeing local politics included the Board of Police and elected officials. In 1867, the board included Iley Coleman, James Williams, Martin Harmon, Marshall Hooks Gregory, and James Mathis. Other officials included Isaac Watkins Scarborough, William Penn Love, John Copeland Lucas, William Van Davis, and James Wallace, who served as probate judge, county treasurer, sheriff, chancery clerk, and circuit clerk respectively.[89]

The first opportunity freedmen had to vote occurred on November 5, 1867. Mississippi voted to hold a state constitutional convention in 1868. Freedmen constituted 57 percent of registered voters with 80 percent voter turnout, solidifying themselves as a viable voting bloc.[90] In Attala, 968 freedmen registered compared to 1,419 whites. General E. O. C. Ord appointed Charles Foster as a registrar in Attala County.[91] The county had 52 percent voter turnout casting 1,293 votes. Edward Coleman stated, "Witnesses say that the negroes would come in several days ahead of time to get to vote, so that when the polls were opened on election day there was such a crowd of negroes standing around that the White men could hardly get in."[92] Given the overall freedmen voter turnout, they likely made up a significant total of Attala's overall vote.[93] Stephen Hahn linked high voter registration and association with the Republican Party to the Reconstruction Acts. Hahn marveled at the level of African American voter participation and their ability to shape state constitutions of the former Confederacy. Hahn stated, "How former slaves accomplished these tasks remains one of the most remarkable, though yet relatively unexplored, chapters in American history."[94] This typical and paternalistic thinking links African American action to federal intervention; however, it omits why African Americans aligned with the Republican Party and how they used the party to promote their agenda. Their efforts are not one to marvel at as a personal or racial achievement. Their actions depicted a group who had long planned how to use their emancipation once the opportunity arose.

Jason Niles represented Attala County at the convention, referred to as the "Black and Tan Convention," beginning January 7, 1868. Niles had the support of both whites and freedmen as the freedmen had "the greatest confidence in his judgment."[95] The convention's ninety-seven delegates consisted of seventy-nine Republicans and seventeen conservatives. Within the Republican ranks were thirteen radicals. Freedmen held eighteen delegate slots, seventeen of which were Republican. One radical and one conservative Republican served within the party.[96] The convention showed Black Republicans' desire to create a landscape where liberation was possible. Republicans pushed a proscription bill to disenfranchise ex-Confederates; however, Black Republicans voted against proscription because they believed that limiting whites' votes would backfire against them. The decision earned skepticism from the delegates as many within the Republican white delegation concluded that freedmen were incapable of understanding politics. James Lynch defended the decision, explaining that disenfranchising whites would create continuous racial conflict, hindering Black progress.[97] Lynch and fellow Back Republicans concluded that the agenda would suffer if they supported a measure that would invite animosity towards them. Jason Niles's views aligned with that of the Black Republicans as he opposed white disenfranchisement, knowing it would prevent ratification.[98] The decision showed a collective Black-liberation consciousness. Freedom and equality remained the goal, not getting even with whites.

In July 1868, Mississippi neared readmittance to the United States. Ratifying the state constitution was the last step; however, this became more difficult than imagined. Fear of "Negro" domination, voter intimidation, and fraud prompted whites to rally and defeat ratification. With the conservative coalition in full force, ratification failed by a 7,630-vote margin. The final vote tally indicated that Black-majority counties favored ratification while white-majority counties opposed ratification. Black counties composed Mississippi's eastern and western regions along the Alabama border and the Mississippi River. White counties encompassed most of the Mississippi interior and coastal region. Attala differed as the only white county to favor ratification. Freedmen likely affected the county's decision to ratify. Attala County voted 989 to 976 favoring ratification. The total number of registered voters at the time of the election was approximately 2,477.[99] The slim margin of victory indicated that most freedmen voted for constitutional passage, given the number of registered freedmen in 1867, while whites approving ratification likely adhered to Jason Niles's proratification influence.[100] One freedman, Parrish Ferguson, experienced the pushback to liberation. Born in 1826 in South Carolina, Parrish once belonged to James A. Ferguson. Parrish

Table 1.1 1868 Mississippi Election Returns			
County	Registered Voters	Approve Ratification	Reject Ratification
Adams	4,624	2,936	834
Amite	1,703	228	1,093
Attala	2,477	989	976
Bolivar	1,880	1,072	157
Calhoun	1,542	103	997
Carroll	4,037	276	2,727
Chickasaw	3,725	971	1,799
Coahoma	1,354	864	114
Choctaw	2,539	277	1,381
Claiborne	2,866	1,696	665
Clarke	2,188	993	835
Covington	688	93	440
Copiah	3,688	556	2,524
Davis	475	132	235
Desoto	4,706	413	2,167
Franklin	1,329	197	756
Greene	330	59	122
Hancock	857	143	404
Harrison	940	231	433
Hinds	5,924	2,869	2,044
Holmes	3,711	1,793	1,207
Issaquena	1,509	1,057	104
Itawamba	1,390	207	683
Jackson	828	123	383
Jasper	1,862	453	1,003
Jefferson	2,731	1,672	653
Kemper	2,313	1,021	953
Lafayette	2,839	298	1,895
Lauderdale	1,282	1,323	1,361
Lawrence	2,085	503	965
Leake	1,451	473	722

Table 1.1 1868 Mississippi Election Returns			
County	Registered Voters	Approve Ratification	Reject Ratification
Lee	3,015	114	1,933
Lowndes	6,135	3,229	2,004
Madison	3,930	2,055	1,190
Marion	755	273	319
Marshall	4,707	1,587	2,279
Monroe	4,754	2,067	1,759
Neshoba	949	172	540
Newton	1,789	115	1,182
Noxubee	4,968	2,978	1,301
Oktibbeha	2,642	1,255	999
Panola	3,805	1,503	1,568
Perry	416	58	228
Pontotoc	2,043	698	929
Pike	2,191	511	1,196
Rankin	2,455	161	1,864
Scott	1,545	291	911
Simpson	972	49	682
Smith	1,078	3	827
Sunflower	1,064	374	301
Tallahatchie	1,675	196	1,031
Tippah	2,797	190	1,621
Tishomingo	3,504	479	1,860
Tunica	1,130	499	109
Wayne	941	394	219
Warren	7,630	4,851	1,316
Washington	3,885	2,733	251
Wilkinson	3,282	2,186	627
Winston	1,512	440	729
Yalobusha	3,640	932	1,963
Yazoo	4,219	1,816	1,490
Totals	153,301	56,230	63,860

Source: The New York Times, July 22, 1868. Reported numbers and actual numbers vary.

reported James to the Grenada sub-assistant commissioner of the Freedmen's Bureau that on November 20, James "shot him through the hip for voting the radical ticket." The violent act caused Parrish to flee the county, leaving behind his wife, Jenny. In addition to shooting Parrish, James refused to pay Jenny for services rendered.[101] Parrish's incident showed the type of backlash that liberation could create and provided a glimpse into what individuals had to overcome in their liberation pursuits.

In the wake of the constitution's defeat, the National Union Republicans came into existence in what William Harris called a conservative attempt to use a Republican agenda until "'nitroglycerin Radicalism' had been destroyed in the state."[102] Conservatives sought political expediency by embracing Black issues. Attala County adopted a moderate Republican platform to ensure Mississippi's reentry into the Union. On June 26, 1869, an interracial meeting consisting of the county's conservative citizen met, chaired by Captain G. P. M. Turner, Democrat. The group met "without reference to race, color, or past political affiliations." Committees assembled and passed resolutions. One resolution accepted Ulysses Grant's Reconstruction plan that would provide Mississippi "a republican form of government," providing universal citizenship and suffrage and rejecting any laws undermining a particular group of people.[103]

Several freedmen gained positions on the executive board during this meeting and gained delegate positions to the future state convention and the senatorial convention (Leake, Neshoba, and Attala). These men included: Ben Ayers, Edmond Clark, C. Comfort, Alfred Frazier, Harry Hardy, Sank Hemphill, Ross McAfee, George Olive, William Snow, Dempsey Taylor, Hosea Taylor, John Thomas, and Sam Wells.[104] The presence of freedmen identifying with conservatives does not fit the typical assumption of the radical African American. Stephen Hahn described the Black Democrat as being dependent on whites for economic survival, coercion, or, quoting Alabama freedmen William Ford, "to keep on the good side of white people, to keep from being interfered with."[105] His analysis lacks nuance regarding party affiliation. Not all Black people were Republican, and within that party not all aligned with the radicals. Black conservatives existed alongside their Black moderate and radical brethren. Assuming that Black people who voted Democratic somehow lacked the sense or power to act as they wished flattens Black people's experiences rather than understanding their decision-making.[106]

Joe Johnson exemplified why a freedman chose the Democratic Party. Born in the District of Columbia in January 1814 to native New York parents,

Joe was kidnapped by a "Yankee" and sold into slavery in Virginia. Joe became a Democrat based on this experience, and "in the dark days of reconstruction wore the 'red shirt' as a token of his fidelity."[107] In Attala, Democrats needed Black support, given thin political margins. Black voters forced the Democratic Party to rethink how they approached their redemption agenda in Reconstruction's early years. As William Harris explained, Black Democratic voters received "whatever favors it may be in the power of our citizens to bestow."[108] Whether die-hard or fair-weather conservatives, the freedmen at the convention kept themselves and their race visible within the local political sphere. They included non-Mississippi natives who worked in the blacksmith, carpentry, and teaching professions. Some of these men, such as Dempsey Taylor and Alfred Frazier, helped African Americans secure educational and business footholds in the following decades.

On July 31, 1869, the National Union Republican Party of Attala County convened. Elijah Sanders, Richard Bullock, W. B. Sanders, Mr. Blackwell, and Rev. John Thomas (the latter two being African American) led the interracial gathering. Members at the meeting pledged their desire for the state to return to the Union and to secure civil and political rights.[109] African Americans witnessed white men acknowledge the need for equality and justice across racial lines, whether or not the intentions were sincere. Rev. Thomas addressed the audience, urging a break from radical Republicans and adopting a belief in equality and justice for all men. During the meeting, the group resolved that Judge Louis Dent was their choice for the governorship.[110] The state Democratic Party chose not to nominate anyone for governor, instead supporting Dent, Ulysses S. Grant's brother-in-law. Grant did not support Dent or the "Conservative Republican Party," and instead supported Dent's opponent, James L. Alcorn.[111] Without Grant's support, the Dent ticket had no chance of victory; however, the Nation Union Republican Party hoped that the presence of Black representation would lead to a sizeable Black turnout. Secretly the party hoped that Black voters would not uncover the party's conservative agenda until the election ended.[112] While Harris depicted African Americans as gullible, he failed to ascertain that African Americans also had personal and collective agendas to execute and understood that obtaining freedom would not happen overnight. Strategically, cooperating with local whites would result in smoother execution of more extensive plans, seeing how it had worked with Black Republicans to get state-funded education approved.

At the National Republican State Convention on September 8, 1869, Alfred Frazier, John Thomas, and C. Comfort occupied three of the eleven delegate slots. One of the three resolutions adopted stated, "We announce ourselves in favor of a liberal system of Free schools, and such equitable distribution of the public school funds as may secure the largest degree of harmony and good feeling among all classes of our citizens." During the convention, Judge Louis Dent's received the gubernatorial nomination with 220 votes.[113] Conservatives within the Republican and Democratic Party met on October 18, 1869, to "ratify the nomination of the Dent ticket and select candidates for the Legislature."[114] Attala County voted for Alcorn by a 1,074-to-564 majority. The county also elected Jason Niles, Rasselas Boyd, and W. S. Rushing to the state house of representatives and senate.[115] While the nonconservative Republicans won vital races, African Americans secured a double victory at the local and state levels. The state remained in control of moderate and radical Republicans while using their "loyalty" to conservative whites to position themselves better to call in political favors.

African Americans ended the 1860s on a high note and moved into the first emancipation decade with the wind at their backs. They emerged from slavery ready to tackle the challenges that littered their liberation pathways. They demonstrated that the slave days were over and that they possessed the ability to advocate and fight against oppressive forces. They made strides in the economic and political arena. Most importantly, whether radical or conservative, the freedmen positioned themselves to have political representation at the state level and political support at the local level. With positive momentum propelling them, African Americans set out to build their Zion.

CHAPTER 2

PICK YO' OWN
DAMN COTTON
BUILDING THE FOUNDATIONS OF ZION

Mississippi returned home when it gained readmission to the United States on February 23, 1870.[1] Passage of the Fifteenth Amendment completed a trio of constitutional amendments that legislatively integrated free and former slaves into America's constitutional framework. Reconstruction aided in liberation; Allen C. Gueizo's *Reconstruction: A Concise History* explained that the "Fourteenth and Fifteenth Amendments to the Constitution empowered the emergence of a black political leadership class." At the same time, the decade marked the first efforts to "redeem" southern states when Democrats began regaining political power.[2] The political battles that defined Reconstruction's later years occurred while African Americans built the institutions needed for personal and racial advancement. Institutions such as communities, schools, and churches provided African Americans a power source to maintain autonomy and visibility. Stephen Cresswell surmised, "Free black Mississippians also found ways of resisting white control. Sometimes they did this by turning inward, building up the institutions of the black community and finding success in a world where whites rarely ventured."[3] Cresswell's assessment lacked understanding of southern society. African Americans did not turn inward; instead, they built their Zion's foundations in whites' open view, sometimes with their participation.

African American institutions challenged the system by shaping the system. Since the federal government lacked the willingness to implement a full-scale plan to bring freedmen to a near-level playing field outside the Reconstruction Amendments, African Americans took control of their situation to create a parallel society that intersected their white counterparts. W. E. B. Du Bois speculated that the Freedmen's Bureau's continued existence would have meant greater African American autonomy. However, from Stokely Carmichael's perspective, liberation would not have been achieved because Blacks would have still depended on an institution controlled by whites.[4] African Americans acted in their best interest, building their home, keeping as much control as possible.

African American landowning exploded during the 1870s as families stabilized and established their way of life. Land allowed for community establishment and the cementing of roots for generations to come. Dylan Pennington's, *The Claims of Kinfolk: African American Property and Community in the Nineteenth-Century South* examined how people transitioned from property to property owners. Although Pennington sought a nuanced understanding of negotiation by shifting the focus of landowning away from mere resistance, he failed to understand that African Americans sought land to resist redemption to property status.[5] As Pennington stated, "For white southerners, emancipation was a revolution in property."[6] Pennington's word choice accurately defined the liberation/redemption battle. Former slaves never lost their economic value, and as property they remained a source of wealth that white planters would not relinquish. For the former slave, they faced two stark realities, either possess property or risk white landowner domination.[7] Colonel Samuel Thomas stated, "The whites know if a negro is not allowed to acquire property or become a landholder he must return to plantation labor . . . this kind of slavery is better than none at all."[8] Determination to keep former slaves landless could not prevent an entire race from obtaining land. Former slaves needed only one white person to sell them land, not the entire race. They had the opportunity to buy good land because white sellers lacked the choice to whom they sold land, resulting in former slaves taking advantage of white people's economic misfortunes.[9]

African Americans earned the land they acquired. Alexander Crummell stated, "The freedmen of this country, on coming out of bondage, began at once all the laborious activities which their needs demanded, and which were required for securing a foothold in this land."[10] Securing land through the federal government ranged from limited to impossible as the federal government failed to pass legislation to redistribute land. As Claude F. Oubre discussed, the Freedmen's Bureau failed to oversee the Homestead Act, which created difficulties for freedmen families to obtain land.[11] Land availability became plentiful in Attala County after speculators purchased large tracts of property in Kosciusko under the assumption that a railroad connecting Canton to Kosciusko would bring economic prosperity to the region. However, the railroad did not bring the type of economic fortune that people in business hoped.[12] The subsequent bust opened the door for African Americans to purchase land.

Land and liberation are inseparable from one another. Building a homeland was neither free nor inexpensive. African Americans financed their purchasing activities with monies earned since emancipation. As discussed in the last chapter, freedmen families work for various kinds of compensation (crop share, cash, food). Between 1865 and 1870, they transformed their earnings into wealth (Table 2.1). Attala's Beat 4 had the most significant number of wealth holders and the highest amount of wealth. The beat, which had a Black majority, comprised 36 percent of the county's total African American wealth. Attala's Beat 5, which had a sizeable African American population, also contained sizeable wealth. African American wealth existed in several counties throughout the Central Mississippi region (Table 2.2). Attala African American families held $83,612 in combined real estate and personal property. Counties with Black-majority populations held more wealth than those in white-majority counties. Attala ranked first among non-Black-majority counties and fourth overall among neighboring counties.

African Americans translated wealth into landowning and community building. Land represented the opportunity to reclaim the notion of a homeland, where they could yield greater autonomy. Understanding how African Americans accumulated their wealth in tandem with diminished white economic positioning gives a nuanced perspective of African American landownership. One of the county's first Black landowners was James Henry Carr. On November 11, 1869, James, along with his white father, Alfred, acquired land from Minerva Peeler, Nancy Peeler, and Elvira Brunt, three white women.[13] Early land transactions were interracial. Former slave owners and non-slave owners dealt with the former slave in a capacity beyond negotiating labor. These encounters transcended race as green was the color

Table 2.1: 1870 African American Wealth in Attala and Neighboring Counties				
County	Real Estate	Personal Estate	Total Wealth	Racial Composition
Attala	$16,931	$66,681	$83,612	40.25
Carroll	$21,690	$124,261	$145,951	54.88
Choctaw	$17,370	$37,766	$55,136	26.27
Holmes	$25,900	$162,595	$188,495	68.28
Leake	$23,085	$26,565	$49,650	35.37
Madison	$37,395	$202,798	$240,193	72.27
Winston	$26,302	$26,293	$52,595	37.88
Totals	**$168,943**	**$646,959**	**$815,632**	**47.89**

Source: 1870 United States Federal Census. These numbers are from household reporting wealth.

Table 2.2: 1870 African American Wealth in Attala by Area			
Area	*Wealth Holders*	*Total Wealth*	*Percentage of County Wealth*
Beat 1	19	$1,740	2.1
Beat 4	221	$30,505	36.5
Beat 5	72	$19,760	23.6
Township 14	27	$13,615	16.3
Township 15	47	$7,539	9.0
Township 16	50	$10,453	12.5
Totals	**436**	**$83,612**	**100**

Source: 1870 United States Federal Census

that mattered. Both groups obtained what they desired: African Americans the green of the earth and whites the green of money.

The opportunity was there for the taking, and with the capital in hand, they met the seller's price. Beginning in the 1870s, African Americans began purchasing land in large quantities (Table 2.3). Based on a sample of land transactions during the decade, they purchased 2,261.9 acres of land, paying $25,805. On average, they paid $11.41 per acre. Land purchases included individual and combined efforts. Men made up most landowners; however, women landowners emerged in the later years, and their contributions to their husbands' ability to purchase land warrant additional inquiry (Table 2.4). Landowners such as Columbus Patterson, Robert Burt, and Lewis Jamison's wealth accumulation began with their labor contracts. Other landowners such as William Ashford, Robert Vanlandingham, and Grandison Thompson did not sign labor contracts and worked independently since emancipation.

Table 2.3: Some 1870s Black Landowners		
Landowner	Acres	Price
Columbus Patterson & Isom Kern	200	$800.00
Willis Jamison	150	$800.00
Nicholas McLemore	40	$235.00
William Ashford	120	$590.00
Jackson Presley	165	$835.00
Henry Huffman	120	$2300.00
George Munson	160	$800.00
Lewis Jamison	120	$7500.00
Straughter Nash		$550.00
William Spivey	320	$640.00
Robert Burt		$250.00
Thomas Jamison	10	$835.00
Grandison Thompson		$1100.00
Robert Vanlandingham	200	$3200.00
Totals	1605	$20435.00

Source: Selected Attala County Land Deed Transactions

Table 2.4: Acres Purchased and Expenditures			
Decade	Acres	Expenditures	Price Per Acre
1870	2,261.9	$25,805	$11.41
1880	1,467.3	$6,721.22	$4.58
1890	1,247.1	$5,670.50	$4.55
1900	1,541.0	$8,211.08	$5.33
Totals	6,517.3	$46,407.80	$6.47

Source: Attala County Land Deed Books. Base on Selected Transactions.

For some former slaves, landowning carried a more profound feeling of independence and reclaimed personhood. When Lewis Jamison purchased land, it concluded a journey that involved witnessing his family's separation within the plantation setting. Lewis, son of Willis and Margaret, belonged to Henry Jamison, along with several siblings. Henry gave to each of his sons Steve, James, and Hugh a slave. The slaves, Gabriel, Solomon, and Sam, were children of Lewis and his wife Mary.[14] Lewis and Mary remained on the Jamison plantation after slavery. Lewis contracted his labor to William Hugh Jamison, earning twenty-five dollars in 1865, while Mary contracted with Hugh Jamison, receiving support. Mary worked as a cook for the Jamison family, which she also served during slavery, taking care of the white Jamison children.[15] Lewis purchased 120 acres of land for $7,500. The land transaction details noted that Lewis paid with fifteen cotton bales, priced at five hundred dollars each.[16]

Beyond acquiring land, these purchases represented families securing the essential foundation to build community. William Ashford's land purchase signaled the end of a long journey, where his family lived under constant

Isom Kern (Courtesy of the
author via Teonne Daye)

Straughter Nash Sr. (Courtesy of Peggy T.
Rush)

Buffalo. Children of Franklin Anderson Carr with
Hattie Mae Presley Lee and Oprah Winfrey (From *The
Star Herald: The Twentieth Century: A Pictorial History
of Kosciusko, Mississippi 1866–1999*, submitted by
Katherine Carr Esters. Courtesy of Jo A. Baldwin.)

threat of separation. William's family remained intact throughout slavery, despite having several slave owners. He journeyed from Fairfield, South Carolina, where his grandfather Jacob Ashford had multiple owners. The first ownership change occurred in 1815, when George Ashford Jr. willed Jacob to his son, George Ashford. Jacob then became the property of George Jr.'s brother, James Ashford. Between 1815 and the recording of James Ashford's will on September 9, 1833, Jacob married Sylvia. According to James's will he bequeathed Jacob, Silvy, and their increase to George DeBelle Ashford. When George DeBelle died with no offspring, Jacob's family, which included three sons, Bartholomew, Wade, and Nathan, became John Rabb Ashford's property. During Winter 1852, John moved his slaves to Winston County,

Mississippi.[17] John died in 1856, and his brother, James Ashford, came into possession of John's slaves. John's 1856 slave inventory identified Jacob's family: Wade, Nathan, Silvy, Sarah, and her four children Caroline, Bill, George, and Fan.[18] Once free, Sylvia took her family to Attala County, where they established roots in Williamsville and Kosciusko. Other Black families, including the Nash, Vanlandingham, Brooks, and Dodd families, soon purchased land in the community.

Williamsville was one of several communities with a strong African American presence. Others included Greenlee, Springhill-Mallet, Center, Little Hill, and Zama. While these communities were interracial, the Buffalo Community stood as an all-Black community. Buffalo's origins begin with Jackson Presley, an ancestor of Oprah Winfrey. In 1871, he allowed freedmen to use his log cabin as a church, the Buffalo United Colored Episcopal Methodist Church.[19] Jackson laid the foundation for a community that served as a haven for several African American families. The following year Nicholas McLemore, a blacksmith, purchased twenty acres of land from James A. Groves on March 11, 1872. The area became known as Blackjack, a neighborhood within the community. Nicholas, born Nicholas Woods in 1800 in North Carolina, became a slave of John McLemore of Carroll County. On January 10, 1874, the community expanded when Jackson paid eight hundred dollars to J. T. and Charlotte Hammond for 120 acres of land.[20] On November 4, 1878, he purchased five acres of land on which the local church stood.[21] He purchased thirty acres from the board of trustees of the episcopal fund and church property of the Protestant Episcopal Church of the Diocese of Mississippi.[22] He donated the land to the Buffalo United Colored Episcopal Methodist Church. Jackson's brother-in-law Henry Huffman purchased 120 acres, solidifying the community's African American ownership. The area expanded when Roland Hazley and his sons-in-law, Charley Funches and George Adams, simultaneously purchased three hundred and twenty acres of land adjacent to and surrounding Nicholas McLemore's land.[23]

ATTALA COMMUNITIES

In the first years of emancipation, the educational landscape had yet to take shape. By 1866, half a million African Americans acquired literacy and education in some capacity a year after emancipation, regardless of

Blackjack. Mary McLemore Evans (courtesy of the author)

Blackjack. Harriet Adams and daughters Lillian, Emma, Nina, and Tennie (courtesy of Shedralyn D. Pullum)

Estes. Family of Lewis Estes (Courtesy of Jeremy Chestnut)

their age. Two years after emancipation, African Americans had constructed approximately twelve hundred schools that consisted of approximately fourteen hundred teachers and nearly seventy-eight thousand pupils. By 1869, the number of schools and pupils doubled.[24] School, like the church, worked to decolonize the mind. The county's white citizens also expressed interest in Black education. In Attala County, the development of African

Center. Branch and
Alma Kern Family
(Courtesy of the author,
from the Blanche Kern
Photograph Collection)

Pleasant Hill (Courtesy of the Archives
and Records Services Division, Mississippi
Department of Archives and History)

Buffalo (Courtesy of the Archives and Records
Services Division, Mississippi Department of
Archives and History)

American schools included white interest. Horace Mann Bond discussed
that following the Civil War, pragmatic whites saw value in educating African
Americans. Their motive was to provide education to prevent the Northern
advocates from returning to the South, pushing their education agenda.[25]
In April 1867, prominent white citizens met to discuss the "establishment of
a school for education of negro children." Those in attendance "advocated
the importance and absolute necessity of establishing such schools, not
only in the town but throughout the entire county."[26] The motive driving
white interest likely stemmed from what Christopher Span explained as
an understanding that the educated Black man would soon vote and that
whites should be the ones to teach them in order to control their vote.[27]
Their position contradicted dominant education narratives at the time,

which objected to any freedmen education, and the planter class's belief that education would "spoil the n----r for work."[28]

During the 1868 convention, Black Republicans focused on state-funded education. It made sense to hold both the state and nation responsible for educating freedmen, serving as a form of reparation. George Stovall introduced an amendment to the education article that would create a separate school system for Mississippi. The Black delegation opposed the amendment. They understood that creating an institution based on racial ideology would undermine the purpose of the system itself. Although they did not publicly support a mixed school system, knowing it would hurt the overall education article, they used their influence with the Republican delegation to defeat the Stovall Bill and have the issue taken up by the future legislature. Democrats, who wanted Black delegates as political allies, discontinued their opposition to the education article. Adopted into the constitution was a "uniform system of free public schools, by taxation or otherwise, for all children between ages of five and twenty-one years."[29]

There is a wealth of scholarship about African American education but a lack of exploration into Black teachers, administrators, and students who provided and lived education; the schools' impact; and those who benefited from their gained knowledge. African American teachers paved the way for the current and future generations. The growing number of schools required teachers to operate them. Between 1870 and 1880, Attala's teaching population ranked third among its seven bordering counties. Historians such as James Anderson, Adam Fairclough, and Christopher Span detailed what education meant to African Americans and their routes to obtaining that education; however, they do not provide information about the teachers themselves. Since education represented the opportunity to undo the psychological brainwashing of slavery, former slaves wanted Black teachers in Black schools to guide their children's education. They knew that white teachers and integrated schools could not achieve this goal in the same manner as the Black teacher who could articulate the community's vision.[30] Ben James and Alfred Frazier served as the county's earliest known teachers. Ben James, born in 1820, came to Mississippi from South Carolina. He lived in Beat 4, which had Attala's only known African American officeholder, Isaac Teague, who sat on the school board.[31] Ben taught school in this area and likely across the county. Alfred Frazier was born on October 16, 1851, in Arkansas. He moved to Mississippi and lived with Caroline Stone and her family outside of Kosciusko.

and began teaching school at a young age. David Austin, Esther Kimes, George Murff, Wilson Wigley, and Isaac Williams also joined the teaching profession during the decade. These teachers represented what James D. Anderson described as local Blacks building and sustaining community schools.[32]

African Americans pushed to develop a community-controlled educational system. Christopher Span discussed that the 1870s were a critical decade for African American school development.[33] In 1870, Vicksburg hosted the First Baptist Missionary Convention. The intersection between church and education served to fuse two institutions needed for liberation. While Mississippi's constitution required state-funded education, African Americans planned accordingly, using the church as additional support. In *Under Their Own Vine and Fig Tree: The African-American Church in the South 1865–1900*, William Montgomery stated, "The churches assumed a prominent role in planning for and implementing programs of personal and racial uplift through education. As one of the few institutions that was able to provide organization and cohesion within the southern black population in the immediate postwar years, they were in a position to perform many useful functions on behalf of education."[34] The number of Black churches in Attala grew during the decade. African Americans formed ten churches: Buffalo, New Hope, Silas Grove, Soul's Chapel, Rocky Point, Smyrna, White Plain, Mount Zion, Wesley Chapel, and Palestine. Several of these churches also had a school of the same name.

Reverend H. P. Jacobs espoused a vision of collective education so that the race could participate in the new society rather than returning to their former enslaved state. He stated,

> I now come to the subject of education, and what I believe to be the destination of the colored race. To elevate that race, and to save it from idolatry and corruption, we must educate. Corruption follows hand in hand in the path of ignorance, and to prove this, had the Southern people been educated up to that high and moral standard that should characterize the civilized world, all this war and devastation, and carnage, would not have happened in our midst. But instead of that, they were educated to believe that they were the peculiar and favored work of God's hand, and that the poor African race was born to be their slaves. That made them believe that a negro had no rights that a white man was bound to respect. But we praise God, from whom

all blessings flow, we find in the face of all that heathenish teaching, that slavery is dead and as such we all ought to be engaged together in building up the old waste places.[35]

In 1871, Mississippi's state-funded educational system commenced (Table 2.5). On March 1, 1871, Hon. H. Musgrove, the auditor of public accounts, received the earliest educable school records for Attala County from James H. Alexander, the first superintendent of public education. Attala's school system consisted of ten subdistricts with 6,303 students. African Americans composed 39.81 percent of that population. Enrollment mirrored the 1866 county racial composition. The early enrollment numbers for both races were on par with the state average for that year, which stood at 40.68 percent for African Americans and 59.32 percent for whites.[36] Educable records for 1872 (Table 2.6) captured the broader Central Mississippi region. The number of white children attending school outpaced African American children. The increased enrollment stemmed from white-majority county data availability and decreased African American enrollment in most counties from the previous year.

African Americans went a step beyond having space where education took place. They gained control of their educational institutions. On March 14, 1871, Judge Samuel Young coordinated with John Cottrell, Fred Jennings, and Dempsey Taylor (the latter three being African American) to establish Kosciusko's colored school. Young laid out the conditions to the Attala County's board of school directors. The trustees and their successors could use the Goodman Road property to construct buildings for educational and religious purposes. Cottrell, Jennings, and Taylor served as the school's trustees. Cottrell, Jennings, and Taylor directly communicated with Attala County's superintendent of education regarding educational matters. At the time of the school's opening, the three men held community status. Cottrell worked as a laborer and possessed a two-hundred-dollar estate. Jennings, a carpenter, had an estate valued three hundred fifty dollars. Taylor worked as a carpenter and had an estate valued at five hundred dollars.[37] Samuel Young's gesture showed complications in post-slavery race relations as Young was a former slave owner of over twenty slaves. Samuel Young, born August 2, 1832, came from Allegany, Pennsylvania. Young's parents died during the first few months of his life, and he spent his early years in an orphanage. Samuel Young arrived in Kosciusko on September 1, 1850, with his brother William. Between 1855 and 1857, Young became a constable and lawyer. In 1870, he became chancellor of Mississippi's

Table 2.5 1871 Central Mississippi School Enrollment				
County	African American	White	Total	African American Population
Attala	2,509	3,794	6,303	39.81
Carroll	5,592	3,901	8,493	54.07
Madison	1,985	1,609	3,594	55.23
Montgomery	2,740	3,804	6,544	41.87
Totals	**12,826**	**13,108**	25,934	47.75

Source: Mississippi Educable Children Records. Records for Choctaw, Holmes, Leake, and Winston not available.

Table 2.6 1872 Central Mississippi School Enrollment				
County	African American	White	Total	African American Population
Attala	1,859	3,436	5,295	35.11
Carroll	3,138	3,248	6,386	49.14
Choctaw	1,170	3,861	5,031	22.26
Holmes	5,221	2,770	7,991	65.34
Leake	1,186	2,807	3,993	29.70
Madison	2,751	2,196	4,947	55.61
Montgomery	2,032	3,220	5,252	38.69
Winston	1,328	2,342	3,670	36.19
Totals	*18,685*	*23,880*	*42,565*	*41.63*

Source: Mississippi Educable Children Records.

13th district.[38] Besides his being a slave owner, there is no evidence of prior personal or working relationships with African Americans.

The Kosciusko colored school, first referred to as Sam Young, represented what African Americans envisioned. As Christopher Span described it, "schools established by and for them as a chief means of achieving independence, equality, political empowerment, and some degree of social and economic mobility—in essence, full citizenship."[39] Span captured African American psychology as it pertained to what education meant to the race. Education served as a gateway, which provided a roadmap to liberation. After Judge Samuel Young's death, the school remained under African American leadership, including George Bullock, Wilson Gerrin, and Asa Simpson.[40] The principals, who represented the highest-quality individuals, included Alfred Frazier, the first principal. His successors included Albert B. Poston,

Thomas B. Wheeler, John Wesley Bain, and William Wendell Phillips. These men represented the next generation of African American leaders. They carried the school into the twentieth century. They positioned it as a future staple in the African American community for those who followed until school integration in 1971, a century after its founding.

Attala County opened thirty-four African American schools during the decade and an additional seven schools catered to both races.[41] The number of schools matched the county's racial composition and echoed the 1867 meeting of prominent whites seeking to provide town and rural schools. Whether those individuals followed through with their plan is unknown; however, one cannot assume that African Americans played a minor role in creating their educational infrastructure. While historians focus on the unequal distribution of funds and supplies between the races, they overlook what each school building meant to the community it served. Each building represented a space where old and young minds could receive the necessary education to function in society and chart their course. By the end of 1871, there were 860 African American schools comprising nearly forty-two thousand students.[42] The former slaves understood better than anyone that without education, freedom had no value. While educational equity became institutionalized in the 1880s and beyond, such efforts to curtail Black education resulted from African Americans' concerted efforts to institutionalize education within their community.

Community Schools

1871 marked a turbulent year in Mississippi state and local politics. Jason Niles resigned his House seat and accepted a judicial appointment to Mississippi's 13th District Court. The radicals maintained their political stronghold, electing John C. Lucas to Niles's seat.[43] John Lucas previously served as Attala's sheriff, a position he first obtained in 1865 by appointment via Governor Sharkey. He maintained the position until 1870.[44] In 1871, Governor James Alcorn resigned the governorship to run for the United States Senate, succeeding Hiram Rhodes Revels, the first-ever African American senator. As African Americans pushed for more rights, the state found itself facing a major political issue, equality in public accommodations. Both Governor Alcorn and his lieutenant governor, the

Mallet (Courtesy of the Archives and
Records Services Division, Mississippi
Department of Archives and History)

Little Hill (Courtesy of the Archives and Records
Services Division, Mississippi Department of
Archives and History)

future Governor Ridgley Powers, deferred the issue instead of seeking
to focus on "material progress" and "reform," which eased the fears of
conservatives and moderate Republicans who feared "social equality."[45]
The fight for social equality pushed Mississippi beyond a point of no return,
birthing the state's infamous color line.

Legislating the Social Equality Bill, which granted citizens access to all
public accommodations, including parks, hotels, and theaters, between 1870
and 1871 introduced feelings supporting and objecting to a color line not
only in Attala County but also in the entire state.[46] As George Frederickson
surmised, the "cornerstone" of the white mindset was the belief that racial
equality was unnatural.[47] The uproar caused by the Social Equality Bill
paralleled the growing racial tensions in the county. On May 26, 1870,
Frank and Elijah Wood, white, murdered and mutilated Joel Harmon and
his nine-year-old son as they returned home from Goodman (Holmes
County), where Joel made purchases. Authorities captured Frank and Elijah
in Opelika, Alabama, and returned them to Kosciusko for trial.[48] Although
racial prejudice likely served as motivation for the crime, Blacks' emergence
as economic competitors threatening working-class whites' socioeconomic
standing gives a likely idea as to why Harmon and son lost their lives.[49]

White citizens believed the Social Equality Bill threatened the racial
hierarchy and paved the road for miscegenation.[50] African Americans also
possessed mixed feelings about the bill. The *Weekly Clarion* published African
American senator Robert Gleed's proposal for the amendment to the bill
legislated towards incorporating the Aberdeen and Elyton Railroad Company.

That no distinction shall be made between the citizens in traveling on said railroad. Any president, conductor, agent, clerk, or other person or persons making any distinction between the citizens of this state, traveling on said railroad shall be deemed guilty or a misdemeanor, and, on conviction thereof, shall be fined in a sum not to exceed five thousand dollars, nor less than one thousand dollars, and imprisoned not to exceed one year nor less than six months, or both in the discretion of the court having jurisdiction.[51]

However, Gleed's personal feelings towards social equality differed. The *Weekly Clarion* published Robert Gleed's response to what Gleed considered a misrepresentation of his position on the Social Equality Bill first reported by the *Columbus Index*. The paper later published "Letter from Senator Gleed," in which Gleed's rebuttal stated,

I notice in your issue of the 20th inst., an article headed, "Work for the Social Equality advocates," in which my name is used and I am sorry to say that I am placed in a false attitude before the public. . . . I now take this time to state that, I personally, give myself no concern whatever of the white man, his hotel, railroad coach, nor his table. My only trouble with the white man is keeping him away from me and mine. . . . "Social Equality," is something that you need have no fear of my advocating, for I am too much of a man . . . to attempt to force myself upon any person or race, that does not want my association. We will have (if desired) our own hotels, churches, farms, stores, boats, shops, factories, wives, children, &c. We want pay for our labor and the protection of the law. Give us our rights as American citizens and you will have after that, no cause or complaint against us.[52]

Robert Gleed's contrasting political and personal views illustrated Mississippi's ideological divide about race. Gleed did not see his liberation coming at whites' expense; however, many whites only understood their freedom to be at African Americans' expense. African Americans wanted equal rights based on citizenship, whereas many southern whites saw equality of any kind as a threat to their nationhood. Alcorn vetoed the bill, seeking an acceptable bill that pleased Black moderates and white Republicans.[53] At the local level, Attala County represented one area with white support for the Social Equality Bill. The stance of Rasselas Boyd, son of former Attala and Wilkerson County legislator Gordon Davis Boyd, on the Social Equality Bill polarized its white citizens. In several newspaper accounts, white citizens criticized Boyd's vote for the Social Equality Bill, accusing Boyd of saying, "He would as soon ride by a colored man in the cars as a white man."[54]

Whites opposing the bill showed their reluctance to accept social and political change and their disdain for "race traitors." In Attala County, the Social Equality Bill marked the first openly stated calls for segregation, primarily to protect white women from Black men. The emergence of African Americans as social equals threatened white sensibility and fueled white paranoia regarding "Negro" domination. The county's white conservative citizens believed that segregation would limit Black social mobility.[55] The legislation highlighted the paradox of whites and Blacks living in the same space. Both groups could not exist as autonomous, liberated entities. Whites saw the advancement of the former slave as social equals as the final nail in their redemption. Possessing whiteness no longer had any value if both races held equality in all aspects of daily life.

Vigilantes and bushwhacks existed in Attala County before the Civil War and the Ku Klux Klan emerged afterward. The earliest known attack of a vigilante group against an African American occurred in 1867 when "ruffians" of the Burt & Co. gang hung Jack Winters. His murder resulted in civil authorities taking no legal action.[56] When the county's official Ku Klux Klan formed is not known; however, Coleman described its members as seventy-five "of the best men in the county." Their purpose was to maintain order amongst "obstreperous" Blacks and whites. Quoting one Attala Klansman regarding the organization, "Things would have been absolutely intolerable without the Ku Klux."[57] While Coleman chose not to disclose the members' names, membership likely included the same men who participated in slave patrolling. Hosea Taylor encountered the Klan when they stopped by his home looking for a Black man named Orange. In his interview with Hosea Taylor., Coleman recalled the following story.

> "Uncle Hose" went to the door and saw in the yard a lot of "spirts", each one riding a horse. The horse would walk around but scarcely made any noise, their feet being muffled with bags and cloth. One of these strange beings rode up towards "Uncle Hose". His form and that of the horse was completely covered with white sheets, with queer letters and

figures on them, looking pretty scary to "Uncle Hose". He had a very large head, with a large nose located on the side of his face. His eyes were out lengthwise and altogether, the figure presented a gruesome appearance. In a low muffled voice the Spirit said that he had come from the Old World and that he was "mighty dry", and had no water since the battle of Shiloh. The darkey went out and brought him a large gourd of water, which he drank down at one gulp. Bring me a bucket of water said the spirit, "I'm thirsty". He proceeded to drink all of it, likewise the second and the third. His comrades, twelve in number, were also thirsty and wanted a little water. Each of them also proceeded to drink the contents of two or three buckets Their capacity for water seemed unlimited. As they drank the old darkey "heard their insides rattle and it "rattled like a lot of sheet iron or something like that". Finding that the negro they wanted was not there, they departed as silently as they had come.

The Klan's goal was to instill fear into Black peoples so that, as Coleman stated, "In this way the negroes became afraid of them. They would frequently ride around at night and this would have the desired effect.[58]

The Ku Klux Klan were the physical embodiment of fear most whites had about losing control over the former slave. Mississippi's Ku Klux Klan wanted to control Black people in the economic, social, and political interests of the Democratic Party, the business class, and those seeking to return the South to its pre-Reconstruction days. The enemy was anyone who posed a threat to white rule.[59] Reconstruction benefited African Americans in eradicating the Ku Klux Klan as a formal organization. Federal troops aggressively went after Klansmen, sparked by the Meridian Riot that occurred in March 1871.[60] In Attala, the United States Cavalry caught two Klansmen, one named Jennings. They tied a rope around his neck and lifted him twice to get the other members' names. Facing a possible violent outbreak from the other Klan members, the cavalry ended its inquest.[61] Federal troops arrested five men, W. D. Hunnicut, Isaac Chesnut (minor), J. D. Massie (minor), Robert Higgs, and Caleb Kellum. The troops took them to Jackson. The *Semi-Weekly Clarion* attested, "They were arrested of no crime that they know of, unless it be upon suspicion of being Ku Klux." The individuals from Beat 5 represented the political spectrum. Hunnicut was a conservative, Chesnut's father was a radical, and Higgs and Kellum had no known political affiliation.[62] The presence of federal troops to handle the Ku Klux Klan provided African Americans some protections. Six years prior, federal troops came to Attala following the assassination of a German-born Jew named Abraham Sternberger, who wanted to assist freedmen in asserting their rights.[63]

Future Attala resident Peter Cooper of Winston County provided congressional testimony regarding his encounter with the Ku Klux Klan. Peter worked as a schoolteacher and shoemaker. He testified during a period of violence against schoolteachers. Many African American schools in Winston, Noxubee, Monroe, Choctaw, Lowndes, Pontotoc, Lee, and Chickasaw succumbed to violent attacks, and teachers endured heinous crimes like murder, persecution, or expulsion from the county.[64] Peter taught school from Monday morning to Friday night. One Friday night around 1:00 a.m., thirty-seven members of the Ku Klux Klan arrived at his home. Upon learning he was not present, they broke into his home, burned his books, destroyed his shoemaking tools and clothes, and stole thirty-three dollars. Cooper did not state why the Ku Klux Klan targeted him, as he received no warning. The Klan destroyed the school, and Peter quit teaching a week later. He relocated to Macon in Noxubee County.[65] Peter later relocated to Kosciusko and worked as a shoe repairman; however, no records indicated a continued teaching career.

The Fifteenth Amendment granted African American men the right to vote, and radicals viewed suffrage as the "culmination of a lifetime of reform." In contrast, other entities viewed suffrage as "an alternative to prolonged federal intervention" and "a means of enabling blacks to defend themselves against white abuse, while relieving the nation of the responsibility." The right to vote, as Richard Yates stated, "will finish the negro question; it will settle everything connected with this question. . . . We need no vast expenditures, we need no standing army. . . . Sir, the ballot is the freeman's Moses."[66] Despite the optimism the amendment bought, voting alone could not secure liberation. By late 1871, Attala's political climate shifted. Although Republicans successfully filled Niles's seat with J. C. Lucas in 1870, the victory signaled the end of Republican victories. As the African American political agenda took shape, Redeemers worked to restore Mississippi to its glory days. On October 10, 1871, Attala County conservatives held a convention. The convention's purpose was to regroup and nominate viable candidates to win congressional seats in the next election. The convention's first declaration stated, "That sinking all minor differences and petty jealousies about party names, we hereby declare ourselves to be the opponents of Radicalism in every shape and form."[67] The resolution indicated a unified white conservative effort where one had not been prior. Boyd became the first individual Democrats targeted. The October 26, 1871, edition of the *Weekly Clarion* reported the following: "The Kosciusko Leader is after R. Boyd, the legislative tom-wit of Attala County, with a very sharp stick. Don't treat him so. If it is continued, the Rads will have to send Bro. Jim Lynch up "to put him in his little bed."[68] In the November election, Attala County proclaimed itself redeemed as Democrats won the majority by 212 votes. Rasselas Boyd lost his bid for Senate, losing to Daniel Lafayette Smythe.[69] Democrats regained political control despite African Americans having 1,013 registered voters, which would indicate conservatives gaining enough Black support in addition to high voter turnout, decreased African American turnout, or possible voter intimidation and fraud.[70]

1872 marked another rollercoaster year in local and state politics. The Social Equality Bill died after the legislature failed to override Alcorn's veto, failing in the Senate by a 15–14 vote.[71] Rasselas Boyd's Senate loss likely impacted the Senate's balance of power and the bill's eventual demise. With one political battle over, the presidential election was on the horizon. Attala Republicans, notably Boyd and Samuel Young, backed Horace Greeley, the Liberal Republican candidate.[72] Liberal Republicans saw a time for change as "they believed that when a party's objective was accomplished, new political parties should organize around the next great idea."[73] As Andrew Slap discussed, although Greeley lost, the impact of the campaign signaled the demise of Reconstruction, including "the party's retreat from its commitment to protecting the rights of Southern freedmen."[74] African Americans understood that their loyalty to the Republican Party did not equate to the party's loyalty to them. Justin Behrend examined the positive qualities that drew African Americans to the party; however, he glossed over African American dissatisfaction.[75]

Black Republicans met at the Southern State Convention of Colored Men and considered abandoning the Republican Party. However, they declined because it could risk the progress made at that point. They channeled their dissatisfaction into progressive action and used their influence to push for civil rights legislation in addition to equal funding of education and access to education.[76] Adelbert Ames acknowledged on different occasions the impact that Black Republicans had in directing state affairs. In his speech to the

United States Senate on May 20, 1872, Ames stated, "The carpet-baggers and the colored men are the controlling element of the Republican party" of Mississippi. "They controlled it when [Alcorn] was nominated and when he was elected to the Senate," Ames contended, "and they control it now, as the actions of the late [party] convention [which demanded a state civil rights bill] shows."[77] African Americans continued to show their political potency when Ulysses S. Grant won reelection. Grant carried Mississippi, including Attala County, by two hundred votes. "The negroes all voted," as the *Semi-Weekly Clarion* stated.[78]

Before the November election, Black citizens voiced their perspective on the upcoming election and what it meant to Black peoples. On September 11, 1872, Loyal League leader Peter Williams, along with his posse, rode through Attala's Newport Community making bold threats and referencing a violent attack towards white citizens regarding the November election. Constable Daniel Ocain quoted Williams saying, "You white people are down upon the loyal league, and we are down upon you, we have stood your opposition long enough, and we will give you white people hell this fall." Ocain stated Williams told his comrades "to sharpen their swords, that it would come to this and the sooner the better." Williams bragged that no law enforcement but President Grant could take him down.[79] Peter Williams represented what most whites feared, the uncontrollable "Negro," and the inevitable race war.

Despite Grant's reelection, changes in public attitudes, economic downturn, and new political faces accelerated the winds of change. African Americans began losing political control at both the state and local level, echoing what other southern states had already experienced with Democrats regaining political power. Although Adelbert Ames defeated James Alcorn in the 1873 gubernatorial election, Attala County went for Alcorn. The conservatives also dominated the legislative races and monopolized the county offices. The *Weekly Clarion* marked the victories "a grand jubilee."[80] In 1874, the *Vicksburg Herald* described Attala as a "white county, [which] has white officers, and its affairs are managed with honesty and economy," and quoting the *Kosciusko Star* stated, "While blood-shed and riot is rife in those localities ruled by vice and ignorance, we are happy to say that peace reigns supreme throughout our borders; and this is always the case where honest and capable men are put at the head of affairs."[81]

The white-line strategy ended Republican rule and restored power to the Democrats,[82] echoing Justin Behrend's analysis that "all across Mississippi in the summer and fall of 1875, white-line Democratic clubs organized and began to lay the groundwork for a coup d'état. The planned takeover of the state government depended on numerous local campaigns against Republican officeholders and voters."[83] Months before the 1875 November election, Attala Republicans met on August 16. D. C. Wasson served as chairman, with Stephen Elias Wilson and Alfred Frazier serving as secretaries. The meeting's purpose was to support Jason Niles's congressional bid and his son Henry Niles's bid for district attorney. The *Weekly Mississippi Pilot* described the meeting as "one of the largest ever held in the county, showing that the Republicans of the county enter upon the canvass with a determination to win."[84] Despite party support for Jason Niles, who ran against conservative Otho R. Singleton in Mississippi's Fourth Congressional District, Niles had fallen from political grace and was viewed as a political pariah.

The *Canton Mail* published the following from the *Vicksburg Herald* regarding Niles: "Poor old Jason Niles, the wretched renegade who disgraced Himself by voting for Grant's Force Bill at the last session of Congress, is wandering about in the Fourth District looking out for a re-election. If there is a white man in the district who is shamelass [sic] enough to vote for Jason Niles, after he voted . . . to give Grant the power to pin the people of Mississippi down with bayonets, he deserves to be kicked by a drunken negro from one end of the district to the other."[85] In a debate held on October 9, 1875, the *Daily Clarion* ripped Niles and praised Singleton for his performance. Singleton attacked Niles for supporting the Force Bill, betraying the county's white citizens, stating, "Niles is done for in Attala."[86] Niles received 1,215 votes to Singleton's 1859. Democrats elected David Thomas Guyton, Joseph K. Shrock, and Sylvanus T. Oldham to the House and Senate. With Niles's defeat, the county's Black Republicans had no county representation in political office. At the state level, the house of representatives possessed a seventy-seven-seat majority, ninety-six to twenty-three. The twenty-three Republicans included one Independent Republican and two fusion Republicans. African Americans held fourteen seats, which included ten Republicans, one Independent Republican, two fusion Republicans, and one Democrat. In the Senate, Democrats held a thirteen-seat majority, twenty-five to twelve. African Americans held five Republican seats.[87] Restoring power did not entail African Americans ceding the control and power they had accumulated. The Redeemers faced African Americans emboldened with citizenship and expecting the privileges it carried. The transformation of the former slave to citizen irritated most whites because, as Minnesota's Senator William Windom stated, "The black man does not excite antagonism because he is black, but because he is a citizen, and as such may control an election."[88]

With the Democrats in firm control of the state legislature and county offices across the state, the South positioned itself to redeem the Old South into a New South, a new white nation. As the decade ended, the *Kosciusko Star* published the following regarding the Democratic Party.

> The moving of the political waters will soon again begin. The great principles that achieved the deliverance of the people from the ungodly rule of Radicalism in 1875 will be maintained in this county. Though there are a number of candidates from the various offices, at present, still when the Democracy of the county, in convention or primary election, shall say who are to be the candidates of the party in the ensuing campaign, all others, like good Democrats that they are, will bow with becoming grace to the will of the majority and enter into the enthusiastic support of the nominees. Each will subordinate his private opinions and personal preferences to the harmony of the party, the peace and quiet of the people and the general public good. "Independents" (only a modest name for Radicals) will find but little encouragement in Attala.[89]

These words reflected non-Democratic success since 1875. Henry Clay Niles ran for Congress in 1877 as an Independent, finishing tied second with David Thomas Guyton to Frederick M. Glass. Glass received 1,233 votes to Niles's 1,180.[90] Attala County's return to Democratic rule appeared as a legitimate shift in political power. No one political party had ever dominated the county since 1850. The infusion of former slaves as voters gave Republicans small majorities. The county had no recorded actions of voter-related violence. Since the early Reconstruction years, the county's voting environment reflected a democratic process as

> the voters were formed in a long line, two abreast, usually two white men followed by two negroes, and marched by a window and handed their votes in from the outside. Ropes were stretched at a distance of forty feet from the window, just wide enough to allow two to march abreast. There was no other way of reaching the window, except by

forming in the line between these ropes. In this way there was very little intimidation of votes. Such means were not resorted to as a general thing, although it is said that the negroes were fooled a lot of times by allowing the white men to inspect their votes after they were in the line. This was, however, very exceptional.[91]

The South had achieved some redemption regarding removing the federal government; however, they now had to contend with a familiar and more formidable opponent. Mississippi's violent persona existed but was quelled during the federal occupation. However, once free of their Northern irritant, Mississippi lapsed back into its Wild West ways. Most of the state was a frontier before the war and did not undergo urbanization during the federal Reconstruction. African Americans waited too long and worked too hard to fold because the federal government's Reconstruction program failed. Rather than Reconstruction's end representing a delaying of liberty, as Bradley Bond surmised, or the "Fall of Democracy," as Justin Behrend contended, Reconstruction's end served as a point in the liberation era reinforced African Americans were solely responsible for their liberation. As the state moved entered a new decade, they would continue pushing forward and building on their gains outside the political arena.

With Democrats returning to political power and national interest shifting away from civil-rights initiatives, African American life continued. They did not idly sit to observe the agenda of new political regimes. Churches, schools, and communities pushed forward and furthered their missions, especially educational advancement. African Americans took advantage of the education system as a means of racial progression and advancement.[92] This push, by the middle of the decade, solidified white fears of education's impact. White attitudes towards education had little influence on African American attitudes towards their educational aspirations. The white majority in Mississippi objected to African American education and wanted to control African American schools' educational content to maintain the white social order.[93] The planter class objected to African Americans obtaining education for different reasons than the social order challenge. They needed African Americans in the fields; however, African Americans' growing commitment to education meant that there would be fewer bodies in the fields and more in the classrooms.[94]

Referencing education, Jay Stowell stated,

The "forbidden fruit" had become the one thing African Americans supremely desired. There was little or no attempt to take over the property of former masters; slight was the concern for material possessions so long as there was a rag to cover the body, a crust of bread to eat, or a shelter of any sort available; the supreme passion was the passion for learning. The school was the one thing needful, and the ability to read and write was the golden key to unlock the riches of the world.[95]

Education represented mental decolonization. African Americans seized what former slaveholders had aggressively withheld and what many post–Civil War whites objected to or took for granted. Objections only emphasized education's importance. According to the Commissioner of Education Report (Tables 2.7 and 2.8), African American school enrollment outnumbered white enrollment for the remainder of the decade, with 1877 being the exception.[96] The Commissioner of Education Report's available statistics indicated that African American students in public schools had higher enrollment and monthly attendance than white students.

Educational pursuits signified education's role in the liberation narrative and its place in post-slavery Zion. School enrollment and attendance numbers indicate a passion for a race to learn and grow. While Christopher Span framed the 1870s as necessary in Black education, he also doubted their participation in the system. He stated, "The dramatic growth in black student enrollment is somewhat misleading, however, and should be approached with caution. This development is only an indication of the increased educational opportunities of black Mississippians following the state's readmission into the Union. The dramatic increase in enrollment offers very little information regarding the type or quality of schooling black children received during these formative years."[97] Such statements undercut Black-liberation efforts. Span downplayed or lacked knowledge of Mississippi's African American education class. Because Span's work marginalized Black educators and students' lived experiences, he missed the opportunity to learn who educated African Americans and how during these formative years.

Freedmen and women set out to build a home that laid the foundations for growth and advancement. While they sought societal inclusion, they began building a self-sustaining home that could withstand large-scale societal decay. Cesaire examined in *Discourse on Colonialism* how a civilization must

Table 2.7 Mississippi School Enrollment, 1875–1879			
Year	African American	White	Total	African American Composition
1875	89,813	78,404	168,217	53.39%
1876	90,178	76,026	166,204	54.26%
1877	76,154	84,334	160,488	47.45%
1878	104,777	101,201	205,978	50.87%
1879	111,796	105,957	217,753	51.34%
Totals	472,718	445,922	918,640	51.46%

Source: Report of the Commissioner of Education for the year 1880 and Report of the Commissioner of Education published in 1883 and 1884.

Table 2.8 Mississippi Monthly School Attendance, 1875–1879			
Year	African American	White	Total	African American Composition
1875	74,265	65,065	139,330	53.30%
1876	68,580	65,384	133,964	51.19%
1877	55,814	63,943	119,757	46.61%
1878	88,660	82,566	171,226	51.78%
1879	91,809	88,750	180,559	50.85%
Totals	379,128	365,708	744,836	50.75%

Source: Report of the Commissioner of Education for the year 1880 and Report of the Commissioner of Education published in 1883 and 1884.

solve its own problems of which it is the source and adhere to the very rules and guidelines that governs its people. If a civilization fails to do so, it is a decadent, sick, and dying civilization.[98] The South represented dying civilizations because the Union failed to address the issues that plagued the region; therefore, despite African Americans seeking societal inclusion, they understood the necessity of creating a home base that would best serve their interest until the broader society positioned itself to be a nation for all peoples. African Americans began building their Zion individually and collectively, with and without white cooperation. The decade was not one spent solely on the cottonfields. African Americans began building the foundations of community necessary to establish a stable and legitimate home. The pace at which they laid the groundwork and constructed their post-slavery home showed no hesitation or confusion about their agenda. Their continued upward trajectory showed that Reconstruction's end did not mean African American slowdown. The race relied on themselves more than the federal government. The next chapter analyzes how Attala's African American liberation efforts took full flight, setting the stage for racially motivated actions designed to punish African Americans as they pursued their quests for liberation.

CHAPTER 3

TAKING FLIGHT
MOVING TOWARDS A LIBERATED ZION

The 1880s represented a decade where African Americans continued building their homes, communities, and institutions while reaping past work benefits. In the wake of Democrats returning to political power and the former Confederacy having the privilege of home rule, African Americans did not wither. They continued with their several missions and pushed the expected boundaries, asserting their citizenship as they defined it. The Democratic Party unified around the principle of white supremacy, a concept that swept the party into power during the latter years of Reconstruction. African Americans found themselves on the defensive and sought ways to remain politically viable. In April 1880, the Attala Republicans selected delegates to the state convention on May 6 in Jackson. Of the ten delegates selected, African Americans occupied four positions: Fred Jennings (Beat 1), John Thomas (Beat 2), Alfred Frazier (Beat 3), and Emanuel Huffman (Beat 5), in addition to George Munson, who held an alternate position. They served alongside Henry Clay Niles, Samuel Conly, Spencer Guess, Amos Richardson, John Sanders, Calvin Clements, and Joe Thompson, who served as an alternate. The delegates to the state convention had instructions to cast their vote for James Blaine for president.[1] Blaine's primary opponent was James A. Garfield. Garfield once stated he had "a strong feeling of repugnance when I think of the negro being made our political equal and I would be glad if they could be colonized, sent to heaven, or got rid of in any decent way. . . . But colonization has proved a hopeless failure everywhere."[2] African

Americans now held the power to use their political presence to vote against an individual espousing such views. In May, the convention took place and included powerhouse political figures including Blanche K. Bruce, James Hill, and John Roy Lynch. Following the convention, records do not provide evidence of active Black participation in Attala for much of the decade, a trend that changed in the decades that followed.

The Democratic Party secured political victories when they subdued African Americans and their allies from political power; however, restructuring life to reflect racial-superiority ideals proved more difficult. As early as 1875, the county's political leaders endorsed the color line; however, despite this endorsement, a color line was not firmly established.[3] Segregation faced opposition from both sides of the racial aisle.[4] Some whites did not want to risk the cordial relationships established with "good" African Americans. As Du Bois summarized in *Black Reconstruction in America*, whites invented the color line to deny Black people their freedoms; however, Black people countered their actions.[5] While some African Americans did not wish to fight segregation to avoid the risk of diminishing the socioeconomic and political relationships they had built with whites, African Americans also rejected segregation in its entirety, and some saw no need to push for integrating spaces unwelcoming to them.[6] Pro-segregationists had limited control of segregating everyday life because African Americans had their vision of the "New South" that did not conform to a southern white agenda. Throughout the process of permanent racial separation, circumstances arose in which racial code "violations" between African Americans and whites occurred, resulting in social exchanges that challenged the color line's concept and intent.

Leon Litwack explained that African Americans were not content with whites referring to them in racial terms; therefore, African Americans disregarded the social norms and racial etiquette of the slave era.[7] Liberation did not mean integration but the freedom to choose where and how to operate in society. African American women played a pivotal role in shaping the color line and the politics of racial etiquette.[8] In households containing mixed-race children, Black women held white men accountable for their children and household. While it is easy to assume these men were noble and honorable, Black mothers secured their children's legitimacy and stability. Ceele Johnson-Carr, Jeanette Atkinson, and Artie Rainey legally obligated their white partners to acknowledge and provide for their families.

Ceele Johnson and Alfred Carr (Morgan Freeman's great-great-grandparents) had an interracial family stemming from slavery. Ceele Johnson, born in April 1824 in Tennessee, belonged to John Johnson (Johnston), a Tennessee farmer. He bought Ceele to the Ethel township in the 1840s. Through the Johnson family, Ceele met Alfred Carr. Born in 1800 in North Carolina to parents of French nativity, Alfred worked as a farm laborer for John Johnson.[9] Between 1847 and 1856, Ceele gave birth to Alfred's children: James Henry, Alexander, Franklin Anderson, William Erastus, and Elizabeth.[10] Following slavery, Alfred and Ceele continued to live as a family. The household included Green, Dewitt, and Luiza, Ceele's children born during the war years, not fathered by Alfred. The 1870 census listed the oldest children as white. The 1880 census referred to Alfred and Ceele as a married couple, listing Ceele as the household's head and Alfred as the husband. Alfred retained his white status while Ceele and their children held a mulatto racial status.[11] Before the 1880 school year commenced, parents and guardians registered their children with the county's superintendent's office. Alfred listed himself as the parent/guardian for Ceele's three youngest Johnson children but did not list the children as Carr. Their interracial family demonstrated that law could not dictate family formation or activity. Upon Alfred's death, the family buried him in the Carr Graveyard, which became integrated as other Black families used it for burial. Mississippi law prevented integrated cemeteries.

Alfred was not an anomaly. During the late 1860s, Jeanette Atkinson and Richard Bullock began a relationship that produced four children, Mary, Mattie, Eliza, and James. Richard Bullock was born in South Carolina. By 1841, he settled in Attala County, where he owned as many as fourteen slaves between 1840 and 1860.[12] By 1880, Jeanette and Richard lived as neighbors, likely sharing a household, given their shared children and Richard's advanced age. Unlike Alfred, Richard did not claim Jeanette's children born in slavery, namely Emily, Richard, Lee Anna, and Mariah. In the same 1880 school registry, Richard registered his and Jeanette's children in the Mallet School and listed the children as Bullock.[13] When Democrats regained control of county offices, Richard became a leader within the party. Richard's presence provided his children the possibility to escape societal hardships and use the Bullock name to navigate the changing political times. The Bullock children lived a life that reflected their father's influence. They received an education, owned land, the daughters married educated and politically active men, and the children used their father's name in their adult life. Richard did not

Franklin Anderson Carr (From the *Star Herald:*
The Twentieth Century: A Pictorial History of
Kosciusko, Mississippi 1866–1999, submitted by

Alfred Carr (Courtesy of Virginia Clark)   Katherine Carr Esters. Courtesy of Jo A. Baldwin.)

extend his paternity as freely as Alfred, nor legally as did Aaron Whitaker
Guyton. The latter publicly acknowledged his mixed-race children and his
mistress while legally incorporating them into his white family.

Aaron Whitaker Guyton, born on November 22, 1808, in Pendleton, South
Carolina, never married or had children with white women.[14] Aaron owned
two slaves, Sarah and Patsy, with whom he had sexual relationships producing
four children, Caroline, Pinckney, Elijah, and Adeline. Following slavery,
Aaron contracted with Sarah and his children, paying them collectively
fifteen dollars a month. Aaron had a relationship with Artie Guyton. Between
1866 and 1878, their relationship produced seven children: Andrew, James,
Casey, Maggie, Anna Black, Simon, and Isaac. Aaron lived with his children
Pinckney and Elijah, who carried his last name. Towards the end of his
life, he lived with his mistress, Sarah, and her husband, Green Russell. On
December 5, 1881, Aaron filed his will with the Attala County Chancery
Court. The document's first provision called for Artie Rainey's "colored"
children to receive land, two choice mules, one wagon, and a year-long
supply of corn, meat, and other supplies. Aaron provided the children with
household furniture and farm tools for the continued operation of the farm.

Harriet Rice Adams
(Courtesy of LaShawn Speed, MA)

In the will, Aaron did not explicitly claim the children as his own. However, the likelihood that a white man would legally provide for children with whom he had no connection is not high. Aaron provided Artie's children legal recognition as Aaron's nephew, J. W. S. Guyton administered the will.[15] Aaron's descendants came to occupy a unique position in Attala society as their Guyton relatives rose to political prominence as lawyers and politicians, notably David Thomas Guyton.

Black women complicated the social order via interracial relationships.[16] They exploited white men's lustful desires and empowered themselves by using their counterpart's power for self and family advancement. Anna Julia Cooper discussed Black women's marginalization as a socially constructed process that stemmed from the domination that men (white men) asserted over their lives. White men perceived themselves to have complete domination over women, including women's mobility within the public and private sphere. Although white men crafted the myth of the hypersexual, immoral Black woman, Black women saw that they could use their sexuality to their advantage. Sex became a tool to acquire freedom.[17] In the post-emancipation era, Black women used sexual relationships with white men to challenge their social, economic, and political marginalization. These relationships represented the race, gender, class, and sexuality power intersections that favored Black women. White men had the power in these concubine-type relationships and could refuse to honor any obligation without consequence.[18] However, in these situations, African American women possessed leverage and power over their white partners. Ceele, Jeanette, and Artie produced their partner's only children. The men had no white spouse or legally recognized white offspring; therefore, the only heirs to carry forward their father's surname lay with the Black woman. African American women represented more than baby-making machines and disposable bodies. The mixed-race class was more than fatherless bastards or a "particular" class of Negroes. Together, Black women and mixed-race children represented a threat to the redemption agenda. Although Black by law, they possessed an outlet to a white power source, and as James Baldwin stated in *The Fire Next Time*, "The only thing that white people have that black people need, or should want, is power—and no one holds power forever."[19] Mixed-race peoples could not obtain the white status without passing; therefore, using a combination of skin color and power connections, they acted in ways that positioned them as untouchable by the white community at large.

African Americans pushed the boundaries of social acceptability beyond sexual relationships and extended them into labor relationships. Bettie Howard, a white housekeeper, lived in the home of George and Harriet Adams. The Adams, an African American family, lived in the Blackjack neighborhood. George W. Adams, born on February 12, 1848, worked as a farmer. He also belonged to the Buffalo United Methodist Church. Harriet (nee Rice), born July 15, 1853, was of mixed Native American and European descent. She lived a quasi-free life until age five when her grandfather, Leonard Rice, died, and his widow enslaved her and her mother and brother. During the time of Bettie's presence in the Adams' home, they had three children, Tallulah (Lillian), David, and Kate.

Mary Ann Eliza "Bettie" Howard was born on February 11, 1839, in Alabama.[20] She was the daughter of William Howard and Martha Rebecca Malone. Bettie's grandmother, Judith Malone, raised her.[21] As an adult, Bettie worked as a housekeeper, finding employment and residence in 1868 with Judge Samuel Young.[22] According to a letter Samuel Young wrote in 1871, Bettie possessed an impeccable reputation. Young wrote,

> I now sincerely pray for wisdom, and commit myself body and soul together with my sacred earthly charges my own and brother's family, not forgetting Miss Bettie Howard who has been in my house as a member of my family for three years past. She is one of the best women I ever saw, amiable, kind affectionate and useful. She is a treasure in my household and my heart goes out to her as to one of my children, or as I imagine it would be to a sister.[23]

While Young's words may reflect speaking fondly of a sweet nanny, his words reflected his affections towards a white woman. Following her tenure with the Young family, Bettie became the Adams' housekeeper. African Americans with live-in housekeepers were a growing trend in the Buffalo Community. Nicholas McLemore employed two women, Clara Curtis and Jane Coleman, and Wesley Adams employed a servant, Charley Bullock (Oprah Winfrey's great-grandfather). George and Harriet also employed an African American servant named Andy Ashford. Unlike the Adams, these families employed only African American servants. There is no clear-cut evidence that can answer the question of what circumstances led Bettie to live and work in the Adams' household; however, based on existing evidence, George and Harriet's economic and social standing put them in a position to hire Bettie.

Bettie Howard was more than a poor-white-trash woman. She had connections to a political power source, a commonality shared with Harriet. During this time, Harriet's first cousin was prominent judge William Van Davis. The connection to the law could explain how an arrangement not only occurred but also endured no backlash. As a white woman, Bettie had more to lose. She risked her reputation and self-respect by placing herself in a position that blurred, if not flipped, racial and class normativity. She positioned herself as a social equal to Black peoples, and as the Adams' employee, they held authority. As Thavolia Glymph stated, "In the antebellum period, white women were clearly subordinate in fundamental ways to men, but far from being victims of the slave system, they dominated slaves."[24] The working dynamic between the two women comes into question. How did Bettie respond to orders given by Harriet? Did Bettie address Harriet as "Mrs. Adams?" Did Harriet address Bettie by her first name or address her help as "Aunt Bettie?"

One may surmise that George and Harriet viewed Bettie as another employee despite her race, or they hired Bettie to break the societal expectation of Black women as domestic help. On January 20, 1867, Harriet's mother Frances contracted with L. A. Webster to work as a housekeeper.[25] Witnessing her mother perform domestic duties likely played a role in Harriet not wanting her children to see domestic services as their only option in life. Stephanie Shaw explained that mothers and fathers alike understood the type of exploitation that Black women faced in domestic and non-domestic work; therefore, parents sought to provide their daughters with enough formal education to escape those conditions.[26] The formal education

George W. Adams (Courtesy of Jerone Garland)   George W. Bullock (Courtesy of Trenace V. Ford)

Wesley Chapel church as built in 1881, circa 1934 (Courtesy of Mary Van Ford)

that Shaw discussed was schooling; however, George and Harriet's situation represented parents giving their children a formal education in the game of life. An indication that this approach worked showed through their daughter, Tallulah. Tallulah became a teacher and married a teacher. Tallulah's oldest daughter operated a grocery store, and their youngest daughter became both a teacher and an administrator. Bettie Howard's case stands as the only example of such labor arrangement; however, within the broader liberation theme, George and Harriet represented how a liberated society could look and function.

Black labor began to shift away from cotton production as their primary source of income, and the decade saw the birth of the Black merchant class. In 1880, Mississippi produced 963,111 cotton bales. Attala County was one of twelve counties and the largest cotton producer in the short-leaf pine and oak upland region, producing 15,285 cotton bales.[27] Attala County's white laborers raised 8,613 cotton bales, compared to 5,924 bales African American laborers raised.[28] Although one may associate Black labor and cotton, the land boom of the 1870s continued, with more African Americans purchasing land in the 1880s. As landowners, they controlled their crop production. White laborers producing higher amounts of cotton should not be shocking given that most yeoman farmers were sharecroppers, and as Harold Woodman stated, "No respecter of race, tenancy involved more whites than Negroes; indeed, tenancy rose more rapidly among whites."[29] Farmers, in general, began to shift from cotton production; as William B. Dana noted in his 1878 study that farmers increased the amount of food grown, allowing them to become less dependent on lenders.[30] Although cotton played a key role in countless African Americans' lives, it was not always "king."

Crop diversity indicated a shift from cotton to other cash crops. As a Louisiana newspaper stated, "Southern farmers would never be prosperous so long as they concentrated their entire effort on cotton growing."[31] By 1880, Indian corn accounted for approximately 91 percent of Mississippi's agricultural output at 21,340,800 bushels. Attala County produced the most Indian corn in the short-leaf pine and oak region. The county produced 413,532 bushels. Other crops grown in the county included 66,106 bushels of oats, 6,981 bushels of wheat, and 66,782 bushels of sweet potatoes.[32] Farmers in Attala County prospered as the *Kosciusko Star* reported in 1883 that "farmers of that vicinity are more prosperous now than at any time since the war. During the coming season they will raise a large amount of corn and meat."[33] The statement pointed to crop yields from 1882, about which the *Kosciusko Star* stated, "Those farmers in our county who raised corn are receiving $1.20 per bushel for it as the wagons leave their cribs." and "the wheat crop in Attala is not large, but the yield per acre is very good. Oats, however, are superabundant."[34]

Farming represented an organic southern occupation, the one occupation most freedmen/women had the most expertise and skills in. African American farmers knew the value of cash crops stemming from labor-contract payments. As independent farmers, African Americans controlled the totality of their harvest.[35] Elizabeth Bethel painted a similar portrayal of African American farmers in the Promised Land community in Abbeville, South Carolina. Farmers in the community developed an economic strategy that centered on subsistence farming and less on cotton production. The rationale was that de-emphasizing cotton cultivation correlated to economic independence.[36] As Bethel stated, "Through this strategy many of them avoided the 'economic nightmare,' which fixated the status of other small-scale cotton growers at a level of permanent peonage well into the twentieth century."[37] Bethel highlighted the African American farmer as possessing the freedom to choose how to diversify their labor. Some understood the necessity to use their land and labor to propel themselves beyond the status quo. In Attala County, Black farmers such as Caleb Stewart, Alexander Carr, James Carr, Scott Raiford, Scott Fletcher, John Winters, and George Eubanks rose to prominence for their agricultural successes. African Americans showed that cotton was not their king as it was for others. The freedom to produce crops and raise livestock of choice was a farmer's dream.

Beyond agriculture, African Americans expanded into other areas of business. Former slaves took their skills and translated them into profitable occupations, while others learned skills to create businesses. They created an economy that included grocery stores, hotels, jewelry shops, blacksmithing shops, and other businesses. Attala County's business economy rebounded shortly after the Civil War. The earliest advertisements in local papers featured white businesses such as D. B. Comfort, Atkins & White (drug and medicine), Simon & Bro., W. D. Sneed & Co. (dry goods), Thomas L. Ford and Sam Sanders (confectionary). Other businesses included shoe shops, saloons, restaurants, and hotels.[38] African American businesses openly competed with their white counterparts. Bradley Bond stated regarding attitudes toward Black labor, "Common knowledge among contemporaries held that the closer a white man stood to African Americans in matters of economics, the more jealously he defended his tenuous status as a free man."[39]

African Americans did not allow white self-reassurance to come at their expense. They built a working middle-class that insulated their community while pushing the boundaries of integration. In most rural towns, the town square served as the business hub. The town square consisted of the courthouse and business surrounding the courthouse on four sides. African Americans such as Alfred Frazier operated businesses amongst whites within and near this space. On November 28, 1881, Jason Niles detailed a fire that destroyed sections of the town square, including Alfred Frazier's grocery store.[40] Frazier's grocery store existed alongside white grocery stores. His business integrated the county's physical environment and possibly its social environment if it equally served both a white and Black clientele. Frazier's store stood alongside Sneed's store, Dr. Lee's store, Andrew Jobes's bank, Joe M. Smith's retail, Eugene Jennings's grocery, Breyer's shop, Greenwald's store, Tobe Boswell's drugstore, Saw and Carr's grocery, Frank Harper's grocery, Ike Scarborough's Law Offices, and Edward's grocery house.[41]

Without any redistribution of wealth coming soon, African Americans played the capitalist game to advance their upward mobility.[42] The Black business class provided goods and services to both races. As one of two Black jewelers, Frazier also operated a watch repair store, the other being Seaborn Spikes.[43] Asa Simpson was the county's first Black grocer. His store's location was adjacent to the town's square, where he also operated a hotel for African Americans.[44] Frazier also served as a prominent figure in education and politics, making him a triple threat for liberation. Simpson worked primarily in farming before venturing into entrepreneurship. Ted Ownby's *Dreams in Mississippi: Consumers, Poverty, & Culture, 1830–1998* omitted the African American business class, choosing to limit African Americans as beholden to white-operated general stores, which assumed that Black peoples did not operate businesses. Ownby concluded, "Further isolating African Americans from the process of spending and shopping was the fact that so few of them were involved in selling goods. With virtually no access to credit, African Americans were slow to become store owners."[45] Ownby's analysis lacks insight into African American life and the measures the race took to acquire capital, which stemmed from being business-minded. In Ownby's explanation of the African American business owner, he stated that having a space that served for leisure and commerce while shopping without an outsider status was the primary motivation.[46] This perspective, while valid, portrayed Black businesses as responses to white exclusion rather than as pushing an economic agenda that provided the African American business class the opportunity for new avenues of wealth accumulation. African Americans benefited from their Black business class that included Jim Mallett, Sol Jamison, and Thomas Griffin, who opened grocery stores. Sol Jamison's business success earned him a sterling reputation among local whites.[47] Mary Alice Alston, Alexander Jones, and Howard Huffman joined the growing list of Black entrepreneurs in the twentieth century.

Reverend Charles A. Buchanan (From the *Western Age* [Langston, OK], April 23, 1909)

The way Black businesses operated shows that Frazier and Simpson's stores did business with both Black and white customers. George Bullock's barbershop possessed an interracial clientele. George Bullock, born to Mary Bullock in October 1865, became a barber and went into business with William N. Dorrill and opened a barbershop. The year the shop opened is not known. George placed advertisements in the *Kosciusko Star* that read "GEO BULLOCK THE BARBER SOUTH SIDE SQUARE. A good shave and a good Hair-Cut are what you require and want."[48] According to the *History of Kosciusko*, his patrons kept their shaving mugs at the shop displaying their names and initials.[49] Bullock competed with a white barber, J. E. Compton, who came to Kosciusko from Copiah County. Compton hired Alex Webber, reported as "the swiftest manipulator of the razor who ever struck Kosciusko."[50] Black capitalists forced whites to see them in a different color: green. Black people as economic competitors served as the catalyst for violence and even death. Whether such incidents happened to Kosciusko's Black business owners remains unknown.

Churches remained a strong presence—seventeen churches of the Baptist, Methodist, and Presbyterian denominations organized during the decade. In 1880, Wesley Chapel formed amidst a 13 percent decline in Black membership in the Mississippi Conference, attributed to the Northern exodus.[51] Some Black peoples chose to build Zion beyond their immediate post-slavery home. As Nell Irvin Painter explained, "Black people . . . struck out for their freedom, real freedom . . . left home on the strength of their faith in their ultimate deliverance from the terrorists and extortionists of the white South."[52] In January 1879, in what newspapers described as "Liberia fever," Reverend Parson Marshall of Holmes County led forty African Americans from Attala and Choctaw Counties in their hopes to find a new home in "this supposed land of Canaan."[53] In April 1880, the *Kosciusko Star* reported to the *Weekly Clarion* that "ninety-nine more poor deluded negroes took the train at this place bound for Kansas."[54] John Marcus Nevils served as the church's first pastor. Alfred Frazier, Hanson Huffman, Isaac Coulter, and Allen Smith served as the church's first trustees.[55] Born in February 1848, John Nevils came from Monroe County, where he joined the Methodist Conference in 1872. After serving churches in Holmes, Pontotoc, and Alcorn Counties, John came to Kosciusko. During his first tenure, Wesley erected a church at a point that was "perhaps the highest hill in Kosciusko to erect their church,"[56] giving the members a literal elevated sense of belonging.

Churches provided more than spiritual and moral guidance. Churches exposed congregations to some of the brightest individuals the race had to offer. During the decade, several influential pastors passed through First Baptist, shaping the institution as a social and political pillar of Kosciusko's African American society. All came from an educational background, ranging from high school to college, serving as teachers before their ministry. Harrison L. Young, born on May 1, 1852, served as the second pastor. A native of Abbeville, South Carolina, Harrison was brough by Sam and Amy Young to Vaiden, Mississippi, in 1858. He received his early education in night schools in Vaiden and the Winona public schools. After graduating from Jackson College, he became pastor at Mt. Zion Baptist Church, where he grew the church by two hundred members. His success led to First Baptist Church seeking his leadership.[57] John H. Nichols, the third pastor, was born on June 2, 1859, in Pickens, Alabama. As a child, he came to Macon, Mississippi, after being sold. Once emancipated, John obtained education at a Quaker school, working for a Quaker teacher. Nichols began teaching, earning the title "best teacher in Noxubee county, Miss." After being ordained, he attended Roger Williams University for further theological studies. His work with the Kosciusko First Baptist Church came during a period in which Nichols helped organize several churches and Sunday schools, including baptizing four hundred African Americans.[58]

John Wesley Bain's Teacher's Contract (Courtesy of Cheryl Bayne)

Charles Buchanan used his position as pastor to embark on a change agenda. Born on February 22, 1860, to John and Ann Buchanan, near Brooksville in Noxubee County, Charles did not have consistent education. He attended school when the opportunity presented itself. By age eighteen, he became an educational professional and later taught in Winston County. While teaching, Buchanan received his call to the ministry. He received his ordainment in Mt. Calvary Baptist Church, which led him to New Garden Baptist Church in rural Attala. Upon becoming the preacher at First Baptist, succeeding John H. Nichols, Charles tackled the intemperance issue.[59] First Baptist Church hosted the sixteenth annual session of the General Baptist

John Wesley Bain
(Courtesy of Cheryl Bayne)

Missionary Association of Mississippi. During the session, the former pastor and corresponding secretary, John H. Nichols stated, "We must do something for our school, or build a house; much dissatisfaction prevails about the school. We need to be more united. Many district associations are making efforts to build schools in their midst, so that the usefulness of our Education Board is much impaired. I think it well for each district to carry on education in its own way . . . We know that education is a great and powerful lever, and every one should have it."[60] The education advances made in the prior decade remained central to the community agenda, taking a more political stance within the church.

African American women gained a more significant presence in the church during the decade. First Baptist Church hosted the annual meeting for the Women's General Baptist Missionary Society. The Women's General Baptist Missionary Society became the first organized group led by African American women within the state's Baptist Church organization. During the fourteenth session of the General Baptist Association held in Canton on October 20, 1886, Reverends I. L. Crawford, T. L. Jordan, and Brother J. J. Spelman discussed the topic "Women's Work." The discussion led to them creating a committee consisting of J. J. Spelman, H. Woodsmall, C. A. Buchanan, A. Reed, and S. P. Martin "to take under consideration of propriety of effecting a temporary organization for Woman's Work."[61] The first executive board consisted of the following women: Addell McLaughlin, Mrs. J. F. Boulden, and Mrs. W. S. Foote.[62] African American women acted on instinct rather than permission and organized to provide "intellectual, moral and spiritual progress of the Negro Baptist of Mississippi."[63] Collier-Thomas explained that the rise in Black women's presence stemmed from their complaining of a lack of activity within the church beginning around 1880.[64]

The organization's second annual meeting took place at the Kosciusko Baptist Church, with thirty-eight societies and forty-one delegates. Despite the organization's long history, the second annual meeting provides one of the few detailed meeting agendas. During the meeting, women gave speeches, preached sermons, and presented papers. In her paper, Sister H. E. Moody stated, "Woman is ever ready to soothe the disconsolate, cheer the cast down, and inspire with vigor, hope and life the soldier of the cross. . . . woman has a position of power which we fear she does not always use. . . . We hope that the time is not far distant when she shall recognize and claim her position."[65] Annie Allen, R. D. Valentine, and Laura Alexander also presented at the meeting. In addition to these meetings providing a space for which African American women could display their intellectual capacity, the meetings demonstrated the financial value they brought to the church. The second annual meeting raised $146.75. The amount combined with the $95.85 raised during the meeting totaled $242.60.[66] Black women were pivotal to the church and eventually began independent religious pursuits; as Collier-Thomas stated, "As women organized and developed programs and became master philanthropists, they gained skills in their ability to lead."[67] In the decades to follow, Black women's roles within various churches and organizations expanded.

African Americans made significant use of the public-school system to seek personal and racial advancement (Tables 3.1 and 3.2).[68] During the 1880s, they demonstrated their educational desires through school enrollment, attendance, and the growing number of Black teachers. The 1880 state census indicated an increase in Attala County's African American school enrollment compared to the previous decade. African American enrollment outpaced white enrollment throughout the 1880s.[69] The *Clarion* emphasized that the number of students enrolled lagged the total number of educable students. African American students in public schools had higher monthly attendance than white students, indicating the seriousness with which African Americans took education. Forty-eight percent of African Americans and 44 percent of white school-age children did not attend schools, which prompted a call for compulsory attendance since tax dollars paid teachers' salaries. Despite African American students making up the school-going majority, Mississippi hired more white teachers. The state employed 3,314 white teachers and 2,644 Black teachers, putting the student-teacher ratio for whites at 27:1 and 39:1 for Blacks.[70] Attala County echoed state enrollment trends. According to

Table 3.1 Mississippi Total School Enrollment, 1882–1885				
Year	African American Enrollment	White Enrollment	Total	African American Enrollment Percent
1882	109,630	104,451	214,081	51.21%
1883	141,398	125,598	266,996	52.96%
1884	149,373	129,647	279,020	53.53%
1885	125,633	101,655	227,288	55.27%
Totals	526,034	461,351	987,385	53.24%

Source: Report of the Commissioner of Education for the year 1880 and Report of the Commissioner of Education published in 1883 and 1884. 1885 Statistics published in the *Clarion Ledger*, August 19, 1885.

Table 3.2 Mississippi School Monthly Attendance to Enrollment by Race, 1882–1885						
Year	African American Attendance	African American Enrollment	African American Attendance Percent	White Attendance	White Enrollment	White Attendance Percent
1882	89,537	109,630	81.67%	82,985	104,451	79.45%
1883	85,517	141,398	60.48%	68,946	125,598	54.89%
1884	99,127	149,373	66.36%	85,294	129,647	65.79%
1885	103,114	125,633	82.08%	91,454	101,655	89.97%
Totals	377,295	526,034	72.65%	328,679	461,351	72.53%

Source: Report of the Commissioner of Education for the year 1880 and Report of the Commissioner of Education published in 1883 and 1884. 1885 Statistics published in the *Clarion Ledger*, August 19, 1885.

the 1885 educable children record, of the 5,291 children between the ages of 5 and 21 in Attala County, 3,892 (74 percent) were African American, and 1,399 (26 percent) were white students.[71] African American's attention and dedication to educating their children proved that education was more than a Reconstruction phenomenon.

Racial attitudes towards education showed a key difference between the races. For African Americans, education represented mental decolonization and a pathway to becoming a better person. By utilizing education, they elevated their status as individuals and as a race. As whites downplayed or ignored education, their status as a people remained stagnant or declined. The call for compulsory attendance likely stemmed from the smaller than expected white student enrollment, and as the *Clarion* stated, "The white people pay most of the taxes, probably nineteen-twentieths, the colored people get most of the school money."[72] Similarly, throughout the slave era,

African Americans did most of the work, and white people received all the money. The complaints made by white citizens reflected the sentiment that whites now footed the bill for Black liberation pursuits.

Education anchored Black liberation. The elevated Black person only fueled the tension between the races, especially lower-class whites and middle-class African Americans. Redemption, as a politic and mentality, centered on political office, and most whites fell through the cracks as political power was pointless unless the entire group benefitted and advanced. Bradley Bond explained that middle-class reformers of the late nineteenth century sought to include poor whites in the evolving new order, focused on commerce and industry while holding onto the old southern creed. Education became a vehicle by which to elevate white students at Black students' expense.[73] Mississippi curtailed African American educational spending as legislators emphasized promoting white. Constitutionally, Mississippi had to provide public education to all residents ages 5 to 21; therefore, politicians sought ways to finagle educational funds to diminish financial obligations to African American schools. The solution rendered was to create one adequate white school system rather than have two substandard school systems (one for each race).[74]

As Black peoples advanced their education agenda, Mississippi racialized its educational system, pushing it towards a separate but unequal framework. Diminishing funding towards Black education became a solution to advancing white education. In 1884, Mississippi sought to institute statewide teaching examinations. Bradley Bond and Horace Mann Bond gave two differing perspectives explaining overall motivation. Bradley Bond examined teaching certification as a way to professionalize and uplift white students. Horace Bond explained the racist intent of teaching certification. Officials designed the examinations to assign pay grades; therefore, they manipulated the system to assign African American teachers lower certifications resulting in lower pay. The state spent less money on African American teachers and used those dollars for white educational use.[75] Given that part of the new social order did not include elevating African Americans to equal status, educational reform centered on promoting white education, improving white education quality, and changing white citizens' attitudes towards education. In 1886, statewide teaching examinations commenced. Teachers scoring above 75 percent earned certification, and those below that mark taught lower grades. The examinations revealed that teachers were not suitable for teaching. D. E. Sullivan, Leake County superintendent, stated, "A large number of test-takers failed even to complete half of the exam, testimony to the intellectual poverty of those who intended to teach in Mississippi schools."[76] Leake County, having a white majority, indicated that white teachers provided subpar education to white students.

In Attala County, one of the first teachers hired under the new state requirements was John Wesley Bain. Born to Joseph and Martha Bain, John received his early education in the Cooks Mill school district. On June 15, 1886, at age 15, he signed a contract to teach in the New Zion school, earning thirty dollars per month. It was one thing for a teacher to appoint a student within the classroom to assist; however, it was another for a school system to employ an individual in a contractual capacity. According to oral-history accounts, John Bain possessed extraordinary mathematics skills. John's salary would later become an issue as it rivaled that of white teachers. In the certification era, African American teachers showed how the educational foundation propelled them to meet the requirements necessary to obtain certification. Wiley Jackson Brooks grew up impoverished without many educational opportunities. Brooks concluded that without education, he would have limited life choices. After attending Alcorn A&M College, he taught in Carthage and then moved to Attala County. He taught at Cedar Grove. Wiley married fellow teacher Hattie Burt, a student of Jackson College.[77] Their marriage produced three children who later became teachers. John married Lillian Adams, a schoolteacher. These marriages ushered in an era of husband-wife teaching households that would come to symbolize Attala's political and social middle-class.

Scholars obsess over what white schools had that Black schools lacked, thereby overlooking the purpose of schools and education. Many African Americans made the most of their education and parlayed it into careers that allowed them to pay it forward to members of their race. Christopher Span questioned the quality of Black education without examining the students these schools produced. James and Caroline Byas raised a family of professionals, all of whom received their early education in Attala County. Their sons Andrew, John, Thomas, and Arthur became doctors. Their daughters Carrie and Lucy graduated from Rust College.[78] Robert Tecumseh Burt, son of Robert Burt and Sylvia Sanders and Wiley Brooks's brother-in-law attended school in Kosciusko. He graduated in 1887. Between 1887 and 1892, he attended Jackson College and Walden University. Robert enrolled

Reverend Wiley Jackson
Brooks (From *The History of
Negro Baptists in Mississippi* by
Patrick H. Thompson, 1898)

Dr. Robert Tecumseh Burt
(Courtesy of the Department
of Special Collections and
University Archives, W. E. B.
Du Bois Library, University of
Massachusetts Amherst)

Dr. Jacob Clinton Tadley
(From the *Nashville Globe*,
June 24, 1910)

in Meharry Medical College in 1893, graduating in 1897. He undertook post-graduate studies at Harvard University between 1901 and 1904.[79] Burt later returned to Kosciusko to deliver a commencement address. Burt's contemporary, Jacob Clinton Tadley, was raised by his mother, Mary Rimmer. He acquired the surname Tadley later in life as early records indicated him as Jacob Rimmer. He received his early education at Sam Young. Jacob wished to become a physician. His mother dressed him in dresses so that he would remain at home. Jacob took the initiative and ran away to fulfill his dreams. Life on his own proved difficult as he struggled to find food and shelter. Jacob made his way to Nashville, Tennessee, where he enrolled in Meharry Medical College. On March 29, 1907, he graduated from Meharry Medical College in the largest graduating class at that point, meeting Booker T. Washington, who gave the commencement address.[80] To question African American educational quality undermines the entire educational movement the race embarked on during and after slavery. The low quality of white education did not mean lower quality for Black peoples. The need to defund Black education to uplift white education showed how whites viewed Black education, one that was more developed and advanced.

As education pushed the race towards liberation, white ruffians continued to hinder the positive race relations county residents built. This hindrance stalled the trajectory of many African Americans. Attala was never a beacon of racial harmony; however, men such as Jason Niles, Samuel Young, and

Rasselas Boyd created a standard for how some African Americans believed that white citizens should behave. No subset of a race controls everyone within its umbrella; thus, violent acts ensued. Prior to the 1880s, the last headlining interracial incident occurred in May 1879 when Elijah Wood—previously arrested for murdering Joel Harmon—James Seals, and three or four masked men held George Love at gunpoint after demanding entry into his home. George escaped, and Wood and Seals, arrested two weeks before this incident for terrorizing African Americans, were arrested again. Due to a lack of eyewitnesses, the court held over their case. The same day that the judge postponed the case, eight men "visited the same place, and fired off their guns to the terror of the negroes." The *Kosciusko Central Star* stated, "The lawless acts being perpetrated in the northwestern part of this county are highly criminal, subversive of peace, security, and prosperity, and should be stamped out with the full weight of the law."[81] An affront to Black liberation was the justice system's inability or refusal to provide judicial consistency and justice in interracial matters as they did in intraracial matters.

Jordan and Dora Teague's murder and trial showcased liberation and redemption within the justice system. Twenty years after freedmen testified to bring justice to Sam Winters, African Americans continued to testify in court. In December 1886, Jordan Teague exercised his civic duty and testified before the Attala County grand jury regarding stock theft. His testimony led to the arrest of white men, namely Head Bailey, Cicero Bain, W. H. Brown, Joe England, Chris Hovers, Brooks Story, Eugene Story, Will Story, and Emmett Thompson. Regarding African American participation and presence in criminal court, Melissa Milewski stated, "They had little choice in their participation in the court system."[82] Such statements fail to realize how African Americans viewed themselves and their role as citizens. One must be willing to accept the power of the Black mindset and its desire to enact its citizenship within the same democracy as whites. Jordan's action sparked retaliation that likely served as an intimidation tactic as well as an expression of disgust that most lower-class whites held towards higher-class African Americans.[83] On December 22, the accused men formed an armed posse and went to Jordan's home claiming to possess a warrant. Once inside the Teague home, Jordan grabbed an ax to defend his personhood, which escalated to the mob shooting him.[84] Dora also suffered several gunshot wounds; however, she was able to identify her shooter.[85] Their children provided law enforcement with their statements. On December 27, police arrested Eugene and Brooks

Story. Cicero Bain cooperated with officials and surrendered the names of all others involved in the murder. The Story brothers and Joe England faced further grand jury action, whereas the others were each arraigned on five hundred dollars bail. By December 29, the accused murderers entered prison, leading to public outcry. Law enforcement officials did not drop the charges in the effort to rid the county of "this species of lawlessness."[86] The public outcry and prosecution did not mean sympathy towards African Americans. Some white citizens wanted to control the race's harmful elements, while others likely saw prosecuting the white men as an affront to racial supremacy.

Cicero Bain faced trial for the Teague murders. The trial began in March 1888 with jury selection and witness examination. Whether Jordan Teague's children testified during the trial is unknown. During the trial, a typical court session could last until midnight. On March 19, both sides presented closing arguments. The jury found Cicero Bain not guilty. Juror Jim Clark explained that Jordan Teague and his wife were not dead; therefore, no murder took place, and Judge Cothran upheld the verdict.[87] Unlike the Samuel Winters case twenty years ago, the all-white jury delivered a verdict based on a ridiculous rationale. The case represented the limitations liberation efforts faced as they pertained to the law. Although Jordan and Dora's accusers faced trial, white citizens sent a message that they would protect their own. Prioritizing racial obligation over justice exemplified the liberation struggle that many Black Mississippians faced. African Americans found ways to deliver justice for themselves in some instances. In September 1880, Samuel Hawthorne, an Irish grocer, murdered a white man, last name McGee, in Vicksburg. His trial consisted of a twelve-member African American jury. The jury sentenced Hawthorne to a life sentence at the state penitentiary. As the *Magnolia Gazette* reported, "This is the first case in Mississippi in which a white man has been convicted by negroes." The paper further stated, "The jury is said to have exhibited every evidence of marked attention and brought in their verdict intelligently."[88] The rationale that exonerated Cicero Bain demonstrated the lack of judicial efficiency and fairness of all-white juries.

"Colorblind justice" applied to situations where white women were the victims. In such matters, whiteness experienced vigilantism in the same manner as Black individuals. In June 1887, James Webb, a Louisiana native, murdered his wife, Mary, leading to his arrest and conviction. They lived near the Newport Community, where he worked as a machinist. Before leaving on what was to be a two-week trip, Webb purchased strychnine and calomel and insisted that his wife take the calomel upon doctor's instructions. After consumption, the wife became ill, and Webb refused to seek medical assistance. Webb's wife died shortly after, and the authorities jailed him without bail. On June 22, at 2:00 a.m., fifty masked men broke into the jail and took Webb outside the Kosciusko town limits, where they hanged him "with a plow line, which was tied to the rail on the trestle."[89] Following charges of assaulting a white child, authorities arrested Jim Mitchell in the Newport community. The night of his arrest, "a mob of infuriated citizens" "hanged and shot" Mitchell for a crime deemed "most damnable."[90] These incidents showed the value white men placed on white life compared to Black life and their disregard for the judicial process.

As the decade ended, African Americans found themselves in solid positioning. For many, their Zion took shape as dictated by their efforts. D. M. P. Hazley, Thomas McLemore, and Isaac Presley secured space for the Masonic Lodge. African Americans showed their rise in economic status through consumerism. Alex Anderson, Reverend G. A. Griffin, and Asa Simpson purchased pianos from Long & Gulledge in Jackson.[91] For men like Asa Simpson, purchasing a piano indicated that his business ventures produced the wealth necessary to make the purchase. Pianos were a fixture in the homes of the county's Black middle-class. Social gatherings took place throughout the county, providing fraternity and comradery beyond the walls of the church or established fraternal order. Farmers in the Center Community held an annual hog-raising contest. Seventeen men participated in the contest that awarded the farmer with the largest hog. In 1888, Elam Meek won with a twenty-three-month-old hog that weighed 615 pounds. Meek won an overcoat, valued at seventeen dollars. Each member contributed one dollar towards the coat's purchase. Referencing the hog contest, the *Tupelo Journal* commented, "Both white and colored farmers in every county in the State might imitate, with profit to themselves, the commendable example of the colored men referred to above."[92] Buchanan spoke to Kosciusko white citizens regarding their role in bolstering race relations. In an editorial written on November 11, 1889, Buchanan wrote of his visit to Grenada. He stated that "the colored people love the whites—but not without a cause." Buchanan identified that white support of colored education, religion, and mercantilism and their respect of "respectable colored people" were factors in the city's colored citizens' respect for the "good white citizens." Buchanan criticized Kosciusko's white citizens, stating, "While we have as good white people here in Kosciusko as anywhere, they have not yet spent their thousands upon our school building. We have a very good house, but it is too small to give accommodation to all."[93] Buchanan used his position to pressure whites in the county to measure themselves against whites in other areas. His actions showed his courage to holding white citizens accountable for pushing the state forward. His actions underscored an understanding that white action had the potential to affect the pace of African American advancement.

African Americans stretched their wings and began taking flight, showcasing what they could do and would do to seek and obtain true freedom. They reaped and enjoyed the fruits of their labor while continuing to build and improve the necessary individual and collective infrastructure needed for liberation. They lived their lives according to their individual notions of life, liberty, and the pursuit of happiness. The decade also exposed the crosswinds of change that threatened to slow or halt full flight. The reactions of white citizens indicated an unwillingness to relinquish notions of racial superiority, and thus a need to assert themselves as masters of the southern domain. The decade saw the beginnings of discriminatory educational policy stemming from African American use of state-funded education and continued denial of justice. The next chapter explores the obstacles African Americans faced in the form of disenfranchisement and continuing educational inequities, and how African Americans organized themselves to meet the challenges head-on.

CHAPTER 4

UNITED WE STAND

ORGANIZING IN THE DECADE OF WHITE SUPREMACY

The quest for African Americans to be a better people and race required that they obtain the highest citizenship levels. Citizenship represented liberation's final frontier. Citizenship transformed the former slave into an American citizen—the status entitled them to the same rights and privileges afforded to their white counterparts. At the same time, society did not acknowledge the tenant farmer, the convict, the vagrant, or any individual under their control. However, white society could not ignore the citizen who possessed autonomy and independence.[1] The 1890s were a decade in which African Americans found themselves both defending their post-emancipation gains and cementing their institutions as part of the county's societal landscape. They moved towards collective organizing to present a united front in the face of racial violence and shrinking civil rights. The gains made in decades prior prompted a more robust, more visceral anti-Black response. Shawn Alexander's *An Army of Lions: The Civil Rights Struggle before the NAACP* captured the struggle to produce effective organizing amid a collective sense of urgency and frustration. Although Alexander focused on the national scale, his work showed the transition from small-scale and individual effort to larger-scale organizing initiatives.[2] To start the decade, Black-controlled institutions such as churches, schools, and the press organized to combine resources for continued advancement. As African Americans organized, so did whites, as Mississippi pushed to use legislative measures to curtail African American advancement, especially as it pertained to voter suppression and disenfranchisement. Historians view the 1890s as the decade that consolidated white supremacy through disenfranchisement and Jim Crow. These bookends define the Black experience not only in Mississippi but across the South. From a local perspective, the decade represented the desperation to affirm white supremacy, which southern whites had failed to do since their takeover of southern politics.

C. Vann Woodward explained that the erosion of Black rights and Republican interests in protecting big business resulted in Blacks supporting elements of the Democratic Party. Fusion politics weakened Republican power in once-dominated areas. Democratic and Black Republicans ran on a single ticket. Democrats gained votes, while African Americans gained political offices and continued access to the ballot. As Vernon Wharton explained, fusion occurred infrequently and in areas with large Black and small white populations. African American dealings with the Democratic Party reflected Hanes Walton Jr.'s conclusion that Black Republicans were less effective at the state level due to the party's weakness and unwillingness to support the Black peoples who gave them their majorities. Beatty asserted that African Americans had few options, as a people without a legitimate party casting their votes for anyone who pledged to support equality before the law.[3] The latter part of the 1880s saw some movement toward independent party politics, including the Populist Party, which African Americans believed would resuscitate the Black political agenda.[4]

African Americans' shifting from the Republican Party prompted the national party's interest in the African American voter, who represented a crucial voting bloc. During Benjamin Harrison's presidential run, the party's slogan stated, "To the supreme and sovereign right of every lawful citizen, rich or poor, native or foreign born, white or black, to cast one free ballot in public elections and to have that ballot duly counted."[5] Harrison's stance of protecting the Black ballot launched the Second Mississippi Plan, designed to ensure legal Black disenfranchisement. In the minds of Mississippi Democrats, legally eliminating the Black vote would halt any federal intervention since the changes did not violate the Fifteenth Amendment.[6] From a local perspective, Democrats had more to be concerned about than federal intervention. As a collective, African Americans identified with the Republican Party and acted to prevent their brethren from switching parties. In the November 1889 election, John Landers voted for the Democratic ticket. His action led community members to surround his home and beat him. The

Clarion Ledger published the following statement following the event: "There is no doubt but that a majority of the colored people of the South would vote the Democratic ticket if they were not afraid of punishment at the hand of their own color."[7] Such actions exposed a mentality of unity expected of the race's members. Years prior, African Americans in Leake County bulldozed a fellow Black man's home for voting Democrat.[8]

Mississippi was the third state to enact voting suppressing or disenfranchising measures. Florida and Tennessee preceded Mississippi. Mississippi took it a step further by creating a three-step voting process through its literacy test, understanding clause, and the poll tax. When Mississippi's Constitutional Convention convened in August 1890, the convention's purpose was to eliminate the vote regardless of qualification.[9] David Thomas Guyton and Frederick Marion Glass represented Attala at the convention. Disenfranchisement existed for two significant reasons: eliminating federal intervention and preventing social equality. Disenfranchisement established a political color line ensuring voting primarily for "whites only." White men would set the rules that would define African Americans' societal position.[10] Because complete redemption relied on a politically nonexistent African American, the 1890 convention showed the impact liberation efforts had on white politics, which now reached the constitutional stage.

Historians' discussion of the constitutional convention focuses extensively on the actions of Isiah T. Montgomery, the lone African American at the convention. He served as the "unofficial" leader of Mississippi's Black peoples. His acquiescence to the proposed changes signaled endorsement by the entire race, evidenced by his statement, "He hoped blacks would earn the franchise in the future and that he hoped they would be admitted as voters when they did."[11] While historians criticize Montgomery, Montgomery likely saw "accommodating" to an already certain decision from two perspectives. What would happen if Montgomery openly rejected the constitutional changes? The work that African Americans put into their liberation pursuits, including Montgomery's own Mound Bayou, would be jeopardized if Montgomery resisted. Did Montgomery realize that disenfranchising African Americans would be more difficult than white legislators imagined? Knowing the progress African Americans made since slavery made it impossible to eliminate an entire race from the ballot box.

Technically speaking, whites could not disenfranchise African Americans with the stroke of a pen because the metrics used to obstruct suffrage rested on assumption rather than fact. Article 12, the Franchise, of the 1890 Mississippi Constitution emphasized two required voting qualifications: poll tax and literacy. The poll-tax provision called for a uniform poll tax, not to exceed three dollars, to fund the common schools. The literacy provision required that after January 1, 1892, all electors be able to read any section of the state's constitution or understand and interpret the constitution when read to him.[12] The "understanding" provision served as a failsafe to bypass white illiteracy while justifying denying Black voters, literate or not.[13] During the convention, David Guyton served on the Franchise Committee. Guyton opposed the educational and property requirement because he acknowledged "the last twenty-five years show that the colored people are capable of acquiring an education." Regarding the property aspect, "they paid taxes in this State on property valued at fifteen million dollars." Despite his opposition, Guyton supported the measures, "believing that it would ensure the great object that all desire—the permanent supremacy of the white race in Mississippi."[14] Guyton understood that African Americans had progressed further than most thought and that whites should not underestimate that progress, likely explaining Montgomery's acceptance of the constitution. Guyton lived in a county where African Americans demonstrated such progress. David Guyton possessed a personal connection to the cause, which he rallied. He had eleven mixed-race nieces and nephews, fathered by his brother, Aaron Whitaker Guyton. They alone possessed education and land. The Beat 4 region, where the Guyton family lived, once comprised the majority of the county's Black wealth.

Charles Chesnutt explained in his 1903 essay "The Disenfranchisement of the Negro" that African American advancement in education, wealth, character, and self-respect created protection against property, poll, and literacy requirements, or what Chesnutt referred to as the first group of voter restrictions. Chesnutt's discussion of the second restriction groups, which included the understanding, employment, and character qualifications, concluded that disenfranchisement was a product of southern whites' ability to interpret African American constitutional compliance instead of African Americans demonstrating constitutional compliance.[15] Ratification of the 1890 constitution boosted southern whites seeking to assert their dominance over African Americans. The constitution built white supremacy into Mississippi society's future framework and served to put African Americans in their societal place legally.

Delegates to the 1890 Mississippi Constitutional Convention (Courtesy of the Archives and Records Services Division, Mississippi Department of Archives and History)

As white citizens organized to hinder Black progress, African Americans increased their organization's efforts at advancement. The church remained the nucleus of liberation. By 1890, Attala County established thirty churches of the Baptist, Methodist, and Presbyterian denominations. Another eight churches formed throughout the decade. Individuals such as Charles Buchanan, Alice Alston, Albert Poston, and William Singleton became central political and social figures during the decade. Baptist church organizations sought to empower their people toward higher goals. Churches combined their talents, seeing that strength centered on unification. On July 22, 1890, the first annual session of the General Baptist Convention met in Greenville. The convention wanted to unite the General Association and the Baptist Missionary Convention. The two bodies merged to form the General Baptist Missionary Convention. The convention's preamble spoke of using religion to unite for the purpose of racial progress in a time of continued oppression.[16] The church intervened to assist those who continued to struggle. Charles Buchanan served several essential roles in the new organization, including an executive position as the Assistant Corresponding Secretary and positions on the Committee on Examination of Letters and College and Schools.[17]

The Women's General Baptist Missionary Society followed suit. At the fourth session held in October 1890 in Yazoo City, the Women's General Baptist Missionary Society discussed consolidation with the Women's General Baptist Missionary Society of the West, which occurred in 1891. Mary Alice Alston, originating member and recording secretary of the WGBMS and current president of the Union District Society, represented Attala County and First Baptist Church in the WGBMS. Mary Alice was born in January 1861 in Oktibbeha County. Orphaned by age six, she relocated to Attala, where at age ten she joined the First Baptist Church. Alice found work as a cook in Isaac and Mary Simon's household, earning enough to pay for her education at Jackson College.[18] During her time within the Women's General Baptist Missionary Society, Alice spoke at conventions, including the Second Baptist Church's sixth session in Noxubee County. She delivered a paper titled "The Best Method of Promoting the Success of the Mission Work" and served as assistant secretary throughout the decade.[19] Alice used her life experience to assist in similar situations. Orphaned herself, Alice involved herself in the mission to create the Aged Women and Orphan's Home, a project originated by Charlotte Fairfax Jones and one about which H. P. Jacobs stated, "We must have an orphan asylum where we can take care and educate our orphan children."[20] Alice worked with George W. Hall, president of the orphan home in Kosciusko, and became the state corresponding secretary and treasurer of the trustees' board.[21] Alice turned her personal experience into an opportunity to provide support for women and children whose life circumstances created an unexpected burden on them.

The Mt. Hope District Women's Convention, organized by Kizziah Clark in October 1889, took its place among the many women-led organizations during the decade. Kizziah was born in March 1837 in Tennessee. The Clark family resided in the Plattsburg township in Winston County. Kizziah obtained an education, and her husband worked as a blacksmith and farmer. The convention included Attala, Winston, Madison, and Leake Counties, giving voice to Black women in areas of lower Black population. The convention's first session occurred in 1890, with Roxie Carter being the only noted position holder as convention secretary. The convention's mission was "giving women will power to exercise their gift in the way of expression and set up objectives to broaden the mission field" and "Inspiring young men and women to become useful citizens in helping christianize the world, and by lifting up the name of Jesus."[22] The convention's mission reflects what Bettye Collier-Thomas explained, that women's religious organizations worked to battle racism and sexism.[23] The moral and spiritual advancement of the Black race played against a social and political environment designed to set the race more than a few steps back.

In 1891, the Ku Klux Klan accosted Charles Edward McMichael, a Neshoba County native. Charles's father was a white Georgia planter named John McMichael and his mother was of Indigenous and African descent and named Sarah Jane McDougal. Charles lived under the protection of his father's name and wealth after his mother worked hard to secure the McMichael name for her children, who were born McDougal. Charles attended and graduated from Haven Institute in Meridian, where he studied education and music. In 1868, Moses Adams, a former slave, opened Haven Institute, which had the distinction of being the only school to have "colored" leadership from its inception.[24] The Klan accused Charles, along with his friend George Kirkland, of openly associating with white women. The women in question looked white but were African American. Charles faced death, but the Klan voted 6–2 to let Charles live; however, George suffered a different fate. The Klan beat Charles and ordered him to leave Neshoba County immediately.[25] Charles's family left the Laurel Hill community, and several other Black families left the area in an event referred to as the "burning of Laurel Hills." Charles settled in Zama, a railroad community in Attala's Beat 5, where he opened and taught school in the Ayers Community.[26] On November 22, 1891, a white mob shot Dan Gladney, a Civil War veteran, landowner, and a registered voter.[27] Law enforcement arrested George Pickle, a leader of the mob. The police then went after the other mob members while protecting Dan Gladney's home.[28] Attala County Sheriff Daniel Lafayette Smythe Sr. expended considerable police staffing to apprehend the violent perpetrators. While guarding Gladney's home, Deputy Daniel Lafayette Smythe Jr. shot and killed an African American man, last name Kennedy, as Smythe cleaned his gun.[29] No prosecutions came from either incident; however, the incidents reflected the continued lawlessness that Mississippi sought to eradicate but allowed simultaneously. Although the origins of the conflict are unknown, the event occurred following the November election. Two men, John Kennedy and J. J. Kennedy voted in said election.

Attala's political allegiance never wavered from the Democratic Party's ideology of power, control, and supremacy. The *Hinds County Gazette* reported the *Kosciusko Star's* statement, "We sink or swim with the democratic party. What it favors we strive for; what it denounces we oppose."[30] The Democratic Party had one central mission: eliminating the Black voter through legal or illegal means, in which Attala participated. Historians make little nuance between suppression and disenfranchisement, which is an entirely different book to be written. While Paul Lewinson questioned the impact that whites had on African American disenfranchisement, he questioned whether disenfranchisement resulted from African American political indifference, apathy, economic standing, illiteracy, a rise in lynching, voting geography, and cynicism. Neil McMillen depicted disenfranchisement more as acceptance of Black peoples' understanding that whites held the ultimate power, which when combined with Perman's assessment that "virtually all African American adult males were disfranchised by the residence, literacy, and poll tax requirements of the new state constitutions,"[31] represented a complete wipeout of the Black Mississippi voter. Black men continued voting during the 1890s in Attala and across the state. These men represented more than the extraordinary "Negroes" whose votes whites controlled. In 1891, Attala's franchise class included 564 African American and 1,987 white registered voters across thirteen districts.[32] Black registrants comprised mostly former slaves, many of whom had an education. As

1892 approached, a litmus test of liberation and redemption played out at courthouses across the state.

The first registration of Mississippi's disenfranchisement era would show if African Americans faltered under the voting requirements. When registration commenced, Attala County had fifteen voting precincts: Ayers, Ethel, Jerusalem, Kosciusko, Liberty Chapel, McCool, Peeler's Mill, Providence, Rochester, Rocky Point, Sallis, Shrock, Thompson School House, and Zilpha. Between 1892 and 1899, 573 African Americans registered compared to 4,463 whites. White registration numbers indicate a fixed system that protected illiterate whites who benefited from their race, not their ability. This is where historians often miss the mark. Instead of obsessing over a rigged system that benefited whites, one must examine the African Americans who continued registering and voting. This perspective provides insight into the complex struggle for liberation and redemption as voting confirmed the effectiveness of landowning, economic independence, education, and community from decades prior.

Demonstrating an ability to read did not guarantee registration, as African Americans had to demonstrate constitutional understanding or interpretation. Even if subjected to this step, they had the ability to pass the obstacle. Five hundred and eight (89 percent) possessed complete literacy (reads and writes), thirty (5 percent) possessed partial literacy (reads only), and thirty-four (6 percent) were illiterate (understands). Those in the understood category signed a special bond rather than a general bond. The number of educated Black men symbolized many southern whites' greatest fear. As Christopher Hager explained in *Word by Word: Emancipation and the Act of Writing*, the idea of literate slaves created fear amongst slaveholders. Literate slaves was liberated slaves who could think for themselves, exchange ideas of freedom, and gain a broader understanding of their current situation.[33] The number of literate Black men (Table 4.1) indicated that they took advantage of their community's educational system. To provide a more nuanced perspective of literacy and voting intersection, the role of women must be examined. When did adult men find time to obtain literacy, if they dedicated most of their time to work? Men likely acquired literacy from their spouses. Malissa Davis taught school in Holmes, Madison, Leake, and Attala Counties. Educated in Madison County, she taught her husband Captain Miller Avery to read and write following their marriage.[34] Several voting households had spouses and children who were literate. While women could

Table 4.1. 1892–1899 African American Voter Precinct Registration				
Precinct	Black Voters	Literacy Percent	Slavery Generation	Freedom Generation
Ayers	45	82	22	23
Ethel	7	100	5	2
Jerusalem	82	94	38	44
Kosciusko	198	98	106	92
Liberty Chapel	17	94	7	10
McCool	51	100	28	23
Newport	14	100	4	10
Peelers Mill	15	87	5	10
Providence	10	100	7	3
Rochester	16	75	12	4
Rocky Point	57	91	27	30
Sallis	36	100	16	20
Shrock	19	84	11	8
Thompson	5	100	4	1
Zilpha	1	0	1	0
Totals	573	87	293	280

Source: Attala County Precinct Voter Registration Books
*One individual had no literacy status. No subsequent information found to verify literacy capacity.

not legally vote, they played an unseen role in fathers, sons, uncles, cousins, and grandfathers being able to add their names to the voting register.

Voting data showed that those born during the slavery era and the emancipation era remained balanced. The continued presence of the pre-emancipation class represented the connected push for liberation that influenced the post-slavery generations. The importance of such balance was the old guard's ability to visibly demonstrate voting's power so that the next generation would have a template for carrying forward. Post-convention registration revealed a full circle from slavery to freedom as families comprising of the former slave and freedom generation registered to vote. These families included Gladney (Daniel, Robert, and Nelson), McLemore (Thomas, Grandison, and Howard), Phillips (Moses and William), and Cole (Warren, George, and John). Witnessing their sons signing the registration books showed fathers that they were baptizing their sons into liberation,

Signature of Thomas Jefferson McLemore (Kosciusko Voter Register Book, June 22, 1892)

Signature of Howard McLemore (Kosciusko Voter Registration Book, August 28, 1893)

rather than whites baptizing them into submission. Leon Litwack argued the Nadir period of southern history was that of white determination to put African Americans in their place; however, Litwack underestimated African American resilience. They did not relinquish what they had worked to obtain. The foundations African Americans built decades prior allowed them to thwart some of the Democratic Party's suppression tactics.

While there is no evidence that the Afro-American League had branches in Mississippi, African American registration patterns demonstrated organizing efforts to lessen the probability of violence and intimidation (Table 4.2). Violence was a proven tactic to maintain the psychological advantage. Beatings and lynching were practical tools to keep African Americans and outsiders in their place. No evidence exists that whites exercised violent efforts to prevent African Americans from voting during the decade. Preventing one or two African American registration attempts would be easier to execute than a larger gathering. Across the various precincts, Black men registered in large numbers simultaneously. Such efforts were unlikely to have occurred by happenstance and likely reflected county-wide organizing so that those seeking registration could do so among their brethren. Given the heightened racial tensions in the county, region, and state, it would be dangerous for a Black man to seek registration in isolation.

Liberation meant the right to make individual choices. Historians take it upon themselves to assume that all Black peoples were political or had an obligation to vote. They fail to assess African Americans choosing to withdraw themselves from political activity. Of the 576 Black registered voters before 1892, 303 did not reregister.[35] Within this group, 187 possessed literacy. These individuals held the capability to pass the literacy test. This

Table 4.2. African American Voter Registration by Date		
Registration Date	*Voters*	*Percentage of Overall Registration*
June 18, 1892	10	5%
July 2, 1892	24	13%
July 4. 1892	20	11%
July 5, 1892	17	9%
July 6, 1892	23	13%
August 28, 1893	12	25%
June 15, 1895	14	11%
June 18, 1895	11	9%
July 2, 1896	21	23%
May 30, 1899	12	14%

Source: Voter Registration Books

nonvoting group possibly grew weary of the ongoing battle and refused to give the ignorant elements of society their time and energy. Members of this group included Gilbert Brooks and George Kern. The November 1891 race riot potentially affected nonregistration in the Jerusalem precinct. Straughter Nash Sr. and his sons, Straughter Jr. and Eddie, were literate landowners who did not register in the years that followed. The constitution disenfranchised African Americans, such as Thomas Gaston, who did not possess literacy and rented his land. He registered prior in the Kosciusko precinct, and his son W. E. T. Gaston, a literate landowner, registered under the new voting guidelines. Given the small number of illiterate men allowed to register, Thomas fit the disenfranchised voter model.

Black Political Class

Kosciusko pushed the envelope further in pushing education and politics to higher pursuits with the creation of Central Mississippi College. Attala County became Central Mississippi's higher education hub when Charles A. Buchanan sought to expand the number of colleges serving African Americans. He wanted a geographically friendly college and one that would provide education beyond the state's borders. Mississippi's catalog of colleges dates from the early emancipation era with Rust College (1866). Tougaloo College

Moses Phillips Sr.
(Courtesy of the author,
from the Annie Harris
Photograph Collection)

William Solomon
Patterson (Courtesy of
Shedralyn D. Pullum)

George Washington
Kern Sr. (Courtesy of
the author, from the
McMichael Family
Reunion Book)

Gilbert Brooks (Courtesy
of Cheryl Bayne)

Thomas Gaston
(Courtesy of Sherron
Campbell)

(1869), Haven Institute (1868), and Alcorn University (1871), Mississippi's first state-funded African American public institution, followed. Mount Herman Female Seminary (1875) served as the first African American institution for women. Natchez Seminary (1877) provided the "for the moral, religious, and intellectual improvement of Christian leaders of the colored people of Mississippi and the neighboring states."[36] Mary Holmes Seminary (1892), built on African American lands, also served African American women. These institutions helped elevate the African American masses while serving as examples of institutional power.

In 1893, Buchanan coordinated with the Baptist State Convention and erected Central Mississippi College in Kosciusko, Mississippi. He served as the institution's first president. The college dedicated itself to training and producing teachers and offered high school and college courses with the following departments: college, normal, college preparatory, training school, and music. [37] Buchanan created an institution served by prominent members of the African American community statewide. The college's board of trustees included Reverends Lincoln N. Williams, Robert Harrington, A. C. Campbell, and schoolteacher Samuel W. Brown. These men represented perseverance and excellence. Robert Harrington was born in June 1840 in Newberry, South Carolina. In 1855, Robert's owner sold him from his parents, Henry and Ann Oneal. His new owner bought him to Mississippi. In 1863, Harrington found God, becoming an ordained Baptist preacher. Harrington met Buchanan at a school that he taught in the Mt. Calvary Settlement in Winston County. Harrington's admiration for him led to him being a founding charter member in Central Mississippi College and his trustee role. [38] Campbell and Buchanan were members of the General Baptist Missionary Convention, where at the sixth annual session, Campbell "spoke in interest" of Buchanan's journal *Preacher and Teacher*. [39]

In 1894, Charles A. Buchanan established a newspaper in Kosciusko called the *Preacher and Teacher*, which reflected his two careers as a minister and professor. Buchanan's paper was the first and only known Black newspaper published in the county. African Americans obtained power based on their ability to produce and disseminate information and knowledge to their people. As Julius E. Thompson stated in *The Black Press in Mississippi, 1865–1900*, "Since the period of American Reconstruction, Afro-Americans in Mississippi have produced several hundred newspapers, more than fifty magazines and journals, and hundreds of pamphlets, newsletters, and other related press materials." [40] Buchanan's paper added to a growing list of Black publications, which led to organizing them into an association. On June 7, 1894, the Colored Inter-State Press Association met in Jackson at the AME church. The meeting represented twenty newspapers, including Buchanan's paper. The convention established itself as a formal organization, adopting by-laws and a constitution. Buchanan served as one of two secretaries for the new organization. [41] The convention acted progressively, pushing an agenda that promoted racial uplift. During the convention, the association passed a resolution supporting Ida B. Wells's efforts in England. [42] Buchanan continued this vein of media activism, using his newspaper as a political tool to promote voting and racial advancement in the following years.

Politics dominated the county between 1895 and 1896. In 1895, Mississippi entered into a contentious battle over the poll tax. The state's constitution called for poll-tax collection to fund public schools. The *Kosciusko Star* published a piece from the *Canton Times* which complained about the poll-tax burden on white citizens. The *Canton Times* stated, "The poll tax being now two-dollars and all going to school fund and being almost entirely paid by the white race is felt, and justly so, to be an onerous and unequal burden upon white men." The piece called for lowering the rate and only those paying the poll tax to have public schools usage.[43] The *Weekly Clarion-Ledger* published William S. McAllister's editorial, which questioned the unequal payment of poll taxes between white and Black citizens and potential legislation mandating poll-tax payment.[44] The poll-tax issue reached the point where counties wanted to amend the constitution so that they "would leave the poll tax receipts in the counties where they were collected."[45] Calls for separating the school fund prompted the African Methodist Episcopal Conference to dedicate time during its conference to addressing the issue. Albert B. Poston of Kosciusko offered a resolution, which O. P. Ross motioned for amendment. The resolution expressed the "necessity for paying their poll-taxes, so there will be no cause existing for the legislature to order a separation of the school fund."[46] Albert B. Poston, regarded as "one of the brightest negroes in the state," served as a Methodist minister and a schoolteacher. As a former member of the state house of representatives from Panola County, he bought political experience to the table. He also served as principal of Sam Young, a position held for the majority of the 1890s.[47]

One argument regarding poll-tax payment was that "any man can make enough in this country to play $1.00 especially when he has a whole family to help him."[48] A mandatory poll-tax payment indicated a need to control one's labor and resources. The question was not affording one dollar, but why did African Americans choose to withhold poll-tax payment? Why would African Americans pay their poll tax if they could not vote? Creating the literacy test and understanding clause did more harm to white citizens than imagined. Because Black voters were disenfranchised at this stage, they could not pay the poll tax that would disproportionately benefit white education. Additionally, paying poll taxes did not guarantee access to the ballot. In Attala County, African American voting peaked between the years 1895 and 1896 (Table 4.3). The *Preacher and Teacher* assessed African American political vitality during this time.

The Democratic party is organized throughout the state. They are drilling their forces with face front and their eyes upon the coming election with hope to carry the state and capture every office from Governor to Beat Constable. The third party is also well organized and intends to cut them off from their expected prize and carry the State for the Populites. Which shall triumph? is the question that now agitates the minds of the citizens, while both parties eagerly watch the result. The Negro who constitutes a part of this great commonwealth and is a tax payer and a voter, belongs to neither of these parties but to a party which is now dead locally. As the Republican party can cut no figure in the politics of the state, is that any reason why the Negro should remain dormant in the state? No.[49]

On November 18, 1895, the *Kosciusko Star* reported November election results. Attala County democrats won control of the board of supervisors. The victory had a more significant impact as it dealt a political blow to populism. The piece made no mention of Republicans or African American voters, instead indicating that "our people, a large majority of whom are conservative and possessed of good sense, can be depended upon after the issues of the day have been discussed before them."[50] The Democratic majority for 1895 was three hundred votes.[51] One hundred twelve African Americans voted in the election. Daniel Smythe Jr. ran for sheriff and lost. Whether Smythe's involvement in the shooting death of Kennedy years prior hurt him with Black voters is unknown; however, it would have been a likely political conversation in Black households. Although local elections had a significant impact, as indicated by who held powerful county positions, national elections gave African Americans a broader platform to advocate for candidates at the state and national level.

1896 represented a watershed year in American politics as it was the first election since the Supreme Court decided Plessy v. Ferguson, a decision that further impeded African American's constitutional rights. A significant act of protest against legal marginalization was demonstrating one's continued presence in the political arena. The 1896 presidential election established itself as the decade's most significant election. Bess Beatty discussed in *A Revolution Gone Backward: The Black Response to National Politics, 1876–1896* that 1896 marked a watershed year because it was the "final battle of the revolution for black equality that began in 1860."[52] In the wake of *Plessy v.*

Table 4.3 Attala County African American Registrations and Voting				
Year	New Registrants	Vote Total	Total African American Vote	Turnout%
1892	178	1331	47	26.37
1893	48	1007	59	26.11
1894	25	1345	43	17.13
1895	121	NA	111	29.83
1896	90	1303	155	33.54
1897	6	NA	6	1.28
1898	23	NA	27	5.50
1899	82	NA	66	11.52
Totals	573		514	18.91

Source: 1892–1895 vote total from the *Kosciusko Star* July 5, 1895. Total African American vote derived from precinct poll books.

Ferguson, African Americans witnessed the birth of legalized segregation. The pursuit of liberation suffered a devastating setback; however, the fight was far from over. African Americans increased their political intensity. They organized and drafted a list of grievances which they presented at the Republican Party Convention. The Colored National Convention pledged their support for the Republican Party. The key issues that propelled their agenda were economics and lynching.[53] In Mississippi, African Americans had enthusiasm going into the election. The *Democrat-Star* reported that "the negro registration in Mississippi is said to be increasing in greater ratio than that of whites."[54]

On October 29, 1896, African Americans and white Republicans gathered at the Kosciusko courthouse for a political rally to pledge support for James E. Everett, the Republican congressional candidate. William A. Singleton, president of the Central Mississippi College, addressed the crowd. Attala County had never witnessed an African American deliver a political address. Singleton's speech urged African Americans to maintain their moral character, be current in their taxes, and vote for their best interests. His speech also demanded African Americans to command respect from their race as well as whites. On November 2, 1896, former Mississippi congressman John Roy Lynch spoke at the Kosciusko courthouse. Lynch spoke on the McKinley tariff and the debate between the gold and silver standard. He urged African Americans to be current in their taxes and to acquire and maintain their property. White citizens praised both speeches for their message to African Americans. They regarded the Singleton speech as one of the greatest speeches they had heard.[55] Black citizens of the county had an added incentive to vote as Albert B. Poston appeared on the ballot. Poston ran as a presidential elector on the Thomas Hill Republican-led ticket. The ticket included Isiah T. Montgomery, R. J. Alcorn, Samuel Blevens, Charles H. Harris, Albert C. Melchoir, James M. Leverette, John W. Randolph, and Emile Engbarth.[56]

Both speeches delivered followed similar themes to Booker T. Washington's Atlanta Exposition address. Both focused on enfranchisement measures such as paying taxes and owning land, both important to clear the now-legal voting obstacles. The speeches did not mention social equality and produced the same acclaim from the white audience as Washington's speech did. By shifting the spotlight from racial organization to individual empowerment, African Americans created a more innovative, more deceptive way to manage Jim Crow politics.[57] African Americans understood the white psyche's politics and spoke in a coded language that provided a blueprint to political liberation while avoiding white suspicion. Most white people grew concerned when Black people rebelled against racial constructions, and such rebellion could disrupt the lives and businesses of white people.[58] Singleton and Lynch advocated for such rebellion but phrased it to give the illusion that they were complying with sociopolitical norms. African Americans found ways to articulate liberation within a white-redemption framework.

The 1896 election provided a positive outlook for the county's African American voters. With 155 votes cast, more Black men voted in the election than any other year during the decade at that point. The African American political presence in Attala County showed no intention to wither during suffrage manipulation. William McKinley won the election, although William Jennings Bryan won Attala with 961 votes to McKinley's 145 votes. Without exit poll data, one can surmise that most African Americans voted for the McKinley ticket. J. E. Everett, backed by the Hill Republicans, received 212 votes (112 Attala). Everett finished third in a four-person race. Democrat, John S. Williams won the seat with 10,475 votes (891 Attala). Populist W. H. Stinson finished second with 2,218 votes (457 Attala), and Republican J. H. Denson, backed by Lynch Republicans, finished fourth with 142 votes (25 Attala).[59] At the local level, Attala County Republicans continued to meet. In December, Lynch Republicans met in Jackson to discuss policy for state

Congressman John Roy Lynch

Republicans following McKinley's inauguration. D. M. P. Hazley and Alfred Frazier attended the meeting. Frazier's political career spanned decades, and Hazley was a rising star in the party.[60]

African Americans pushed each other to keep striving for more despite personal and social obstacles. The liberation struggle was not just a battle with an ever-changing, white-controlled political system responding to Black advancement. African Americans could not sabotage themselves or the broader group with self-inflicted wounds. This point reflected not acknowledging long-term trauma associated with slavery or individual experiences since slavery and pushing a "respectability" politic. However, African Americans were in a fight, one that did not privilege everyone to deal with personal issues, especially at the race's expense. With Reverend Henderson W. Bowen's help, the paper's homiletical editor Buchanan continued to use the press to push his people past idleness and complacency. In 1897, the *Mississippi Farmer* printed Buchanan's words: "Our young men should seek employment and stop lounging around on the streets, fingering over an old guitar. Get a permanent job and go to work—make something and be somebody."[61] The tone the paper expressed echoed a piece published in the *People's Defender* a year prior, which stated that "the best thing for the Negro to do is remain at the place where he was born and raised, where he has already accumulated property, capital, school houses, colleges and the like, and where colored men and women have grown to be statesmen, orators, lawyers, doctors, editors, dressmakers, stenographers, and learned all other various trades and professions formerly known and mastered by the whites only."[62] The press attempted to push a narrative of fight and struggle, understanding the true potential of their people.

Black students in Attala continued to enroll in school at levels near that of whites throughout the 1890s (Table 4.4). The county invested more in white student's education than Black students. The 1890 Mississippi constitution served as a vehicle to reduce state spending on African American education. Focus on the constitution's disenfranchisement clauses overshadowed the state's efforts to derail African American education. The constitution specified that schools with equal term lengths were not required to have equal teachers or services. Mississippi increased its educational expenditures to match growing student enrollment. States granted local officials more considerable discretion regarding fund allocation.[63] In 1894, T. J. Fowler, education superintendent, reduced Black second- and third-grade teachers' salaries from $14 to as low as $10 per month. In 1895, the board of trustees of city schools reported that expenditures for white teachers' salaries totaled $3,080, compared to $600 spent on colored teachers' salaries.[64] Given the disparity, some Black teachers earned the same or more than white teachers (Table 4.4). When T. J. Fowler settled teachers' contracts in 1895, William Phillips, Daniel Hazley, Artemus Rimmer, S. McMillan, W. T. Burnside, Anderson Byas, and Riley Duckett earned monthly salaries equal to or more than white teachers, which eventually led to public outcry.[65]

The Annual Report of the County Superintendent for 1894–1895 noted that the average white teachers' salary was $29.26 compared to the $18.15 Black teachers' salary.[66] Byas, Frazier, Hazley, McMillan, and Phillips earned above the average white pay. Within an educational structure designed to pay Black teachers less, some broke through such barriers. Objections arose along racial lines; however, these objections did not care to consider teachers' quality. James and Caroline (Conway) Byas's son Anderson D. Byas was born on May 9, 1871. As one of twelve children, he attended the county schools until ninth grade, after which he entered Rust College in 1888. While attending college, James began teaching summer courses in Attala County starting in 1890. He graduated from Rust College in 1895, so his higher salary likely corresponded to his educational obtainment.[67] William Wendell Phillips was born on June 13, 1872, in Madison County to Moses Phillips and Annis Lacey. In 1877, William began school under the instruction of the Honorable Samuel P. Hurst. At age ten, William entered high school. He studied under

Table 4.4: Attala County Teachers' Salaries Contracted by Superintendent T. J. Fowler			
Teacher	**Race**	**Sex**	**Salary**
S. McMillan	Black	Male	$30.00
Alfred Frazier	Black	Male	$30.00
William W. Phillips	Black	Male	$30.00
Daniel Hazley	Black	Male	$30.00
Anderson D. Byas	Black	Male	$30.00
Richard R. Duckett	Black	Male	$30.00
Ida Lawrence	White	Female	$30.00
Beulah Teat	White	Female	$30.00
Kate Guess	White	Female	$30.00
Alice Bennett	White	Female	$28.00
P.A. Teat	White	Male	$27.50
Birtie Austin	White	Female	$27.50
Anna O'Briant	White	Female	$27.50
George Sanders	White	Male	$27.50
Dona Ray	White	Female	$25.00
Daisy Mather	White	Female	$25.00
Nannie Glass	White	Female	$25.00
H. L. Skeen	White	Male	$25.00
John W. Bailey	White	Male	$25.00
Allie Campbell	White	Female	$25.00
W. T. Burnside	Black	Male	$25.00
May Black	White	Female	$25.00
E. B. Allen	White	Male	$25.00
Sophia Harmon	White	Female	$24.00
Linda Hanks	White	Female	$24.00
Barbara O'Briant	White	Female	$23.00
Hassie Riley	White	Female	$22.50
Mary Phillips	White	Female	$22.50

Source: The *Mississippi Farmer*, July 7, 1899. Phillips and Hazley would eventually earn thirty-five dollars a month.

M. G. Campbell
(From the *Kosciusko Star,*
September 27, 1895)

Professor Matthew Leroy. At age fifteen, William graduated high school and enrolled at Tougaloo College. Although he could not complete his studies due to personal issues, he began a two-year teaching tenure in Kosciusko between 1890 and 1891. In 1892, William returned to school at Rust College, where he earned his AB degree. After traveling to Chicago, Pennsylvania, and New York, he undertook additional studies at Hampton Institute.[68] Aside from these individuals, African Americans earned significantly less than whites occupying the same role. African Americans earning more than their white counterparts cost Fowler his position, which M. G. Campbell took over. When Campbell assumed the role of education superintendent in 1896, African American teachers "received a smaller per cent of the funds than under ANY of [Campbell's] predecessors."[69] Monthly salaries during this period included sixty dollars for a Hall teacher, forty-five dollars for a first assistant, and forty dollars for other assistants. The Black principal earned thirty-five dollars, and the assistant earned twenty dollars a month.[70]

Overall, African Americans paid the price for pursuing education in terms of monetary compensation. Given the enrollment numbers, Attala County education officials paid most Black teachers and administrators less for working with near equal student numbers (Table 4.5). Black teachers did not idly accept the pay inequity. When the Attala County Colored Teachers' Institute convened in Kosciusko on August 29, 1898, thirty-five teachers attended. The enrollment included nineteen men and sixteen women. The meeting included a few husband-and-wife teacher households such as the Bayne, Henry, and Wheeler families. Professors David C. Hull (white), Thomas B. Wheeler, and J. E. Smith (Black) conducted and managed the institute. Wheeler, a native of Issaquena County, served as current principal

Table 4.5 Attala County School Enrollment, 1892-1896			
Year	African American Enrollment	White Enrollment	Total	African American Enrollment Percent
1892	4,429	4,970	9,399	47.12
1894	4,750	5,115	9,865	48.15
1896	4,728	5,189	9,917	47.68
Totals	13,907	15,274	29,181	47.65

Source: Attala County Educable School Records.

of Sam Young. During the institute, a teachers' association formed. The association consisted of both men and women, including James Smith, Winnie Snow, George Henry, Cooper Dodd, and Artemus Rimmer. The association passed several resolutions, one that called for improved salaries and a second that called for resolutions to be published in the *Mississippi Farmer* and the *Preacher and Teacher*.[71]

Central Mississippi College stood as a reminder of the teaching excellence possessed by Black teachers. In 1897, Jefferson Anderson Jr. became the college's dean. Jefferson, son of Jefferson Sr. and Mariah Anderson, came from Holmes County, near Lexington. His parents, believing in education, supported his normal schooling. In 1880, he entered Alcorn A&M, followed by enrollment at Rust College and Roger Williams University. Anderson possessed exceptional oratory skills, which won him a gold medal in oration following a debate between Roger Williams and Central Tennessee College. Aspiring to become a doctor, Anderson enrolled at Howard University.[72] The college's 1897 commencement attracted many African Americans for the weeklong event that included speakers, exhibitions, concerts, and graduation for eleven students.[73] Buchanan hired the highest quality individuals to operate his school. After Anderson's untimely passing, William A. Singleton, Silas Lynch, and Lillie Singleton served as college assistants to the school, overseeing 120 scholars and three normal students.[74]

NINETEENTH CENTURY EDUCATORS

During a decade dominated by racial tensions, times arose when both races found common ground and unity. While these interactions do not constitute

Charles Edward McMichael (Courtesy of the author, from the McMichael Family Reunion Book)

Anderson D. Byas (From *Beacon Lights of the Race* by G. P. Hamilton, 1911)

Professor Jefferson Anderson Jr. (From *The History of Negro Baptists in Mississippi* by Patrick H. Thompson, 1898)

Professor D. M. P. Hazley (Courtesy of the author)

organizing, they do demonstrate a level of community building from an interpersonal perspective. Michael Ayers discussed that relationships between Blacks and whites were complex. In some cases, they were genuine, a point that Booker T. Washington observed in the South, as he found "at least one white man who believed implicitly in one Negro, and one Negro who believed implicitly in one white man." Harry Crews reflected, "There was a part of me in which it did not matter at all that they were black, . . . but there was another part of me in which it had to matter because it mattered to the world I lived in."[75] Focusing on white society elements that held contempt for Black peoples and vice versa omits genuine interactions between the two groups. George Bullock proved that he would or could work with anyone.

Sam Gant with the Jackson family
(Courtesy of the Attala County Library)

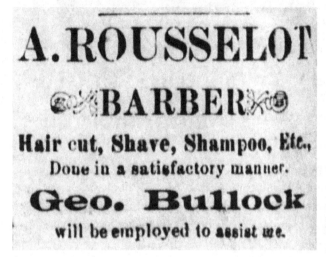

A. Rousselot 1895
Advertisement
(From the Kosciusko
Star Ledger)

Auguste Rousselot purchased Bullock and Dorrill's barbershop, and George remained as Rousselot's assistant.[76]

Born in June 1836 in France, Auguste Rousselot began barbering at age twelve. He immigrated, aboard the Columbian Barque Teresa, to New Orleans in 1854.[77] Auguste moved to Attala County following the death of his wife, Marie. He advertised in the *Kosciusko Star*, "A. ROUSSELOT BARBER Hair cut, Shave, Shampoo, Etc. Done in a satisfactory manner, Geo. Bullock will be employed to assist me."[78] Rousselot gave George prominent space on the advertisement, spelling his name in bold letters likely to remind customers who once patronized Bullock's shop. Rousselot added Andrew J. Hemphill, white, to the shop and advertised both Bullock and Hemphill as equals, advertising them as "two of the best Tonsorial artists of the state."[79] The barbershop served all customers, indicating Rousselot's nonracialized view of southern society, given his French background.

Comfort and Style

Served to all customers alike in the Shaving and Hair Cutting by Andy J. Hemphill and George Bullock, two of the best Tonsorial artists of the state.

A. Rousselot 1898
Advertisement
(From the Kosciusko
Star Ledger)

A. ROUSSELOT.

Elegant Shoe Shining and Polishing.

On June 15, 1897, a photograph captured Frederick Zollicoffer Jackson's sons with Sam Gant, Black. Sam and Doty Jackson hold sticks hoisting a turtle in the photo. Sam Gant was the son of Scott and Celia Gant. Scott Gant worked as a day laborer, and Frederick Zollicoffer Jackson worked as a merchant and owned F. Z. Jackson & Co., which later became F. Z. Jackson & Sons. The Gant and Jackson family's relationship remains unknown; however, the photograph indicates that some cordiality existed between the two families. The captured image does not depict Sam in an inferior position or role but as equal.[80]

Cordial racial relationships extended beyond private interactions and into more public spaces. On September 27, 1898, members of a white Methodist church in Camden, located in Madison County, visited a Black Methodist church in Kosciusko. African American minister Albert B. Poston led the service. Following the service, leaders from both churches decided that Rev. Poston should preach at the white Methodist church the following night. Rev. Poston and his church members traveled to Camden, where both congregations united for Rev. Poston's sermon.[81] The positive interracial meeting demonstrated that some individuals sought to find peace during otherwise tense racial times, regardless of community reaction.

A white congregation turning over their church to an African American minister demonstrated some social and religious equality. The significance extends beyond the interracial gathering and the institution in which it occurred. During slavery, the church represented the battle between control and liberation. Slave owners went to great lengths to control slave worship and their religious instruction. It becomes difficult to ascertain why a white church would relinquish their pulpit to an African American pastor besides acknowledging that despite Poston's race, his ability to preach gospel broke racial barriers. The public, however, was reluctant to accept any racial mixing. The author who reported the story in the *Canton Times* (named "disgruntled citizen") stated, "Now if this is not a bitter pill to be swallowed by the pure blooded Anglo-Saxon who prides himself upon the pedigree of his ancestry and wants to perpetuate it unsullied, tell me the reason why. If other places that boasts of the social standing that Camden does will just follow her example the race problem that has so long been discussed will soon be solved and race distinction sunk into oblivion."[82] At least one white citizen, possibly speaking on behalf of others, saw this incident as an affront to racial supremacy. Social mixing threatened the balance of power, for miscegenation appeared to be the quote's unspoken theme. African Americans were as much responsible for setting the parameters of the southern code. While whites sought to dictate Black action, most refused to understand that Black peoples had no desire to yield to command.

As the decade close, African Americans in Attala County entered the twentieth century in a solid position. Organizing within the church, politics, and education and cordial interracial relationships allowed them to remain relevant as they continued to shape their future's trajectory. However, African Americans witnessed whites organizing to solidify their control of important institutions such as education and voting. African Americans demonstrated that their years since emancipation were well spent. As literate, landowning, and labor-independent peoples, they were a force not willing to relinquish their individual and collective gains. The next chapter examines the heightened tensions between liberation and redemption, setting up a violent battle between the two. As African Americans reached the peak of their forward progression, the white response turned violent, creating a series of back-and-forth actions as individuals and institutions sought to maintain control of their liberation at the twentieth century's dawn.

CHAPTER 5

THERE SHALL BE BLOOD
THE PRICE OF LIBERATION

The liberation struggle continued into the twentieth century. Segregation's legalization, erosion of civil rights, voter suppression, disenfranchisement, lynching, and other cowardly actions were not enough to deter Black peoples. Complacency and fear had no place in the recipe for freedom and liberation. Yes, the county's Black population showed self-determination to achieve an uplifted status; however, achievement, self-determination, and uplift by themselves lacked the permanency of freedom and liberation. Whites witnessed the transition of the subservient slave to the empowered citizen and worked diligently to create a permanent Black second class. Through the setbacks, African Americans continued to push forward, knowing that the backlash they faced stemmed from their progression, not their inferiority.

In the first decade of the twentieth century, African Americans continued making strides in Attala County as white citizens ramped up their efforts to control them. W. E. B. Du Bois said, "The problem of the twentieth century is the problem of the color line."[1] The color line extended beyond Black and white and included red and green. Blood and money played critical roles in shaping the color line and the Attala liberation struggle at the beginning of the twentieth century. As African Americans continued their quest for liberation, white citizens relied on a familiar yet effective tactic: violence. During the opening decade, Mississippi's state politics shifted from the tolerable Governor Andrew Longino to the intolerable and outrageous James Vardaman. During this decade, Attala County resembled a battlefield, capturing state and national attention. African Americans held their ground by defending themselves, their institutions, and their race. Democrats controlled Mississippi's state legislature; however, Republicans occupied the White House. The 1896 election of William McKinley, whom African Americans helped elect, paid dividends. In May 1900, the McKinley administration appointed Daniel Hazley and William Phillips as census enumerators. Hazley and Phillips were active Republicans and established figures in the county and within their community. Despite their standing, the appointment drew immediate backlash. The *New York Times* reported on May 6 that white citizens became outraged by the enumerators' appointment.[2] African Americans held leadership and authority over whites, exposing white people's fear at its most significant physical and mental manifestation.[3]

On May 7, a letter in the *Kosciusko Herald* noted that the white citizens refused to accept the appointment because they believed "this [was] a white man's land."[4] Citizens threatened to lynch both Hazley and Phillips and destroy the county unless authorities recalled the appointment. Both Hazley and Phillips resisted the threats and affirmed that they could fulfill the duties entrusted to them. The outrage reached a point where federal intervention became necessary.[5] On May 9, 1900, Hazley and Phillips lost their federal appointment, thus satisfying the white citizens.[6] The May 11 issue of the *Kosciusko Herald* published a note of appreciation for removing Hazley and Phillips. The note stated,

> The good people of Beats 3 and 4 owe a debt of gratitude to Col. Brooke at this end of the line and also to Senator Sullivan, whose influence with the administration secured such prompt action in the matter. That they feel deeply grateful and will display it when occasion arrives, goes without saying. We are truly glad that the matter has ended this way, violence in any form is to be deprecated; and the temper of the people of Attala county is so well defined in matters of this nature that there was no telling where the matter would have ended, had they persisted in an attempt to discharge the functions of the office. It would be much better for all parties if the aspiring darkies could be made to realize perfectly that THE WHITE PEOPLE OF THE SOUTH WILL RULE THE SOUTH. This principle is as firmly implanted within the minds and consciences of the white people, as is the law of self preservation, and no argument, logic, or sophistry

can shake its adamantine foundation. So jealously do they guard this priceless heritage that the slightest infraction means trouble and it is not a species of trouble that is hard to find, either. But nothing further need be said. The incident is closed so far as these particular coons and the census are concerned and we feel thankful that no serious trouble has arisen.[7]

White Mississippians displayed their fear through their supposed superiority. Redemption could never be complete if African Americans remained uncontrolled. A conclusion that whites might have arrived at was that they could not institute the sort of control they imagined, and the fear they espoused was not as much one of Negro domination as the reality that whiteness had limitations. As Bradley Bond surmised, "The appearance of blacks at the voting booth in 1895 and 1899 proved to the emerging redneck faction that the Constitution of 1890 fell short of removing blacks from a position of influence in state politics."[8] As in previous decades, violence served as the backup mechanism whites used to get their way. The threat of violence showed the weak mentality that several whites possessed as it related to a society in which African Americans held control and power. With Hazley and Phillips serving as enumerators, they would possess a power typically held by whites. Socially, the position would make them equals with African Americans. As census enumerators, they had access to white homes in a nondomestic role (front door access), contact with white women (those in single-parent or nonmale households), professional terms of address ("sir" and "Mr.," not "boy," "uncle," "n----r," or other derogatory names), and obtaining and possessing information about the white community. These social norms anchored the ideology that whites were the superior race. The *Daily Morning Journal and Courier* elaborated this point, stating, "It is unwritten law, but law as effective as if engraved ten thousand times upon statute books, that negroes shall not go into white houses to question the women there about any sort of business whatsoever."[9] From Attala's perspective, its white citizens, who rejected Hazley and Phillips, likely espoused such beliefs and felt that African Americans reached a point where they acted without white permission or dictation.

Attala's white citizens claimed to have no ill will or feelings towards African Americans. Their contentment relied on African Americans remaining in their social and political place and remaining within the white citizens' boundaries.

White citizens made it clear that blurring or crossing those boundaries could result in actions that would not be to African Americans' benefit.[10] Although violence or threats of violence existed long before this incident, the collective resistance demonstrated the emergence of political colonization. Colonization was not merely the relationship between the metropole and its distant colony. It also included the "sociopolitical relationship between a colonial center and the indigenous or transplanted people forcibly brought within the orbit of the colonizer's influence."[11] The backlash to African American census enumerators represented a sociopolitical battle between colonizers and colonized. The United States possessed a double colony. The Union itself represented the nation. Within the Union, the former Confederacy operated as a nation-state within a larger nation. Within the former Confederacy were African Americans who constituted their own nation within southern codified and unwritten law. The circumstances around the African American political appointments exposed the tensions between the federal government and the South, and the tensions between the South and its African American inhabitants. Mississippi, to preserve the nation-state, called upon the Union to assist in controlling African Americans.

Whites reserved violence as a viable second option, the white default. It was the weapon in their arsenal that possessed the most significant impact. Attala County's white citizens expressed this sentiment with their willingness to inflict physical harm, highlighting their fragile mentality. The cracks in that mentality showed a temperamental and childlike response to situations that went against their liking. The federal government supported this infantile mindset by its inaction and choosing to cater to the southern nation-state. The persistent threats of violence and destruction prompted the federal government to withdraw its appointment, thus appeasing the white citizens. Following the incident, newspapers reported no evidence of ongoing racial tensions regarding the matter. The government withdrawing the appointments represented what Oliver Cromwell Cox described as "situations in which there are large proportions of both colored and white persons seeking to live in the same area, and whites insisting that the society is a 'white man's country,' as in the United States and South Africa—the bipartite situation."[12] Backlash spread to other parts of the Mississippi and the South about Black census enumerators. Oliver Campbell and Albert Ballus of Lowndes County, Mississippi, resigned their position following a mass meeting of white citizens protesting their appointment.[13] Three Black census enumerators in Montgomery County resigned their positions. The *Pascagoula Democrat-Star* referenced the Attala County incident related to the Montgomery County situation.[14] White citizens in Atlanta, Georgia, objected to Black census enumerators. In Little Rock, Arkansas, a Black census enumerator had to vacate a citizen's property at gunpoint.[15] Across Mississippi and the South, white peoples met African American progression with resistance and violence.

The November election was the first political event since the census incident. African Americans' continued presence at the ballot box represented the inability for whites to accomplish their suppression/disenfranchisement agenda, echoing David Guyton's concerns regarding the limitations of the poll tax and literacy test. Between April and October, seven African Americans registered to vote, the lowest total since 1897. The poll-tax amendment served as the central issue on the ballot, aside from the presidential election between William McKinley and William Jennings Bryan. Mississippi's efforts to institutionalize unequal school funding continued. A decade prior, David Guyton introduced a clause to be included in the 1890 constitution that stated, "The Legislature shall have power to prorate the school fund paid into the State and county treasuries by virtue of any per capita or property taxation, among the children of the white and colored races, according to the amount paid by each race."[16] After ratification, the common school fund and poll-tax totals were combined and allocated based on educable children per county, which benefited Black-majority counties.

When Andrew Longino became governor, he addressed white-majority counties' issue with distribution practices. Longino pushed the idea that fund allocation should derive from school attendance, not merely the number of educable children. Black children did not regularly attend school in Black-majority; white students in those counties benefited more than white students in white-majority counties. Evidence from previous decades showed that Black children outpaced white children in school attendance.[17] White counties wanted to separate poll taxes from the school fund, and the poll-tax amendment would allow each county to allocate the revenue rather than the state. The amendment passed with relative ease. Attala supported the amendment by a sizeable margin.[18] Attala's African American and white students made up almost the same percentage of the student population (Table 5.1). Enrollment did not reflect the racial composition of the county, which had held a consistent sixty-forty margin.

Table 5.1 Attala County School Enrollment, 1900–1908				
Year	African American Enrollment	White Enrollment	Total	African American Enrollment Percent
1900	4,146	4,712	8,858	46.81
1902	4,755	5,209	9,964	47.72
1906	5,048	5,342	10,390	48.59
1908	5,090	5,382	10,472	48.61
Totals	19,039	20,645	39,684	47.93

Source: Attala County educable school records.

While the poll-tax argument indicated African Americans not paying their fair share, Attala County's poll-tax situation paints a different picture. Poll tax was a confusing political issue. White citizens complained about paying disproportionately more taxes than Black citizens; however, connecting poll-tax payment to voting rendered their complaints tone-deaf. In 1900, the *Star Ledger* published a statistic that Attala County had between 1,500 and 1,600 delinquent taxpayers creating a $3,000 shortfall.[19] The white race could not have it both ways; they could not push for an all-white electorate and demand Black peoples fund their racial practices. The rise of the white primary, enacted in 1902, did not help the poll-tax issue. The primary system excluded African Americans from voting in primary elections, which further marginalized their local and state political visibility.

On March 15, 1901, the *Kosciusko Herald* published the names of delinquent taxpayers, a law passed by the state legislature (Table 5.2). The law required "a list of persons who fail to pay their poll tax before February 1 of each year." The intended impact was "that hundreds will be prompted by pride to do what their duty of citizenship requires, and the public will know who refuse to bear their proportion of the burden of the government."[20] Of the 1,757 names listed on the first published delinquent poll-tax list, 709 were African American. Despite the high number, they made up roughly 40 percent of delinquents compared to the 60 percent made up by white delinquents. These numbers aligned with the county's overall racial composition. Based on these numbers, the white population owed more in taxes than their racial counterparts. The poll-tax debate likely had more to do with local governments wanting to make up the deficits created by those within the white race. The greater the number of white

Table 5.2. African American Delinquent Poll Tax Breakdown by Precinct			
Precinct	*Black Residents*	*Literacy Percent*	*Average Unemployment (Months)*
Ayers	30	57.1	0.7
Ethel	17	52.9	1.2
Jerusalem	53	62.3	0.4
Kosciusko	213	59.2	1.4
Liberty Chapel	31	58.1	0.4
McCool	39	46.2	3.6
Newport	47	34.0	0.0
Peelers Mill	6	83.3	1.2
Providence	14	50.0	0.0
Rochester	19	47.4	0.1
Rocky Point	55	49.1	2.0
Sallis	104	51.0	1.2
Shrock	56	51.8	0.1
Thompson	8	62.5	0.0
Zilpha	17	47.1	0.7
Totals	*709*	*54.1*	*0.87*

Source: Data derived from 1900 United States Federal Census. Not all names could be identified as either African American or White as some names were associated with both races living in the same precinct or names could not be located in Attala County.

men who failed to pay their tax correlated to a more significant deficit since the county spent more per white child.

Further examination of the poll-tax situation allows for a more nuanced analysis of the liberation/redemption fight. African Americans choosing not to pay their poll tax cannot be assumed to have been economically incapable. African American men maintained gainful employment, as their average unemployment was less than one month between June 1899 and June 1900. They worked various occupations such as barber, blacksmith, butcher, carpenter, cook, cotton marker, ditcher, driver, farmer, farm laborer, horsier, laborer, minister, painter, teacher, railroad, servant, waiter, and well-digger, representing both the working and middle class. These men were not educationally deficient. On average, 54 percent possessed full or partial literacy. Legally, county officials could not prosecute African Americans for lack of poll-tax payment. By not paying the poll tax, African Americans showed their rejection of the white power structure. Although publishing delinquent names served to shame citizens, white citizens were likely the target of such shaming because they should have been taking advantage of the laws that legislators changed to benefit them. Neil McMillen focused on the disenfranchised African American and overlooked the nontaxpayer's potential anti-white-supremacist stance. His lack of discussion of poll-tax politics plays into a narrative of the marginalized voter who presented little defense of his Fifteenth Amendment rights. McMillen narrowly referenced slave narratives, where subjects discussed their apathy toward voting that stemmed from white disapproval; however, McMillen's missed the opportunity to examine the intersection of politics and choice.[21]

Charley A. Lovelady was born on March 12, 1859, in Illinois. He lived in Holmes County before moving to Kosciusko, where he worked as a house painter. An educated man, Charley registered to vote on July 2, 1892; however, he never voted. Born a free man, Charley likely possessed the mentality that true freedom had no strings attached. Charley appeared to face no repercussions for not paying his poll taxes. In 1905, he secured work painting the Vaiden courthouse.[22] Later that year, F. W. Devoe & Company put a notice in the *Kosciusko Herald* advertising their paints to Charley. The notice addressed Charley as "Dear Sir."[23] A photograph taken at the turn of the century showed Charley standing alongside Merchant & Farmer's Bank personnel A. E. Atkinson, W. B. Potts, and E. L. Lucas. The photograph also featured George Eichelberger. George was born in March 1869 in South Carolina. Married at age fourteen, George did not receive a formal education, nor did he ever register to vote. He worked as a porter, the position he held at the time of the photograph. Charley and George resided in the same voting precinct. While Charley appeared to be nonpolitical by choice, George represented what the white political machine sought, the legally disenfranchised African American. The photograph represented each man's standing in society: Charley standing equal to his white counterparts, while George's seated position indicates a lower social status.[24]

Attala County reentered the national spotlight with the double lynching of Jim Gaston and Monroe Hallum. On July 20, 1902, in an area known as the Crossroads near the Rockpoint and Natchez Trace roads, Gaston and Hallum died at the hands of a white mob who believed the men led a secret organization whose goal was to incite and inflict violence on white citizens.[25] Evidence that such an organization existed does not exist; however, white citizens linked a previous organization, Peoples Protection, to such activity. Peoples Protection, a Black organization, operated in North Attala. In 1898, organization members William and Emmanuel Jones published and disseminated a report alleging that Jim Short "told the white men of the neighborhood that it was a society to boycott labor and to raise a mob and commit other crimes." The press favored Short, describing him as "one of the best darkies in the county," over William Jones, a teacher who "deserved to be rigidly dealt with."[26] Four years later, in the exact geographical location, violence erupted over similar accusations that Short allegedly made to the white community. The belief that such an organization existed meant that William and Emmanuel Jones told Jim Short's truth. Peoples Protection likely advocated self-defense, which Short relayed as mob violence. White authorities also had a history of sabotaging Black organizations that they could not control. In 1889, Oliver Cromwell went to Leflore County to recruit for the Colored Farmers Alliance. White authorities responded by spreading rumors that the alliance planned an uprising against whites. The accusation led to state intervention, resulting in weapon confiscation and death.[27]

Lynching served to circumvent the legal system. White men used lynching to prosecute, convict, and execute without due process. The practice reenforced white supremacy by demonstrating white power and African Americans' inability to challenge or disrupt said power. Jim Gaston and Monroe Hallum (also known as Monroe McCain) were born in Attala County.[28] They were blood relatives and educated men. Gaston owned mortgage-free land, and Hallum was a registered voter in the Liberty Chapel precinct.[29] The mob acted as judge, jury, and executioner, deciding that Gaston and Hallum were the leaders and sentencing them to death by gunshot. Upon the arrival of police, the mob openly disclosed how the murder unfolded; however, they did not disclose who did the shooting.[30] The initial murder brought no charges as no witnesses stepped forward. On September 13, 1902, the Attala County grand jury "distinguished itself in an unprecedented manner" when its members indicted twenty-five white men for murdering Gaston and Hallum.[31] On January 24, 1903, the *Grenada Sentinel* reported that ten white men, namely A. E. Kierk, A. R. Tucker, Bill Goff, Bob Millner, Jim Green, John Green, Lee Whatley, Jim Whatley, Garrison Carlisle, and Oliver Wasson, were arrested and incarcerated by Sheriff Love in connection to the murders. Noah Lindsey, the eleventh individual, had been arrested prior. The grand jury indicted these men for their participation.[32] As the *Woodville Republican* published, the case marked the first time in Mississippi's history that the lynching of an African American led to trials for white men.[33]

Bill (William) Goff, Lee Whatley, Jim (James) Whatley, and Oliver Wasson lived in the Liberty Chapel Community. Garrison Carlisle and Noah Lindsey lived in the Zilpha Community. The men, except for Bill Goff, had some education, and most owned land by which farming was their chief occupation. Whether or not these men had a formal relationship before the lynching is not known. The mob violence prompted Governor Andrew Longino to intervene and turn the incident into a state issue. Governor Longino launched a diligent prosecution assembling prominent counsel to bring justice and finality to the incident.[34] Andrew Longino served as Mississippi's governor from 1900 to 1904. He attempted to end Mississippi's mob-violence epidemic. He introduced legislation that required counties to financially support families affected by lynching. Longino hoped that the financial burden would prompt local authorities to eradicate mob violence and reduce lynching.[35] Longino was not a civil rights governor. He wanted business and industry to relocate to the state and saw mob violence as a barrier to his legislative agenda. The Gaston and Hallum lynching provided Longino the opportunity to demonstrate his determination to end mob violence.

John Greene was the first man bought to trial, which began on Thursday, March 5, 1903. He entered a plea of not guilty. Lawyers chose fifty men to serve as potential jurors, none being African American.[36] The jury selection took place from March 9 through March 11. The jury consisted of twelve men, namely: Peterson E. Watts, James A. Smith, Anthony Y. Foster, Thomas E. Stingley, Henry C. Miller, Milton J. Girner, W. W. Bond, James S. Belk, John L. Graham, Henry W. Herod, Thomas D. Ray, and Silas W. Brister. The judge's illness postponed the trial's first day.[37] On March 17, 1903, the court granted a continuance, set bail for $750, and provided a security detail for John Green. The term ended without the jury hearing testimony. Noah Lindsey received a $200 bond conditional on his testimony during the next term and any subsequent term until further notice. The final business of the court was to order payment to certain individuals for their services.[38] Constant court delays derailed the state's witnesses' ability to come forth and testify in open court. African Americans Ernest and Green Adams were the state's key witnesses. The witnesses went to Arkansas, and communication with them was lost. In September 1904, the judge ordered the trial removed from the docket. There was no further investigation of the case and no verdict rendered for any of the arrested parties. However, the two-year ordeal was a sizeable expense for the county's taxpayers.[39] The Gaston and Hallum trial mirrored that of Jordan and Dora Teague. While their accused murderers faced trial, the verdict and nonverdict fell short of delivering true justice.

James K. Vardaman's election to the governorship marked the true beginning of Mississippi's white supremacy era. Vardaman, known as the "White Chief," advocated maintaining the white social order at the expense of African American rights. Vardaman had a history in Mississippi politics. Initially unsuccessful in his previous bids for governor, Vardaman distinguished himself with his unapologetic and bold attack on African Americans. In the 1903 gubernatorial race, Vardaman vilified African Americans and, as David Oshinsky stated, "sketched a more ominous portrait in which blacks were demanding social equality, pursuing white women, and committing awful crimes."[40] Vardaman's words reflected his 1903 campaign slogan: "A VOTE FOR VARDAMAN IS A VOTE FOR WHITE SUPREMACY, THE SAFETY OF THE HOME, AND THE PROTECTION OF OUR WOMEN AND CHILDREN."[41] Vardaman resonated with voters in areas where "fear of 'race leveling' was more intense."[42] As governor, Vardaman gave poor whites power to police themselves and deal with African Americans as they saw fit. In his response to lynching, Vardaman stated,

> I can sympathize thoroughly with one whose friend or relative has been outraged or atrociously murdered by a black brute, and I am not going to censure people who act a little indiscreetly under the influence of passion thus aroused, but there is one thing certain, the law must be upheld, and so long as I occupy the gubernatorial chair I shall do all within my power to see that the laws are enforced. The courts must perform their functions. When this is done the people will be satisfied.[43]

Although Vardaman cracked down on the whitecapping phenomena that resurfaced under Longino's administration, Vardaman urged legislation strengthening Jim Crow in public accommodations and reviving Black Code-type laws such as penalties for loafing.[44]

African Americans did not cower under Vardaman. When Charles Buchanan left Kosciusko, he moved to West Point in Clay County, where he continued to publish the *Preacher and Teacher*.[45] Despite physically leaving Attala, he retained close ties. Buchanan continued to spearhead campaigns for Black liberation. In March 1904, Buchanan, along with Louis Kossuth Atwood and G. W. Porter served on a committee to select the venue for the Negro Congress scheduled to take place that August with an estimated attendance of ten thousand.[46] Buchanan used his paper to promote a progressive social and political agenda. In September 1904, Buchanan's advocacy for social equality led to white citizens in West Point forcing Buchanan to leave the city. As stated in the *Columbus Weekly Dispatch*, "Buchanan had been looked upon as a disturber and trouble breeder and no doubt the men of both races who love peace and an amicable relationship in life between the white and black man, will endorse his deportation. . . . The white man is going to rule absolutely the South."[47] The *Water Valley Progress* provided further detail surrounding Buchanan's forcible removal. The paper stated, "C. A. Buchanan, a negro editor of a paper at West Point, who has been advocating social equality, was ordered by the citizens of that town to leave within a specified time. He went. Mississippi has no abiding place for a social equality negro."[48]

Buchanan's encounter resembled a North Carolina incident from November 1898 when, according to the *Columbus Dispatch*, a newspaper office operated by African Americans burned following a publication that "reflected upon the chastity of the women in the state." The article also stated, "There is a lesson in this episode for the negroes of the south. It should be a warning to them to keep out of politics and pursue peacefully their vocations. The South is the white man's country and he will rule."[49] Buchanan's white response indicated that whites read the Black press or recruited other African Americans to report to them any "deviations" from their expectations of normalcy. Charles Buchanan left Mississippi and relocated to Guthrie, Oklahoma. There he began a new paper, the *Oklahoma Safeguard*. Through this paper, Mississippi and Attala County gained a wider audience.

Violence continued to define the Attala County sociopolitical landscape. In November 1905, one of the first race-based incidents occurred involving Black men, white women, and lynch mobs in the Vardaman era. Rufus Ousley faced accusations of writing an "insulting note" to a "respectable young lady." The woman's brother asked Lucius Love and others to assist him in arresting Ousley. On November 29, 1905, the party arrived and surrounded Ousley's home, demanding his surrender; however, Ousley fired a double-barrel shotgun at Love, hitting him twice in the chest.[50] Ousley's actions showed an action rarely discussed. The presence of a white mob did not mean instant compliance. Ousley defended himself, not allowing himself to accept blame for an act he did not commit or where the white woman was an active participant. Ida B. Wells's *Southern Horrors: Lynch Law in All Its Phases* exposed the false rationale of white rape as justification for lynching.

Attala County had no publicized cases of white women accusing Black men of rape; however, at first instance, the response was typical. The mere claim that a Black man acted inappropriately towards a white woman resulted in either death or imprisonment. The next day, while attempting to bring Ousley to justice, a lynch mob killed a Black man named Bob Kennedy, thinking he was Ousley. The mob received no punishment for murdering Kennedy and proceeded in their quest to lynch Ousley.[51] James K. Vardaman issued a cash reward for Ousley's "arrest and conviction."[52] On December 29, a reward for Ousley's capture appeared in the *Star Ledger*. The award totaled $750: $250 for capture and $500 for conviction. Ousley's description read as follows.

> Rufus Ousley is about 5 feet 11 inches high, weighs from 160 to 170 pounds, is 32 years old, wears No. 9 shoe, round face, prominent cheek bones and nose, has a light moustache, walks erect, nervous or restless, with pleasing address, often smiling. A noted crapshooter and all around touch. Was wounded in left side from top of head to waist band of pants with No 4 shot. Any one capturing a negro answering to the above description should communicate with Sheriff J. W. Black, Kosciusko, Miss, at once. The negro was last seen near the Louisiana line going West.[53]

Ousley defended his life by taking a white man's life who threatened his. Ousley was the first known Black man in the county to kill a white man in self-defense. However, his situation was not in isolation. On August 18, 1904, Andy Nash shot and killed Ben Ellington in Thomastown, located in Leake County, after Ellington and his two friends assaulted Nash, thinking he was a white man they had had an issue with prior. Nash took offense to their intrusion, and the situation escalated, and the men seized Nash's horse and planned to beat him. Nash responded by shooting at the party, striking Ellington, who died the following day.[54] These men were not what Leon Litwack would call "baptized" in the ways of white peoples. In *Trouble in Mind: Black Southerners in the*

Age of Jim Crow, Litwack discussed societal lines that white citizens drew to dictate African American life. He stated, "Fear of violating those boundaries—unintentionally or as perceived by whites—haunted black men and women in their daily routines, compelling them to act with extreme caution in the presence of whites."[55] He further elaborated, "The slightest deviance from the racial code, no matter how unintended, could produce immediate concern in a black person."[56] Akinyele Umoja examined the rebellious African American through the lens of the "Bad Negro." The Bad Negro defied the color line and refused to defer to white peoples. Such individuals had a reputation for threatening the stability of the social order.[57]

Like Litwack, who overemphasized the white ego and underestimated the Black mindset, Umoja begins and stops his analysis of the Bad Negro from the perspective of the southern white mindset. African Americans did not fear whites in the manner that is commonly displayed. People like Ousley and Nash were not anomalies but individuals who fully understood the ramifications of their actions and acted upon them anyway. The race could not advance if those within the race allowed fear to dominate them. One way to defeat the boogeyman was to kill him. African Americans had the right to protect themselves when forced. African Americans had to see how they lived in a violent society, and freedom resulted from violence.[58] W. E. B. Du Bois supported armed resistance for protection and lambasted those for backing down to the threats and violence white society inflicted upon them.[59] African Americans used violence to shatter the idea that African Americans had a fear of white peoples.

The violent reaction to the Ousley incident occurred months after Charles Buchanan's editorial praising the late Judge Charles H. Campbell. Campbell, brother-in-law of J. A. P. Campbell, was "a citizen far above the average, beloved by the blacks as well as the whites," who was "opposed to mobs and in favor of law and order in both races." Buchanan explained that men like Campbell were "fastly [sic] passing away and it will be the worse for the Negro when this class are all gone," adding "Kosciusko can richly boast of having some of the noblest hearted white citizens in it that can be found in Miss. anywhere."[60] Buchanan saw the potential for solid race relations but placed the onus on white citizens to act in a manner that reflected the actions of upstanding, principled whites who preceded them. Men like Jason Niles, Samuel Young, and Rasselas Boyd passed in the decades prior, to be replaced by leaders who sought subordination more than cooperation.

While Vardaman fanned the flames of racial hostilities, he also set out to eradicate Black education. Booker T. Washington explained in his 1903 letter to Oswald Garrison Villard that Vardaman's election signified white Mississippians' support of diminishing educational opportunities in the same manner that Mississippi was the first state to diminish voting capabilities. Washington called for strong action in response to Vardaman's election.[61] Vardaman did not see Black education's practicality, a point he raised and obsessed over as early as 1899. Vardaman saw that the quality of education in majority-Black counties was better than that in majority-white counties, which crafted his position that state funds be used for the group who paid the most taxes.[62] Vardaman's statement, "Forty years experience had proved that the Negro was unsuited for the same type of education the white man received. Literate Negroes were criminally inclined, and it was folly for the whites to tax themselves to create criminals," underscored his disdain for Black peoples and the idea that whites played a role in providing them an education.[63]

After entering office, Vardaman supported spending more money on common schools, "poor man's university."[64] Mississippi had long instituted an educational caste system that rewarded white teachers and students; however, Vardaman's desire to strip education from African Americans set him apart from his political counterparts. Several African Americans left Mississippi during the early 1900s because of Vardaman's educational views, that education was "not meant for Negroes but white people only." A lack of educational opportunities prompted an exodus to the north, west, and for some even to Mexico.[65] Those who remained added to their educational independence by creating institutions to meet the educational demands of their people without white assistance.

On January 9, 1905, a fire destroyed Central Mississippi College.[66] Fireworks were the fire's official cause. This explanation seems unlikely since the fire occurred during a time when fireworks would not be in use. The more probable cause for the fire was criminal arson; however, there was no further investigation.[67] Professor Isham Harris Hampton served as the college's president during this time. Isham was born in Fayetteville, Tennessee, to Thomas Hampton and Martha Lamb. Harris joined Central Mississippi College following his tenure as principal of the North Alabama Baptist Academy in Courtland, Alabama. The college's destruction did not demoralize African Americans but rather galvanized them to rebuild their institution. On May 10, 1905, the college's trustees decided to rebuild the institution. The trustees described the new college as

> a four-story building this time instead of three as before. A nine-foot brick basement will be built; composed of an engine room, coal-room kitchen, dining room, and a store room. The second floor will consist of a large well lighted and heated chapel, President's office, and four classrooms. The petitions will be moveable so that on special occasions you lift them up, turning all the rooms into one, making the largest assembly room in the city. The two other floors will be used for dormitories. The plan will be steam heated, electric lighted and plenty of water on every floor.[68]

The trustees decided to build a larger and stronger structure that established the college's presence in the city. The new building's price was five thousand dollars. The college raised an additional three thousand to meet the November 1, 1906, completion date.[69], and other individuals raised four thousand. Charles Buchanan (who now resided in Guthrie, Oklahoma) embarked on a fundraising mission throughout Mississippi, making stops in Vaiden, Meridian, Kosciusko, Jackson, Macon, Durant, Pickens, West Station, and West Point. The Mount Hope Association raised $500. While in Kosciusko, Buchanon secured $800. The Second New Hope and Meridian Association donated $41.50. During his trip, Buchanan raised $1,341.50.[70] Since the monies collected included no county or state funds, Central Mississippi College maintained its autonomy.

While efforts to rebuild Central Mississippi College continued, in June 1905 the convention of Baptist churches and preachers met in Vicksburg, Mississippi. Natchez College president S. C. H. Owens spoke on education and the importance of colleges. From this conversation grew the foundation to create an industrial school in Kosciusko. The industrial school would serve the entire state.[71] Rev. Patrick Henry Thompson spearheaded the project. Thompson, son of Milton and Ellen Thompson, was born on March 15, 1864, in Okolona, Mississippi, located in Chickasaw County. Thompson received his education at an early age in the Okolona city schools under Professor J. H. Henderson, his earliest known teacher. In 1883, Thompson became the principal at an Okolona school with 150 students and three teachers under his charge. In October 1885, he entered Jackson College and graduated with high honors in 1887. He taught at Jackson College before attending Virginia Union University in Richmond in Fall 1888. In Spring 1892, Thompson received his bachelor of divinity. From 1892 to 1898, he taught at Jackson College before taking a position at Central Mississippi College.[72] In July 1905, Kosciusko Industrial College's twenty-one board-member committee, headed by Thompson and the General Baptist Educational Convention, became partners.[73]

The Kosciusko Industrial College began operations in late 1905. Like Booker T. Washington, Thompson wanted to transform the Kosciusko Industrial College into Mississippi's own Tuskegee.[74] According to Thompson, "I do not hope to do anything greater than to well establish the Kosciusko Industrial College and make it the Tuskegee of Mississippi, where thousands of boys and girls resort for the development of 'Hand, Head and Heart.'"[75] Thompson's biography in the Mt. Helm Church history indicated that he did not want a Tuskegee imitation but one that would complement Washington's institution for Mississippi's African American citizens.[76] Booker T. Washington's arrival on the national political stage elevated education and its importance to a broader Black global audience.[77] Thompson's industrial college coincided with an international effort to promote industrial education to the masses, which arose during the early-twentieth-century American imperialist campaigns. Washington's stance and promotion of industrial education galvanized African Americans domestically and internationally.

Thompson, chairman of the location committee, chose Kosciusko for the school's location over West Point, Jackson, Canton, Florence, and Vicksburg. Thompson chose Kosciusko based on the understanding that Buchanan, president of the Central Mississippi College's board of trustees, would influence the board to combine the two schools into one institution.[78] On November 30, 1905, Masons laid the cornerstone for the institution's first building. Students attended class in Thompson's home, and the First Baptist Church housed opening exercises during the campus's construction. Thompson, his wife Sarah, and Leona Hampton served as the first teachers. After relocating to a CME church, the school opened Attala Hall on March 30, 1906.[79] Florence Newell and Emma Shorter also joined the faculty. With Kosciusko Industrial College in operation, construction on the new Central Mississippi College began in February 1906, with the cornerstone being laid in May 1906. The college's trustees turned the cornerstone milestone into a statewide event. Dr. E. W. Lampton, grand master of the Mississippi Masonic Grand Lodge, laid the cornerstone, which was followed by a barbeque on the campus grounds. Rev. A. M. Johnson, president of the General Baptist State Convention, and Rev. E. B. Topp, editor of the *Baptist Reporter*, served as guest speakers.[80]

The college served a larger purpose than education. There was a sense of racial unity and pride displayed during the college's reconstruction. Rev. J. A. Marshall stated in the *Vicksburg Evening Press* regarding Central Mississippi College, "there was no School in the state for Negroes that was doing more to lift up the race and train the boys and girls for useful work."[81] The college capitalized on its momentum. The school expanded its curriculum to include courses in typesetting, music, and photography. The Central Mississippi College Publishing Company published its educational journal, the *Central Mississippi College Gazette*, with Lee Ashford as foreman.[82] The college advertised for nine positions, including a president, matron, and seven teachers (two men and five women).[83] H. M. Thompson replaced Hampton as the school principal. His wife, Mary, became the college's matron. H. M. Thompson began his teaching career in Savannah, Tennessee. After he graduated from Roger Williams University, he taught school in Okolona, Aberdeen, and Brooksville. Before taking the president position at Central Mississippi College, he held the position of principal at West Point's Ministerial Institute and High School.[84]

Kosciusko Industrial College represented a counter to redemption. Southern Redeemers had yet to fully establish complete control over the Black population in land ownership, education, and social control. Thompson's goals for his people and his school made it so "the eyes of the State of Mississippi then turned towards this great school and anxiously awaited its development."[85] By February 1906, Kosciusko Industrial College hit its stride, attracting a high number of students. The industrial college joined a growing list of state industrial colleges, including Bogue Chitto Industrial College in Lincoln County and Mound Bayou Industrial College in Bolivar County. The institute showed a promising start, and its first graduating class in 1906 included Oscar C. Thomas, who would go on to graduate from Virginia Union University.[86]

Central Mississippi College graduate and professor Lee Boston Turner wrote in Buchanan's *Oklahoma Safeguard* regarding Black-operated institutions,

If Negroes are ever to become anything more than drudges for other races they must both establish and support more high schools and colleges, and see that they are attended regularly. From time to time wise and good people, inspired by the xpressed [sic] above and realizing that the public schools of the South are inadequate to meet the needs of the Colored people, have established schools of higher grade.[87]

Turner's words reflected the sustained desire for higher education as Central Mississippi College enrollment reached a point that exceeded both expectation and capacity.[88] Both Central Mississippi College and Kosciusko Industrial College educated and produced graduates who had successful careers in business, education, ministry, and medicine. These individuals included Lee Boston Turner, Cassius Alexander Ward, Leroy Dabbs, Jeremiah J. Olive, Thomas Luther Zuber, E. L. Todd, William Brown, James Monroe Coleman, Oscar C. Thomas, Edward Henry, Walter Alexander Zuber, and Patrick Henry Thompson's son Charles Henry Thompson.

Dr. Leroy Dabbs, son of Jack Dabbs and Caroline Hudson, came to Kosciusko from Kemper County. He became a prominent physician after graduating from Meharry Medical College. He specialized in pediatrics and did postgraduate studies at the Children's Hospital in both New York and Chicago. He served in the World Medical Association, formed by the United Nations in 1946. As a member, he travelled to Haiti, Jamaica, Cuba, and Western Europe.[89] Cassius Alexander Ward, son of Lewis and Emily Ward, lived in Holmes County. After receiving his education in Mississippi, he graduated from the Andover Newton Theological School and pastored at the Ebenezer Baptist Church in Boston, the largest Black church in the city. He later became pastor of the Central Baptist Church in Pittsburg.[90] Dr. Thomas Luther Zuber, a native of Starkville, Mississippi, and son of the Rev. John Zuber and Annie Dunlap, attended Central Mississippi College during the few years he lived in Kosciusko. After leaving Kosciusko, Zuber earned his AB degree from Morehouse College, and on April 22, 1913, Zuber graduated from Meharry Medical College.[91] He established the Zuber Clinic in West Point, Mississippi, and served as president of several medical associations that included the North East Mississippi Medical, Dental, and Pharmaceutical Society and the North Mississippi Medical and Surgical Association.[92]

Jeremiah Olive, a Kosciusko native, was the son of Thomas Olive and Eliza Love. After completing his studies at Central Mississippi College, he pastored in Winona, Mississippi, and East St. Louis, Illinois. Olive settled in Cairo, Illinois. As vice president of the Illinois State General Baptist Convention, he helped raise funds to assist the Tulsa race-riot victims. As president of the Illinois State Baptist Convention, he led 160,000 Baptists.[93] He last served the Salem Baptist Church in Champaign before his sudden death in 1937. Charles Thompson came to Kosciusko following his father's decision to teach at Central Mississippi College. In a trial transcript of Sweatt v. Painter, Thompson spoke about his time in Kosciusko. Thompson stated, "I attended an elementary school, private Baptist school in Kosciusko, Mississippi, and graduated from what I thought was a high school." Louis Ray surmised that Black families sent their children to private schools because of the lack of choice for public schooling.[94] Ray failed to discuss that Thompson received his education at schools his father either taught or founded, rather minimizing these Black-operated institutions in comparison to midwestern and eastern colleges and universities. Central Mississippi College and Kosciusko Industrial College served as a stepping-stone for its graduates to pursue higher education. Thompson earned his bachelor's degree from Virginia Union University and later attended the University of Chicago, becoming the first African American to earn a doctorate in educational psychology. After teaching in Missouri, he found a teaching position at Howard University in 1926. Thompson created the *Journal of Negro Education* in 1932, of which he served as editor-in-chief.[95]

Central Mississippi College and Kosciusko Industrial College

African American political presence continued to dwindle at the voting booth; however, they found their political voice in the jury box. Four African Americans, Daniel Webster Turner (Chickasaw County), Alfred Frazier (Attala County), George Pilcher Childress (Choctaw County), and Daniel Mongo Hazley (Attala County), along with nineteen whites, served on the Mississippi state grand jury in the state's Eastern Division of the Northern District. Attala and Chickasaw County had the highest representation; however, Attala was the only county with multiple Black jurors.[96] Three of the four Black jurors were former slaves, with Turner and Frazier living more

Rebuilt Central Mississippi College (From *Multum in Parvo: An Authenticated History of Progressive Negroes in Pleasing and Graphic Biographical Style* by Isaiah Wadsworth Crawford and Patrick H. Thompson, 1912)

Professor Patrick Henry Thompson (From *Multum in Parvo: An Authenticated History of Progressive Negroes in Pleasing and Graphic Biographical Style* by Isaiah Wadsworth Crawford and Patrick H. Thompson, 1912)

Professor Isham Harris Hampton (From the *American Star*, December 19, 1902)

Professor H. M. Thompson (From *The History of Negro Baptists in Mississippi* by Patrick H. Thompson, 1898)

Professor Lee Boston Turner (From *Multum in Parvo: An Authenticated History of Progressive Negroes in Pleasing and Graphic Biographical Style* by Isaiah Wadsworth Crawford and Patrick H. Thompson, 1912)

Charles Henry Thompson, PhD (From *Multum in Parvo: An Authenticated History of Progressive Negroes in Pleasing and Graphic Biographical Style* by Isaiah Wadsworth Crawford and Patrick H. Thompson, 1912)

James Monroe Coleman (From *Multum in Parvo: An Authenticated History of Progressive Negroes in Pleasing and Graphic Biographical Style* by Isaiah Wadsworth Crawford and Patrick H. Thompson, 1912)

Oscar C. Thomas (From *Multum in Parvo: An Authenticated History of Progressive Negroes in Pleasing and Graphic Biographical Style* by Isaiah Wadsworth Crawford and Patrick H. Thompson, 1912)

Reverend Jeremiah J. Olive (Collected by Doris K. Wylie Hoskins. "Salem Baptist Church files–Doris K. Wylie Hoskins Archive," in eBlack Champaign-Urbana, Item #167, http://eblackcu.net/portal/items/show/167 [accessed August 24, 2021])

than five years in slavery. Black jurors in Mississippi were not a novelty, but their presence was not commonplace either. On April 27, 1869, Mississippi African Americans gained access to the jury box. Military Governor Adelbert Ames issued an order stating, "All persons, without respect to race, color or previous condition of servitude, who possess the qualifications prescribed by ... the Revised Code of 1857, shall be competent jurors."[97] Between 1865 and 1895, five known cases of all-Black juries or interracial juries occurred in Mississippi. These cases included both white and Black defendants. The grand jury's presence alone was significant; however, the ability for Black men to criminally sentence white men in the wake of the James Vardaman era added another dimension to the liberation struggle.

Sitting on a jury alone is merely symbolic; however, what the jury decided moves the narrative forward. Bill Barfield (Attala County), Wade Bean, and Willie Ray (Prentiss County) were three white men convicted of violating revenue and postal laws and sentenced to prison. Fayette Mathews (Clay County) was the only African American man convicted and sentenced during this session. Barfield and Mathews committed the same crime; however, Matthews received a lesser sentence. Barfield received ninety days in county prison, suspended because he paid his fine. Matthews received a thirty-day sentence in the county prison.[98] William Philips served as the only Black grand juror during the 1909 October Term. He was one of three jurors from Attala County. During the term, the jury rendered a guilty verdict for Will Rutherford (Attala County).[99] Serving on juries and rendering justice can be classified as one of the best realizations of liberation.

As Hazley and Frazier delivered justice at the state level, an old local case reached finality. Rufus Ousley eluded captured for nearly three years before being arrested in September 1908. His case had not vanished from state memory. At trial, John A. Davis and Allen P. Dodd represented Ousley, while Thomas Sisson and Thomas Guyton represented the state. Ousley's jury consisted of Bartley Thomas Chappell, William A. Crossley, Edward L. Watts, M. J. Moore, John Burwell Davis, George Thomas Galloway, Perry Thomas Simmons, George V. Crook, Luke Wood, Felbrert Ray, James Thomas Woods, and J. H. Armstrong. Ousley's council took measures to ensure a fair trial. They motioned to "quash the indictment and quash the special venire" given African Americans' exclusion from the process.[100] Davis and Dodd recognized that an all-white jury would not fairly judge the evidence, rendering Ousley's fate already sealed. Hazley and Frazier's appearance on the state grand jury did not translate to African Americans securing jury slots in local cases. Jury exclusion allowed whites to control the rule of law, similar to days of slavery and the Black Codes. The all-white jury rendered a guilty verdict; however, they could not agree on punishment. Eleven men favored the death penalty, and Perry Simmons favored a life sentence. The result was that Ousley received life imprisonment, not death. White citizens expressed outrage that Ousley did not receive the death penalty. Fearing a potential mob attack, Sheriff Emmett Carr put Ousley on a train to West Point.[101] Ousley began serving his sentence at the Parchman Penitentiary; however, he escaped the prison in October 1909.[102]

The mob mentality that citizens displayed at the onset of the decade continued during the latter part of the decade. The appetite for revenge showed lynching's impact as a psychological instiller of fear in the African American psyche and the further cementing of white supremacy as both a concept and reality. As Charles S. Johnson discussed in his 1947 work *Patterns of Negro Segregation*, African Americans sought to avoid whites because they understood that nothing good would come from interactions with them—not because African Americans feared them, but because

African Americans understood white people's volatile personality.[103] Regarding color prejudice, Du Bois stated,

> Such curious kinks of the human mind exist and must be reckoned with soberly. . . . They must not be encouraged by being let alone. They must be recognized as facts, but unpleasant facts; things that stand in the way of civilization and religion and common decency. They can be met in but one way,—by the breadth and broadening of human reason, by catholicity of taste and culture.[104]

African Americans knew the ability and power they possessed, and they understood that most within white society would reject them despite likely understanding that African Americans possessed such awareness.

In Du Bois's *Atlanta University Studies on the Negro*, he envisioned African American advancement as a process by which society changed its attitudes toward the race because the strength of its hatred and prejudice towards Black peoples must change by the acceptance of facts over speculation and theories about the Black race that had been proven inaccurate.[105] While Du Bois placed responsibility on whites to use both common and book sense, African Americans long demonstrated that waiting on that to happen would only prolong their liberation efforts. Within Attala's borders, African Americans pushed the boundaries of their liberation, which in some situations led to responses that curtailed their advancement. Most white citizens would not accept Black peoples in an advanced mental, educational, economic, or political state. As the next chapter examines, the first part of the next decade saw liberation and redemption efforts entangled amid the throes of legalized Jim Crow. African Americans and white citizens settled into patterns of maintaining their gains while seeking ways to gain the upper hand in their liberation struggles.

CHAPTER 6

UNFINISHED BUSINESS
LIBERATION AND JIM CROW

The 1910s, or at least their first half, represented a settling-down of Attala society. African Americans and whites laid the groundwork for their liberation and redemption agendas. The fall of the county's Black political class settled into permanency by 1910. Following the census-enumeration incident and the increase in delinquent poll-tax payers, African American political activity plummeted. The South had not forgotten Republican efforts to appoint Black census enumerators. Ahead of the 1910 census, white citizens publicly stating their resistance to Black census enumerators. The *Hartford Courant* published the following in its July 5, 1909, edition.

> Concerned about what they supposed to be the possibility that negroes will be sent into the homes of white residents in the South as enumerators to gather information for the thirteenth federal census, democratic members of Congress will urge President Taft to give instructions that only white enumerators shall be employed in districts south of "Mason and Dixon's Line." Representatives of the southern states in Congress say they have little hope of preventing the employment of negroes unless the President interferes.[1]

The political productivity that positioned men like Hazley and Phillips to gain federal appointments began to disappear in the previous decade (Table 6.1). Forty-one Black men registered to vote between 1900 and 1909.

Table 6.1. Shifts in Black Voter Registration				
Precinct	1892–1899	1900–1909	1910–1915	Total Registered
Ayers	45	1	1	47
Ethel	7	0	0	7
Jerusalem	82	4	1	87
Kosciusko	198	8	6	212
Liberty Chapel	17	4	2	23
McCool	51	3	0	54
Newport	14	0	0	14
Peelers Mill	15	0	0	15
Providence	10	0	0	10
Rochester	16	0	0	16
Rocky Point	57	6	0	63
Sallis	36	8	0	44
Shrock	19	2	0	21
Thompson	5	2	0	7
Zilpha	1	0	0	1
Totals	573	38	10	621

Source: Attala County Precinct Voter Registration Books.

The decade opened with zero new Black registered voters and only twelve new registrants between 1911 and 1915. Instead of simple disenfranchisement, these shifts indicate two plausible scenarios. First, the African American voter was demoralized. Decades of political participation and progress produced a zero-sum game, leading to focus shifting to other areas. Second, whites realized how close they came to "Negro domination" and increased their suppression and disenfranchising efforts. These scenarios may have played out individually or occurred in some combination. Leon Litwack portrayed political withdrawal not as a weakness but rather as a natural reaction to the trauma created by broken political promises. Litwack provided a glimpse into the psychological wear and tore on the human mind without giving whites absolute power in the matter. He examined the impact that African American political activity had on white politics and the impact that white politics had on African Americans.[2]

In 1910, former governor James Vardaman ran for the United States Senate in the first election of senators by popular vote. With nonexistent political

James Vardaman on a campaign stop in Kosciusko in June 1911. Vardaman is pictured standing on the wagon in a suit and no hat. (Courtesy of the Attala County Library)

visibility, African Americans had limited say in electing officers. Even if it had little to no impact on the outcome, their vote had the capacity to sway elections among Democratic candidates. Vardaman, who campaigned on an anti-Black platform, held a campaign rally in Kosciusko. Photographs of the rally show no African Americans present. African Americans remained relevant at the state and national level, where locals Hazley and Phillips remained active. During the contested 1912 Republican Party primary between William Howard Taft and former President Theodore Roosevelt, Hazley and Phillips served as Taft delegates representing Mississippi's fourth district at the Republican National Convention in Chicago.[3]

While political activity decreased significantly, landowning, community building, and education remained central to Black Attala. The landholding class maintained the Black community. They represented the literate, illiterate, wealth-creating, educating, and the politically active and inactive (in varying combinations). By 1910, 13,219 African Americans lived in Attala County, which constituted 5,089 adults. Of the 2,663 Black households, 740 owned land, constituting 14.54 percent of the adult population and 27.78 percent of all Black households.[4] The 740 landowners provided 3,132 African Americans access to land. These individuals resided on the lands and reaped the same benefits and protections as their legal owners. Approximately 30 percent of African Americans had access to land by 1910.[5] In Cicero Adams's household lived his children, stepchildren, and siblings. Cicero Adams's father, Gilbert Adams, left his children land following his death; however, an unpaid debt resulted in lienholder Henry J. Munson pursuing foreclosure. Gilbert's son purchased the foreclosed land through auction, which Cicero purchased "for the purpose of holding it for the benefit of the heirs of his father."[6] The land never lost its significance and importance. The land acquired during this period relied more on intraracial transactions than interracial. Black landowning progressed from the early emancipation years—money from land transactions filtered through Black hands, not white hands or institutions. The parties of the first part received an influx of cash, and the following parties gained the opportunity to create their economic destinies. Intraracial transactions represented one of the earliest examples of African Americans building an economic power base.[7] As Leo McGee and Robert Boone summarized land's impact, "Ownership of land affects one's psychological state, which may be more important, particularly at a time when blacks are attempting to show greater signs of security and independence in determining their own destiny."[8]

Mississippi authorized school consolidation. Counties merged smaller schools into larger schools at greater distances.[9] African Americans benefited little from the state's education policies. As they had done before and since emancipation, African Americans established an educational system to benefit their people. John Henry Hopkins, brother of John Wesley Bain, became an educational powerhouse. Henry graduated from Central Mississippi College and began his teaching career in Attala County before branching out to other areas to spread education. The *Neshoba Democrat* reported that Henry Hopkins proposed building an institute in Neshoba County to spread education to its rural areas.[10] Neshoba County had one known Black teacher, Thad Barrie, but by 1910, no Black teachers taught in the county. By 1920, Neshoba County had three African American teachers. Whether or not this was a direct impact of Hopkins's actions cannot be measured; however, there was push for education before this slight increase in teachers occurred. Henry relocated to Holmes County, teaching in the Goodman school system. Throughout his career, Henry traveled throughout Mississippi, creating new schools for his race. Henry taught school in Tallahatchie County, becoming a fixture in the *Mississippi Sun*. Upon his death in 1940, the *Chicago Defender* noted him as one of Mississippi's most noted educators. Hopkins took his education and used it to advance the cause of his race beyond their current position.[11]

Hopkins's efforts paralleled Mississippi's disdain for Black education. The Department of the Interior Bureau of Education's *Negro Education: A Study of the Private and Higher Schools for Colored People in the United States* (Table 6.2) captured the disparate school spending between the races. Data on teacher salaries and the population of school-aged children six to fourteen from the 1910 census shows that Mississippi spent an average of $11.38 per white child compared to $2.56 per Black child, based on teacher's 1912–1913 school-year salaries.[12] Attala County ranked forty-sixth, paying $1.52 per Black child compared to $4.55 per white child. Attala ranked fourth among white counties in the lowest amount paid per Black child. In 1912, Attala had 6,111 Black and 6,395 white children. The spending disparities reflected a decade-long fight to bolster white education at Black children's expense. Spending was a key area where whites held the advantage. County officials had the power to distribute school funds to their own satisfaction. These numbers reflected the need for independent institutions.

Regarding early-twentieth-century education, Leon Litwack stated, "No matter how it was measured—by the quality of facilities, the length of the school term, financial appropriations, student-teacher ratio, curriculum, teachers' preparation and salaries—the education available to black children in the New South was vastly inferior to that available to white students."[13] In the broad view, Litwack's statement is accurate; however, Litwack overreached regarding inferior education. When Central Mississippi College sought a new teaching staff for its rebuilt institution, their advertisement stated, "Nothing but experienced graduates need apply."[14] Litwack overlooked the work Black teachers put into their craft and the high standards by which they operated. Adam Fairclough followed a similar thought pattern in his discussion of white efforts to blunt Black education. Fairclough emphasized how whites conceived of education and how they "failed to turn black schools into engines for the reproduction of white supremacy."[15] Dating back to the 1890s, Attala's Black teachers voiced their desire for better pay as a means to funnel more money into Black schools. African Americans were not oblivious to local and state spending tactics, thus their need for independent institutions; however, for those attending public schools, Black teachers shouldered the burden of ensuring students in public schools received quality education. Without the same funding as white schools, Black teachers showed their

Table 6.2: County School Expenditures 1912–1913 by Race			
County	White Spending in $	Black Spending in $	County Majority
Alcorn	9.37	2.85	White
Amite	9.50	1.59	Black
Attala	4.55	1.52	White
Benton	9.09	1.93	White
Bolivar	18.22	2.39	Black
Calhoun	5.60	2.44	White
Carroll	11.19	1.88	Black
Chickasaw	10.88	1.56	Black
Choctaw	7.68	1.71	White
Clay	15.41	1.85	Black
Covington	9.79	4.36	White
DeSoto	18.44	2.15	Black
Forrest	14.82	2.91	White
Franklin	9.75	11.55	White
Grenada	17.57	2.58	White
Hancock	8.97	3.29	White
Harrison	14.59	4.43	White
Hinds	23.01	2.35	Black
Holmes	19.59	2.08	Black
Jackson	6.05	0.73	White
Jasper	7.00	2.01	White
Jefferson	22.08	1.86	Black
Jefferson Davis	12.65	2.50	Black
Jones	5.26	6.16	White
Lafayette	9.43	1.97	White
Lamar	7.82	0.63	White
Lauderdale	18.7	3.44	White
Leake	6.02	2.43	White
Lee	4.60	1.58	White
Marshall	11.65	2.00	Black
Neshoba	5.13	3.48	White
Newton	12.65	2.24	White
Oktibbeha	13.97	2.39	Black
Panola	16.23	1.36	Black
Pike	4.88	2.08	White
Pontotoc	7.36	2.31	White
Prentiss	4.72	1.23	White
Rankin	12.91	2.04	Black
Sharkey	3.30	2.09	Black
Simpson	9.95	2.11	White
Smith	9.95	3.01	White
Sunflower	21.43	2.15	Black
Tunica	2.06	2.11	Black
Union	7.08	3.46	White
Warren	20.42	4.51	Black
Washington	25.24	2.86	Black
Wayne	11.97	2.77	White
Wilkinson	12.66	1.53	Black
Winston	9.97	1.97	White
Yalobusha	7.59	1.69	Black
Average	11.38	2.56	

Source: Department of the Interior Bureau of Education. Negro Education: A Study of the Private and Higher Schools for Colored People in the United States, Volume II.

excellence in educating the next generation of community leaders. The twentieth-century Black teacher symbolized the continuation of the "doctrine of equality" and "kept alive the ideal of racial equality and trained another generation of teachers."[16]

The institutional discrimination and racism in the educational system did not hurt Black teachers' quality and willingness to teach in the county. Teachers such as Sarah Phillips, Volina Cooper, and Dovie Turner served as a new generation of teachers within the public-school system. Sarah Phillips taught in the county and city schools, beginning in the latter in 1902. Sarah married William Phillips and joined Sam Young Public School under his leadership. Upon her retirement in 1953, the following statement summed up her career: "We owe much to this grand old woman who has served us to the fourth generation."[17] Volina Cooper got her start in education at a young age. She received her education from Sam Young. In 1900, she lost her mother, but the tragic event did not derail her life. Her earliest teaching positions included serving as musical director of the Baptist Young People's Union and working with Professor G. W. Beauchamp in West Station, Mississippi.[18] She returned to Sam Young and worked under the leadership of William Phillips. Dovie Turner came to Kosciusko from Bellefontaine in Webster County, where her father worked as both a schoolteacher and minister. Dovie began teaching in Europa at the Little Black school.[19] Trained in English and education, she taught at Sam Young and Central Mississippi College.[20] Adam Fairclough stated, "The hardening of white supremacy left black teachers feeling confused, depressed, and vulnerable."[21] Such statements must be nuanced and assessed to individual communities, towns, and counties. Attala County's long history of educational independence afforded its Black citizens levels of autonomy and authority that Fairclough overlooked. Fairclough's image of Black education fits a typical southern setting, where one teacher educates an entire community and is at the mercy of white trustees.[22] Teachers established permanency, allowing themselves to build the infrastructure necessary to shape African Americans' next generation.[23]

In August 1912, the First Baptist Church governing body members filed a lawsuit against their minister, Thomas H. Allen. The governing body accused Allen of causing conflict within the church. James Gordon Smythe defended First Baptist Church, and Thomas Percy Guyton defended Reverend Allen. Thomas was born March 23, 1859, near the Sharon Community in Madison County. His father, Willis, active military, died shortly after Thomas's birth.

Volina (Miller) Cooper (Courtesy
of Cheryl Bayne, from the First
Baptist Church Centennial
Souvenir Book, 1996)

Reverend Thomas H. Allen (From *Multum
in Parvo: An Authenticated History of
Progressive Negroes in Pleasing and
Graphic Biographical Style* by Isaiah
Wadsworth Crawford and Patrick H.
Thompson, 1912)

Overcoming a rough childhood and home life, Allen received his call to
ministry in 1886.[24] Smythe explained in his testimony that this was his
first case involving church matters. Within the context of the case, Smythe
introduced Bettie Johnson, a Black woman who attempted to rally other
Black domestic works to deny whites their washing and cooking services.
Allen's accusations included having a close relationship with Johnson and
also advocating the labor boycotts. Allen's inability or refusal to dismiss
Johnson from the church became central to the case.[25] Bettie Johnson, a
divorced and educated woman, worked as a cook in a private home. She
owned her home and had no mortgage. Bettie's 1912 protest potentially
stemmed from her experiences with her employers. Society's oppression of
African American women allowed them a unique perspective into American
society that afforded them the advantage of creating ideas to tackle issues
from multiple perspectives. African American women used their oppressions
to craft strategies and structures designed to advance the race's causes. They
did not allow the marginalized societal structures to slow their efforts to
prepare the next generation for the struggle of securing equality and justice.[26]
It would be only appropriate for a woman working as a domestic to create a
plan that could make the lives of white women, and through them white men,

uncomfortable. The presence of county officials in a church dispute indicated that white involvement was likely rooted in finding a potential "troublemaker" or surveilling a radical institution, crossing the lines of separating church and state. The church suing Allen brings into question the suit's motive and intended result. The case made it to the Mississippi Supreme Court, which rejected calls to prevent Allen "from performing ministerial duties."[27]

Black women established a foothold in domestic service following slavery. This foothold allowed them to create autonomy. Gerald Jaynes's examination of the black working class through the planter-class efforts to reestablish the slavery economic model failed to analyze how freedmen, and in particular freedwomen, created the African American working class and thus dictating the terms of its operation.[28] Domestic workers served as the backbone of the Black working class, contributing to its independent identity. Terra Hunter discussed African American women's labor as dictated rather than chosen, although she did note that laundresses "had the advantage of accommodating family and community obligations."[29] Domestic workers understood the dependency of former white mistresses on Black labor. Thavolia Glymph nuanced the dictated concept to underscore how former mistresses perceived themselves about former slaves. Glymph stated, "In the antebellum period, white women were clearly subordinate in fundamental ways to men, but far from being victims of the slave system, they dominated slaves."[30] While white women grew accustomed to controlling Black women's labor, Black women sought to benefit from their labor.[31]

Black women's skills allowed them negotiating power.[32] On January 6, 1866, Charlotte Taylor became the first known washerwoman to earn wages when Jason Niles contracted her services. She earned seventy-two dollars.[33] The washerwoman became a profession that allowed Black women the opportunity to control both their labor and life. While not viewed as the most glamorous profession, domestic service fueled the Black working class, giving the next generations the possibility for advancement. Ann Smith, born October 1843 in Mississippi, married Allen Smith, a painter. She obtained an education, joined Wesley United Methodist Church, and became an Eastern Star member. At her death, Eastern Star members from across the state attended her funeral, which included a march of present members.[34] Ann Smith represented how Woodson viewed washerwomen outside their occupational role, explaining that they were active community members who participated in their race's social uplift through the church and service.[35]

By 1900, the county had 104 washerwomen. Washerwomen held steady employment. They worked on average ten out of twelve months, with 59 percent holding employment year-round. In 1910, washerwomen in Attala County represented the largest entrepreneurial class. Seventy-three percent worked on their account, providing them the space to capitalize on their skills without subjecting themselves to the master/slave work model. Eighty percent possessed literacy, indicating that this group did not fit the typical "domestic" model. Within a domestic household, some homes had multiple family members working as washerwomen., who worked as laborers, carpenters, brick masons, and railroad workers. Fifty percent of the washerwomen were married, and 58 percent of their spouses could read, write, or both. Cooks differed from the washerwoman in that they mostly worked for wages. In 1910, 123 women listed cook as their primary occupation. Ninety-eight percent worked for wages in private homes, hotels, boarding houses, or other industries, and 53 percent possessed literacy. Compared to washerwomen, cooks comprised mostly single, widowed, and divorced women. Bettie Johnson's boycott would need the assistance of women such as Lee Anna Evans's and Francis Eichelberger's families. Lee Anna performed laundry services as a private business, including providing service to a local boarding house, and her daughters Magnolia and Georgia worked as cooks for private families. Lee Anna's mother, Jeanette, spent years working as a cook. Francis Eichelberger worked as a private cook for a family, while her daughter, Mary Jane, worked as a hotel cook.

A consistent threat to African Americans was white mobs. On March 10, 1913, a mob shot and hung seventeen-year-old Leander Harmon after he was accused of entering a widowed white woman's home and going into her two daughters' bedroom. On Tuesday morning, the sheriff, deputy, and constable cut down Harmon's body and took Ben Cole into custody, whom Harmon had implicated in the trespassing incident.[36] Little information exists regarding Ben Cole's life. His grandfather Jackson was a landowner, and his father Warren was a voter. At the time of the incident, Ben had a wife and four children. He did not suffer the same fate as Leander. By all accounts, Ben faced no criminal charges, nor was he lynched. The circumstances surrounding this case are sketchy at best. The newspaper account gives the impression that the white girls were alarmed by Harmon and Cole's presence and that an alarm bought attention to the situation.[37] Given that this event occurred at night, the parties involved knew each other, and the widowed

Lee Anna (Atkinson-Evans)
Benjamin (Courtesy of the author)

Francis (Coleman) Eichelberger (Courtesy of Cheryl Bayne)

Georgia Lee (Ashford-Evans) Thornton (Courtesy of the
author, from the Mae Evans Photograph Album)

mother caught them. The same mob that lynched Harmon failed to lynch Cole, who lived another sixteen years following the incident.

Threats existed in nonviolent forms, such as labor exploitation. Kosciusko's white-operated press ran few stories or features on the county's Black citizens, although they had Black subscribers. In rare instances, African Americans used the white press to address a white audience; however, in May 1913, Ned Meredith published a warning in the *Kosciusko Courier* under the headline "Do Not Hire or Harbor My Boy." The warning stated, "I hereby serve this notice on the public not to 'hire or harbor' by boy, Gene Meredith, as he is yet a minor."[38] Ned Meredith, the grandfather of civil rights activist James Meredith, addressed those seeking to exploit his son's labor. Meredith, born in January 1850, worked

Don't Hire or Harbor My Boy

I hereby serve this notice on the public not to hire or harbor my boy, Gene Meredith as he is yet a minor.

                          NED MEREDITH

M 23-3t   his father (col)

Ned Meredith (Courtesy of James Meredith)

Ned Meredith's Notice (From the *Kosciusko Courier*)

as a farmer. Meredith lived in Winston County before relocating to Attala County. Meredith's approach was atypical when he used the white press to make demands on white people. Meredith's need to command compliance with his demand likely meant the act had occurred on recent occasions, prompting Meredith's action. The turbulent year of 1913 closed out with a celebration of excellence. From October 30th through November 1st, the Colored Peoples Attala County Fair took place, "a decided success." The event had exhibitions and garnered good attendance.[39] The fair took place weeks following the African American fair in Louisville, where Reverend Columbus Moody and Professor William Singleton spoke and Kosciusko's band provided entertainment.[40] The fair was an open display of liberation as African Americans showcased the results of their decades-long struggle to define and shape themselves as people and citizens of their county.

Setbacks accompanied progress, and progress possessed multiple facets. The beacons of education, Central Mississippi College and Kosciusko Industrial College, faced catastrophic events. In March 1915, Central Mississippi College burned, destroying the building. For the second time in ten years, the college suffered the same fate.[41] Kosciusko Industrial College fared worse when it ceased operations shortly afterward. Patrick Thompson found difficulty raising the money necessary for running the Kosciusko Industrial College after his efforts to merge with Central Mississippi College failed.[42] While Central Mississippi College reopened, Attala lost Thompson, who left Kosciusko, ending his twenty-year tenure as a county leader. Central Mississippi College continued to serve as the county's only independent school for African Americans.

On November 21, 1916, William Phillips's barn burned. The *Kosciusko Herald* reported that the supposed origins were incendiary, and authorities sought outside assistance from Crystal Springs in Copiah County. Phillips held position and status amongst the county's white citizens. The paper reported he enjoyed "the respect and confidence" and showed the paper's own support, stating, "The white friends of Will Phillips among whom may be counted the Herald and its management, are in deep sympathy with him in his great loss."[43] The person or people responsible for the barn's burning went unreported. It would be unlikely for another African American to burn Phillips's barn, and the lack of a follow-up story likely indicates a white culprit. Phillips's respect from white citizens reflected Booker T. Washington's belief that through education and wealth obtainment, one would find societal inclusion. Although Phillips experienced racial discrimination previously during the census incident and potentially with the barn burning, he had respectable whites' backing. Within a norming Jim Crow society, having support from white citizens served as a barrier for continued liberation efforts against the lower and ignorant white citizens. They served as the greatest threat to Black liberation.

White citizens played a role in assisting African Americans in criminal justice matters. On October 19, 1915, Frederick Z. Jackson, Lemuel D. Jackson, T. H. Wagoner, Dr. Sam P. Sims, Samuel L. Dodd, John F. Allen, Calvin Hall, George H. Wallace, Samuel A. Jackson, and Charles B. Fullilove petitioned to the board of pardons in Jackson. They sought a pardon for Albert Jenkins, a Black man, sentenced to five years in the state penitentiary in 1915 for manslaughter. The men proclaimed Jenkins's innocence. Their petition stated the following.

> The reason that we ask this pardon is because the petitioner was at his own home on the day of the killing and the deceased came there from Leake County and was drunk and raising a disturbance, and was in the act at the time of killing or committing a felonious assault with a deadly weapon upon the person of this petitioner, and had taken possession of his house at the time of the shooting, and had violated the sanctity of his household.[44]

Records provide no connection between Jenkins and the petitioners, all of whom were white, except Hall. Pardon requests were not anomalies as governors received letters for pardons, usually signed by prisoners or their families. In July 1916, Governor Bilbo granted Jenkins, ten white men, and two other Black men a pardon.[45] David M. Oshinsky explained in *Worse than Slavery: Parchman Farm and the Ordeal of Jim Crow Justice* that white peoples seeking pardons for African American convicts held ulterior motives. The imprisoned Black body meant one less worker for a white planter. The pardons had a paternalistic tone, where upstanding white men spoke of the Black convict as an inferior being who had learned their lesson.[46] Jenkins's pardon spoke less to paternalism and more to the fallacy of the criminal justice system. The petitioners did not proclaim Jenkins to be of good character, but rather the victim of a misguided verdict. In February 1920, deputy revenue agents raided Albert Jenkins illicit distillery, for which he faced another trial.[47] Newton's illegal activities provide some insight into his background and the possible connection to the white citizens who sought his release as Jenkins likely served as a revenue source through his distillery. Regardless of motive or ulterior motive, the actions of the white men spoke to what Charles Buchanan discussed in prior years, that Attala's white citizens must act in a manner that promoted equality and justice like the white men of the early emancipation years.

Interracial cooperation continued when the country entered World War I. At the onset of the war, the county's Black citizens organized to aid in the war effort. On April 20, 1917, William Singleton and William Phillips led an event at the courthouse aimed "to show our state and national government where we stand as a part and parcel of the nation's citizenry."[48] A week later, William Phillips and Lee Boston Turner, along with Reverend Jessie W. Winbush and David B. Mallett, called a meeting of Black and white citizens at the courthouse to support Sam Gaston and T. B. Mallett's volunteering their services in the army.[49] The war brought out cordial interracial relations amid a backdrop of rising white nationalism. Black and white citizens gathered on the courthouse's grounds to send off thirty-one Black soldiers to Camp Pike in Arkansas. The soldiers came from both Attala and Leake County. William Phillips led the ceremony, and white citizens including James Smythe, Wiley Sanders, and Col. S. L. Dodd "gave the soldiers some very wholesome advice and spoke words of encouragement to strengthen them in mind and heart."[50]

A committee that included William Phillips, George Hall, George Bullock, James A. Carr, and Lee Boston Turner posted a call in the *Star Ledger* calling for African Americans to contribute to the cause. Phillips reminded his people of their contributions to democracy, stating, "We were true during the revolutionary period, we were true during the Mexican trouble, we were true during the fray between the sections, we answered during the Spanish-American crisis and let us doubly answer now." Phillips added, "A very prosperous year has just passed, and most of us have money, so let us not be unmindful of the fact that our boys along with the whites are within the throes of the enemy; and must fight for victory too.... The quicker we respond collectively just that correspondingly quick victory will be ours; real victory with assured universal Democracy."[51] The call for action led to the formation of the Colored Red Cross, which consisted of eighty-five members.[52] African Americans used the war to remind their race and whites that this democracy belonged to them as much as it did to anyone else. War allowed African Americans to attach their liberation goals to the nation's goals of liberating abroad. This strategy existed long before the existence of the United States. Slaves sought freedom by fighting with the Spanish against England. Lord Dunmore's Proclamation enticed slaves to seek liberation fighting against the colonists, and free and enslaved Black peoples fought against the Confederacy to rid the nation of the slave institution. The cloud of war gave cover to African Americans seeking to use the situation for greater racial gains.

World War I ended the first phase of the liberation era. Approximately fifty years after the war opened the gateway to freedom, another war would launch African American's determination for true freedom into another orbit. As Attala settled into set political, social, and economic patterns, African Americans continued to empower themselves, using similar and new tactics. The fight continued, although the actors changed. The freedmen generation aged and passed, leaving the freedom generations to carry the torch. Education, church, business, and, most importantly, the freedom mentality remained the centerpiece of the Black community. Larger organizations such as the M. W. Stringer Grand Lodge and Eastern Star connected Attala's Black citizens to their brothers and sisters across the state and region. Marriages between prominent families solidified the middle-class that held its ground for the decades that followed. In the fifty years since their emancipation, Attala County's African Americans created the individual and collective spaces necessary to establish themselves as freethinking and self-sufficient people. African Americans were more than people with agency—they acted on their desires, drive, talents, and skills to push against forces seeking to marginalize and control them.

EPILOGUE

Attala County may be an atypical county based on history's interpretation of southern and African American history. It may be one of several locations where the fight for liberation forced society to use the full force of whiteness to slow progression. *Mississippi Zion* aims to demonstrate that everyday actions, whether viewed from the macro or micro perspective, allowed African Americans to secure their rightful place in their community, town, county, state, and nation. Their actions reflected the ongoing fight their enslaved ancestors undertook. The Black liberation mentality empowered African Americans and provoked their white counterparts to respond to maintain their real and imagined powers. The county's Black residents acted to best suit their needs individually and collectively, creating a multistep liberation plan that produced varying results.

African Americans maintained a small presence in the voting arena. In the Ayers precinct, Charles and Zanney McMichael and William and Albert Simmons continued voting during the 1920s, and the Patterson family remained registered voters. In the West Kosciusko precinct, Dovie Turner became the first African American woman to register in 1924. Other individuals included Alfred and Ceele Carr's grandchildren James A. Carr and Frank A. Carr Jr. African American men also pushed the sociopolitical envelope during this period. James William McKinley Carr, Winfrey and Freeman's relative, engaged white people in debate and was a registered voter.

He also encouraged other Black men to exercise their right to vote.[1] McKinley came from a family of active voters; therefore, it would not be unusual to think he would encourage other men of color to become part of the society in which they lived on the political level.

Men like McKinley Carr are not often discussed because this type of man is often viewed as a myth as it relates to Mississippi. The African American man in the South prior to 1960 is sometimes viewed as submissive and afraid. The idea that men would take it upon themselves to not only challenge the white power structure but also to embrace and display their education without the backing of a group or organization seems absurd to many. Not all African American men feared white men or their retaliations.[2] McKinley helped an individual evade arrest by law enforcement because he felt the crime committed was justified. He was not going to allow the law to deal with this individual based on its rules. McKinley also showed the pride that was carried in some African American men. When questioned whether or not he was a participant in vandalism that had taken place during a riot, McKinley not only answered that such activity was beneath him, but he also boycotted the store of the man who asked him the question.[3] African American men such as McKinley were well aware of the capabilities of whites and society as a whole; however, he is an example that buying into that fear only strengthens the power of the oppressor over the oppressed.

During William's tenure, Rosenwald Funding transitioned Sam Young into its second and third iterations, the Attala County Training School and Tipton Street High School. The institution thrived under the leadership of Lee Boston Turner, Thomas Porter Harris, and H. C. Redmond. Black women continued to make their mark on education, ascending to leadership positions. Eva (McLemore) Phillips and her cousins Alice (McLemore) Burkhead and Viola (Bain) Garland became the Jeanes Agent for Carroll and Attala Counties.[4] Lucille Williams (Little Hill), Lessie Hunt (Holsey), Ella Smith (Buffalo), Mary Phillips (Cook), and Eunice Simmons (New Garden) ascended to the principal position.[5] Volina Cooper reported local educational, church, and social happenings to the *Chicago Defender* for two decades until her death.[6] She provided insight into the insular society that focused on teachers, school and church activities, social clubs, parties, and other functions. The world Volina depicted to the *Defender*'s readers did not include the continued struggles of violence the race suffered at the hands of their white counterparts. The murders of John Wesley Bain, Lee Boston Turner's son Martin Turner, and D. M. P. Hazley's daughter Zipporah Thompson showed the continued strained relations between the races. During World War II, Laplace Franceno Turner, son of Lee Boston Turner, applied to the University of Alabama to take a mail course. Dr. Charles Thompson of Howard University disclosed that the university rejected Turner. On June 29, the university's secretary-register Charles Parker wrote to Turner stating, "The laws of this State provide for the maintenance of separate schools for the races," adding that the "institution was established to service the educational needs of members of the white race."[7] Attala remained connected to the broader political currents of the time and would further impact civil rights politics in the decades that followed.

Following World War II, African Americans continued to push their community forward. James Williams created the Central Mississippi Trade School. James Williams, a native of Newton, Mississippi, followed in Charles Buchanan and Patrick Thompson's footsteps, creating an independent institution for African Americans. Isaac Paul Presley Jr. created the Negro Brotherhood of Kosciusko. Isaac Presley left Mississippi and moved to New York, where he co-owned Presley and Allen Supply Company.[8] Upon his return to Kosciusko, he operated a gas station and created other business ventures. The Negro Brotherhood assisted several institutions and organizations, including enrolling students in school and building a recreational center that included courts for tennis, croquet, and basketball, in addition to playground equipment.[9] The emphasis on internal race development echoed the ideology of Dr. Calvin Perkins, president of Central Mississippi College, who stated, "Negroes wanted their own churches and schools, so they could be run just as they wanted them run."[10] Perkins sentiment spoke less to separatism but rather to an understanding that control remained a necessity to achieve liberation.

In Stokely Carmichael's "Berkeley Speech," he posed the question "what are the ways that black people can clear the obstacles placed before them so that society treats them as humans?"[11] Carmichael asked an already answered question. African American liberation permeated the post–Civil War atmosphere. With 250 years of involuntary servitude behind them, the freedman and freedwoman possessed the space to create opportunities to solidify their place in American society as humans, not chattel, and citizens, not slaves. Against the American and southern racial hierarchy's backdrop, the fight for liberation shaped nineteenth-century social, political, and economic landscape and forecasted twentieth-century politics. When Booker T. Washington stated, "Pull yourself up by your book straps," he spoke to African American reality. Waiting on white society to atone for its wrongs and cede power that rested on an ideology of privilege and oppression would do nothing. If Black peoples wanted liberation, they would have to empower themselves to take personal and institutional power from their former masters and the current forces attempting to entrap them in a permanent subservient state.[12]

African Americans did not view emancipation with rose-colored glasses. They possessed no grand illusions that the same society that held them captive or allowed their captivity would openly embrace them. The color line did more than separate the two races; it tied them together. African Americans and whites sought autonomy and freedom; however, the societal structures implanted long before emancipation created a post-slavery society that nullified the belief that the races could live equally alongside each other. The white population eroded civil rights to hamper African American liberation and cement white redemption. Rather than falling into complacency, African Americans increased their efforts to retain their citizenship status.

On October 1, 1962, James Howard Meredith, Attala County native, integrated the University of Mississippi. His historic act occurred almost fifty years after his grandfather, Ned Meredith, forbade the exploitation of his son's labor and seventy years after his grandfather, William Solomon Patterson, registered to vote under Mississippi's restrictive voting laws. Meredith's act came a century after Duncan Patterson, the family's last slave owner and father to some of Meredith's family members, chaired the committee at the Conservative Union Men meeting, which supported slavery. James Meredith's action cannot be limited to a specific political movement but was the continuation of the liberation struggle that his ancestors participated in decades prior. During his 1966 March Against Fear, Meredith continued protesting southern racism and challenges to African American voting. Meredith's assassination attempt prompted civil rights leaders to complete his efforts. During this march, the call for Black Power, coined by Willie Ricks and immortalized in historical and contemporary memory by Stokely Carmichael, changed the trajectory of the modern civil rights movement.[13]

Attala County's role in shaping Mississippi's history and, to a more considerable degree, that of the United States stemmed from African American's everyday liberation efforts. The quest for freedom, equality, and recognition varied from person to person, resulting in successes and failures. These individual and collective successes and setbacks shaped the broader social and political structures within a given community, county, or state. The African American experience is a diverse experience that mirrors and contradicts how historians traditionally explain African American life in the United States, particularly in the Deep South. The negatives cannot overshadow the positive actions in the first fifty years of emancipation because, in most cases, the negatives stemmed from a backlash to forward progress.

As Kwame Ture and Charles Hamilton explained, the foundations of freedom lay in forcing the greater society to accept peoples' identity that society sought to oppress.[14] After all, "Freedom is an attitude, a principle that operates perhaps most visibly in spite of resistance. Without resistance, without the restraint of physical or metaphysical shackles, without the tyranny of our passions, without the necessity of unwavering discipline to negotiate difficult tasks, without the body's decay, the mind's fallibility, how would any of us discover our capacities, our freedom, in spite of those obstacles, in spite of slavery, colonialism, the social pressure to conform?"[15] These individuals showed that African Americans had only begun to fight for the liberation that would one day translate into the freedom their African ancestors lived in their motherlands.

APPENDIX A

~

AFRICAN AMERICAN REGISTERED VOTERS, 1892–1915

Year	Name	Occupation	Literacy	Precinct
1892	J. M. Gregory	Laborer	Reads & Writes	Ayers
1892	Marshall Gregory	Laborer	Reads & Writes	Ayers
1892	Green Hill	Laborer	Reads & Writes	Ayers
1892	Jack Hill	Farmer	Reads & Writes	Ayers
1892	John Hill	Laborer	Reads & Writes	Ayers
1892	Solomon L. Jamison	Laborer	Reads & Writes	Ayers
1892	S. N. Jamison	Laborer	Reads & Writes	Ayers
1892	Scipio Lee	Farmer	Reads Only	Ayers
1892	T. H. Moore	Farmer	Reads & Writes	Ayers
1892	A. H. Patterson	Laborer	Reads & Writes	Ayers
1892	Peter Patterson	Laborer	Reads & Writes	Ayers
1892	William H. Patterson	Laborer	Reads & Writes	Ayers
1892	Louis Shumaker	Farmer	Reads & Writes	Ayers
1892	W. R. Spivey	Laborer	Reads & Writes	Ayers
1892	Wiley Spivey	Laborer	Reads & Writes	Ayers
1892	F. A. Alston	Railroad	Reads & Writes	Ethel
1892	R. C. Campbell	Farmer	Reads & Writes	Ethel
1892	J. S. Gaston	Farmer	Reads & Writes	Ethel

Year	Name	Occupation	Literacy	Precinct
1892	B. F. Washington	Laborer	Reads & Writes	Ethel
1892	Henry Young	Laborer	Reads & Writes	Ethel
1892	Charles Beamon	Farmer	Reads & Writes	Jerusalem
1892	Frank Beamon	Farmer	Reads & Writes	Jerusalem
1892	H. M. Clark	Farmer	Reads & Writes	Jerusalem
1892	John W. Clark	Farmer	Reads & Writes	Jerusalem
1892	R. B. Clark	Farmer	Reads & Writes	Jerusalem
1892	J. J. Cotton	Farmer	Reads & Writes	Jerusalem
1892	Quitman Cotton	Carpenter	Reads & Writes	Jerusalem
1892	J. V. Dodd	Farmer	Reads & Writes	Jerusalem
1892	Moses Dodd	Farmer	Reads & Writes	Jerusalem
1892	S. M. Dodd	Farmer	Reads Only	Jerusalem
1892	Lewis Ellington	Farmer	Reads & Writes	Jerusalem
1892	Allen Fletcher	Laborer	Reads & Writes	Jerusalem
1892	David Fletcher	Laborer	Reads & Writes	Jerusalem
1892	Scott Fletcher	Farmer	Reads Only	Jerusalem
1892	Wade Fletcher	Farmer	Reads & Writes	Jerusalem
1892	William Fletcher	Laborer	Reads & Writes	Jerusalem
1892	Green Gilliland	Farmer	Reads & Writes	Jerusalem
1892	J. S. Gilliland	Farmer	Reads & Writes	Jerusalem
1892	Irving Gilliland Jr.	Farmer	Reads & Writes	Jerusalem
1892	Nelson Gladney	Farmer	Reads & Writes	Jerusalem
1892	Robert G. Gladney	Farmer	Reads & Writes	Jerusalem
1892	Enoch Hannah	Farmer	Reads & Writes	Jerusalem
1892	Isaac Hanna	Farmer	Reads & Writes	Jerusalem
1892	John Holsey	Farmer	Reads & Writes	Jerusalem
1892	Charlie Jamison	Farmer	Reads Only	Jerusalem
1892	William H. Jamison	Farmer	Reads & Writes	Jerusalem
1892	John Mallett	Laborer	Reads & Writes	Jerusalem
1892	Andrew McCoy	Farmer	Reads & Writes	Jerusalem
1892	George W. Nash	Farmer	Reads & Writes	Jerusalem
1892	Thomas H. Nash	Farmer	Reads & Writes	Jerusalem
1892	W. T. Newell	Farmer	Reads & Writes	Jerusalem
1892	William S. Patterson	Farmer	Reads & Writes	Jerusalem
1892	James Pool	Farmer	Reads & Writes	Jerusalem

Year	Name	Occupation	Literacy	Precinct
1892	Henry Rayford	Farmer	Reads & Writes	Jerusalem
1892	Jeff Rayford	Farmer	Reads & Writes	Jerusalem
1892	J. R. Rimmer	Farmer	Reads & Writes	Jerusalem
1892	Allen Ross	Laborer	Reads & Writes	Jerusalem
1892	T. R. Ross	Farmer	Reads & Writes	Jerusalem
1892	Henry Ryals	Laborer	Reads & Writes	Jerusalem
1892	Shepherd Scurlock	Farmer	Reads & Writes	Jerusalem
1892	Isaac Shuler	Farmer	Reads & Writes	Jerusalem
1892	H. T. Thompson	Farmer	Reads & Writes	Jerusalem
1892	John H. Winnick	Farmer	Reads & Writes	Jerusalem
1892	Anthony Adams	Laborer	Reads & Writes	Kosciusko
1892	Gilbert Adams	Laborer	Reads & Writes	Kosciusko
1892	Tom Atwood	Farmer	Reads & Writes	Kosciusko
1892	J. M. Baccus	Clerk	Reads & Writes	Kosciusko
1892	M. V. Baccus	Mechanic	Reads & Writes	Kosciusko
1892	Jackson Blumenburg	Laborer	Reads & Writes	Kosciusko
1892	Aaron Bryant	Farmer	Reads & Writes	Kosciusko
1892	Walter Bryant	Farmer	Reads & Writes	Kosciusko
1892	Charles A. Buchanan	Minister	Reads & Writes	Kosciusko
1892	George Bullock	Barber	Reads & Writes	Kosciusko
1892	Fred H Bunton	Minister	Reads & Writes	Kosciusko
1892	W. T. Burnside	Teacher	Reads & Writes	Kosciusko
1892	George W. Burt	Farmer	Reads & Writes	Kosciusko
1892	Louis Burt	Laborer	Reads & Writes	Kosciusko
1892	Franklin A. Carr	Farmer	Reads & Writes	Kosciusko
1892	R. B. Clark	Farmer	Reads & Writes	Kosciusko
1892	Robert Comfort	Laborer	Reads & Writes	Kosciusko
1892	Peter Cooper	Shoemaker	Reads & Writes	Kosciusko
1892	Isaac Coulter	Farmer	Reads & Writes	Kosciusko
1892	Washington Collier	Farmer	Reads & Writes	Kosciusko
1892	Robert Dickens	Farmer	Reads & Writes	Kosciusko
1892	Sylvester Dobbs	Laborer	Reads & Writes	Kosciusko
1892	Alex Dodd	Farmer	Reads & Writes	Kosciusko
1892	Rice Dodd	Farmer	Reads & Writes	Kosciusko
1892	Joe D Douglass	Mechanic	Reads & Writes	Kosciusko

Year	Name	Occupation	Literacy	Precinct
1892	F. K. Eubanks	Farmer	Reads & Writes	Kosciusko
1892	Alfred Frazier	Jeweler	Reads & Writes	Kosciusko
1892	Wiley Gage	Farmer	Reads & Writes	Kosciusko
1892	W. E. T. Gaston	Laborer	Reads & Writes	Kosciusko
1892	Wilson L. Gerrin	Mechanic	Reads & Writes	Kosciusko
1892	Isaac Godwell	Laborer	Reads & Writes	Kosciusko
1892	A. Hammond	Laborer	Reads & Writes	Kosciusko
1892	Leonard Hammond	Minister	Reads & Writes	Kosciusko
1892	Dawson Hardy	Laborer	Reads & Writes	Kosciusko
1892	Dempsey Harper	Laborer	Reads & Writes	Kosciusko
1892	D. M. P. Hazley	Teacher	Reads & Writes	Kosciusko
1892	John Hazley	Laborer	Reads & Writes	Kosciusko
1892	Willis Hazley	Laborer	Reads & Writes	Kosciusko
1892	Marshall Hill	Laborer	Reads & Writes	Kosciusko
1892	Joe Johnson	Laborer	Understands	Kosciusko
1892	Jael Jones	Laborer	Reads & Writes	Kosciusko
1892	C. B. Keaton	Minister	Reads & Writes	Kosciusko
1892	Albert Kerr	Laborer	Reads & Writes	Kosciusko
1892	W. H. Kerr	Laborer	Reads & Writes	Kosciusko
1892	Robert Lampley	Farmer	Reads & Writes	Kosciusko
1892	J. C. Leonard	Minister	Reads & Writes	Kosciusko
1892	Henry Mallett	Farmer	Reads & Writes	Kosciusko
1892	Miles McAdory	Farmer	Reads & Writes	Kosciusko
1892	Thomas J. McLemore	Brick Mason	Reads & Writes	Kosciusko
1892	William Miller	Porter	Reads & Writes	Kosciusko
1892	William M. Miller	Farmer	Reads & Writes	Kosciusko
1892	Sank Moore	NA	Reads & Writes	Kosciusko
1892	Johnson Nash	Laborer	Reads & Writes	Kosciusko
1892	John M. Nevils	Minister	Reads & Writes	Kosciusko
1892	L. S. Newell	Laborer	Reads & Writes	Kosciusko
1892	Albert B. Poston	Teacher	Reads & Writes	Kosciusko
1892	Jim Riley	Farmer	Reads & Writes	Kosciusko
1892	W. S. Riley	Farmer	Reads & Writes	Kosciusko
1892	Artemus Rimmer	NA	Reads & Writes	Kosciusko
1892	R. C. Roby	Farmer	Reads & Writes	Kosciusko

Year	Name	Occupation	Literacy	Precinct
1892	Ruffin L. Shepherd	Mechanic	Reads & Writes	Kosciusko
1892	Seymore Singleton	Laborer	Reads & Writes	Kosciusko
1892	Joe Simpson	Clerk	Reads & Writes	Kosciusko
1892	Allen Smith	Painter	Reads & Writes	Kosciusko
1892	J. E. Smith	Teacher	Reads & Writes	Kosciusko
1892	Seaborn S. Spikes	Jeweler	Reads & Writes	Kosciusko
1892	Caleb W. Stewart	Farmer	Reads & Writes	Kosciusko
1892	Joseph C. Terry	Farmer	Reads & Writes	Kosciusko
1892	Nelson Terry	Farmer	Reads & Writes	Kosciusko
1892	Jordan Thompson	Blacksmith	Reads & Writes	Kosciusko
1892	F. A. Tipton	Farmer	Reads & Writes	Kosciusko
1892	James H. Tipton	Farmer	Reads & Writes	Kosciusko
1892	Ed Veazey	Farmer	Reads & Writes	Kosciusko
1892	F. W. Winters	Farmer	Reads & Writes	Kosciusko
1892	Jordan Winters	Farmer	Reads & Writes	Kosciusko
1892	William P. Winters	Farmer	Reads & Writes	Kosciusko
1892	Judge Yelvington	Farmer	Reads & Writes	Kosciusko
1892	James Adams	Teacher	Reads & Writes	Liberty Chapel
1892	D. B. Gaston	Farmer	Reads & Writes	Liberty Chapel
1892	Dewitt C. Johnson	Farmer	Reads & Writes	Liberty Chapel
1892	Green L. Johnson	Farmer	Reads & Writes	Liberty Chapel
1892	John H. L. Kimbrough	Farmer	Reads & Writes	Liberty Chapel
1892	A. D. Nash	Farmer	Reads & Writes	Liberty Chapel
1892	Howard Peeler	Farmer	Reads Only	Liberty Chapel
1892	D. D. Alston	Farmer	Reads & Writes	McCool
1892	J. R. Ashford	Farmer	Reads & Writes	McCool
1892	William W. Ashford	Farmer	Reads & Writes	McCool
1892	A. J. Dotson	Farmer	Reads & Writes	McCool
1892	J. L. Dotson	Farmer	Reads & Writes	McCool
1892	J. N. Dotson	Farmer	Reads & Writes	McCool
1892	Riley R. Duckett	Teacher	Reads & Writes	McCool
1892	W. M. Hallum	Laborer	Reads & Writes	McCool
1892	Geet Hemphill	Farmer	Reads & Writes	McCool
1892	P. P. Knox	Farmer	Reads & Writes	McCool
1892	Willie Potts	Laborer	Reads & Writes	McCool

Year	Name	Occupation	Literacy	Precinct
1892	E. Shumaker	Farmer	Reads & Writes	McCool
1892	B. F. Sisson	Farmer	Reads & Writes	McCool
1892	Joe Barr	Farmer	Reads & Writes	Providence
1892	George Rimmer	Farmer	Reads & Writes	Providence
1892	T. R. Rimmer	Farmer	Reads & Writes	Providence
1892	T. R. Ross	Farmer	Reads & Writes	Providence
1892	Henry White	Laborer	Reads & Writes	Providence
1892	James Ratliff	Farmer	Reads & Writes	Rochester
1892	W. T. Dodd	Teacher	Reads & Writes	Rocky Point
1892	Joe B. Harvey	Farmer	Reads & Writes	Rocky Point
1892	Haywood Love	Farmer	Reads & Writes	Rocky Point
1892	Thomas Olive	Farmer	Reads & Writes	Rocky Point
1892	Charles Crawford	Laborer	Reads Only	Sallis
1892	R. C. Dickens	Farmer	Reads & Writes	Sallis
1892	Price Ellis	Farmer	Reads & Writes	Sallis
1892	L. C. Lowery	Laborer	Reads & Writes	Sallis
1892	Virgil McPherson	Farmer	Reads & Writes	Sallis
1892	R. R. Rimmer	Farmer	Reads & Writes	Sallis
1892	George W. Sallis	Farmer	Reads & Writes	Sallis
1892	Richard Teague	Farmer	Reads & Writes	Sallis
1893	Charles E. McMichael	Teacher	Reads & Writes	Ayers
1893	George Collins	Farmer	Reads Only	Jerusalem
1893	R. B. Dodd	Farmer	Reads & Writes	Jerusalem
1893	J. D. Rimmer	Laborer	Reads & Writes	Jerusalem
1893	G. W. Wilkes	Farmer	Reads Only	Jerusalem
1893	Robert Burt Jr.	Laborer	Reads & Writes	Kosciusko
1893	Burton Cade	Laborer	Reads & Writes	Kosciusko
1893	J. W. Coleman	Minister	Reads & Writes	Kosciusko
1893	Charlie Cottrell	Farmer	Reads & Writes	Kosciusko
1893	John Wesley Coulter	Laborer	Reads & Writes	Kosciusko
1893	Simon Davis	Farmer	Reads & Writes	Kosciusko
1893	J. H. Fortune	Farmer	Reads & Writes	Kosciusko
1893	S. W. Fortune	Laborer	Reads & Writes	Kosciusko
1893	Moses Hazley	Laborer	Reads & Writes	Kosciusko
1893	James Huffman	Laborer	Reads & Writes	Kosciusko

Year	Name	Occupation	Literacy	Precinct
1893	Alexander M. McGlown	Teacher	Reads & Writes	Kosciusko
1893	Howard McLemore	Laborer	Reads & Writes	Kosciusko
1893	Fred Munson	Farmer	Reads & Writes	Kosciusko
1893	J. P. Moore	Farmer	Reads & Writes	Kosciusko
1893	R. G. Moore	Laborer	Reads & Writes	Kosciusko
1893	Henry Murff	Farmer	Reads & Writes	Kosciusko
1893	Joe Riddle	Farmer	Reads & Writes	Kosciusko
1893	James W. Simmons	Farmer	Reads & Writes	Kosciusko
1893	Jordan Simpson	Farmer	Reads & Writes	Kosciusko
1893	T. L. Thompson	Farmer	Reads & Writes	Kosciusko
1893	R. L. Watkins	Farmer	Reads & Writes	Kosciusko
1893	G. C. Bridges	Laborer	Reads & Writes	McCool
1893	E. D. Hanna	Laborer	Reads & Writes	McCool
1893	Butler A. Ashford	Farmer	Reads Only	Providence
1893	Willis Connor	Laborer	Understands	Rochester
1893	William Lucas	Farmer	Reads Only	Rochester
1893	Jim McMillan	Farmer	Understands	Rochester
1893	H. F. Moore	Laborer	Reads & Writes	Rochester
1893	Solomon Moore	Farmer	Understands	Rochester
1893	W. A. Moore	Laborer	Reads & Writes	Rochester
1893	Matteson Guess	Farmer	Reads & Writes	Rocky Point
1893	M. J. Weaver	Farmer	Reads & Writes	Rocky Point
1893	Richard Culpepper	Farmer	Reads & Writes	Sallis
1893	William Culpepper	Farmer	Reads & Writes	Sallis
1893	Randall Dickens	Farmer	Reads & Writes	Sallis
1893	Abe Eubanks	Laborer	Reads & Writes	Sallis
1893	J. Fullilove	Farmer	Reads & Writes	Sallis
1893	James Golden	Farmer	Reads & Writes	Sallis
1893	Buck Harmon	Farmer	Reads & Writes	Sallis
1893	Johnny Johnson	Farmer	Reads & Writes	Sallis
1893	Buster Ware	Laborer	Reads & Writes	Sallis
1893	Robert Wyse	Farmer	Reads & Writes	Sallis
1893	A. P. Magrone	Farmer	Reads & Writes	Shrock
1894	J. L. Wheeler	Minister	Reads & Writes	Jerusalem
1894	J. G. Wilkes	Farmer	Reads & Writes	Jerusalem

Year	Name	Occupation	Literacy	Precinct
1894	William Black	Laborer	Reads & Writes	Kosciusko
1894	John Fondren	Laborer	Reads & Writes	Kosciusko
1894	Bias Fulton	Farmer	Reads & Writes	Kosciusko
1894	Charles Garrett	Blacksmith	Reads & Writes	Kosciusko
1894	Edmond Hanna	Laborer	Reads & Writes	Kosciusko
1894	John H. Hopkins	Laborer	Reads & Writes	Kosciusko
1894	Alex Jones	Laborer	Reads & Writes	Kosciusko
1894	Albert S. Munson	Farmer	Reads & Writes	Kosciusko
1894	Clinton Olive	Laborer	Reads & Writes	Kosciusko
1894	Simon Olive	Laborer	Reads & Writes	Kosciusko
1894	George R. Tucker	Barber	Reads & Writes	Kosciusko
1894	Emmett Kimbrough	Laborer	Reads & Writes	Liberty Chapel
1894	John Kimbrough	Laborer	Reads & Writes	Liberty Chapel
1894	Elijah Ellis	Farmer	Reads & Writes	Newport
1894	B. Greer	Farmer	Reads & Writes	Newport
1894	James Jones	Farmer	Read Only	Rochester
1894	Henry Beaty	Farmer	Reads & Writes	Rocky Point
1894	J. C. Cook	Farmer	Reads & Writes	Rocky Point
1894	Alex Dodd	Farmer	Reads & Writes	Rocky Point
1894	Henry Palmer	Farmer	Reads & Writes	Rocky Point
1894	William Perry	Farmer	Reads & Writes	Rocky Point
1894	Jack Towers	Farmer	Reads & Writes	Rocky Point
1894	Wilson Dickens	Farmer	Reads & Writes	Sallis
1895	Dave Brookshire	Farmer	Understands	Ayers
1895	George W. Cole	Farmer	Understands	Ayers
1895	Bazzil Griffin	Farmer	Reads & Writes	Ayers
1895	J. A. Griffin	Farmer	Reads & Writes	Ayers
1895	Jim Hill	Farmer	Reads & Writes	Ayers
1895	Levi Huffman	Farmer	Understands	Ayers
1895	Thomas J. Kern	Farmer	Reads & Writes	Ayers
1895	Andy Lee	Farmer	Reads & Writes	Ayers
1895	J. H. Medley	Farmer	Reads & Writes	Ayers
1895	William S. Patterson	Farmer	Reads & Writes	Ayers
1895	H. Sallis	Farmer	Reads & Writes	Ayers
1895	William A. Simmons	Farmer	Understands	Ayers

Year	Name	Occupation	Literacy	Precinct
1895	J. W. Winters	Farmer	Reads Only	Ayers
1895	Morris Winters	Farmer	Reads & Writes	Ayers
1895	T. W. Winters	Farmer	Reads Only	Ayers
1895	W. H. Winters	Farmer	Reads Only	Ayers
1895	Jordan Tucker	Farmer	Reads & Writes	Ethel
1895	C. G. Ashford	Farmer	Reads & Writes	Jerusalem
1895	William P. Ashford	Farmer	Reads & Writes	Jerusalem
1895	William W. Ashford	Farmer	Reads & Writes	Jerusalem
1895	Willie Chestnut	Farmer	Reads & Writes	Jerusalem
1895	John Cole	Farmer	Reads & Writes	Jerusalem
1895	Warren Cole	Farmer	Reads & Writes	Jerusalem
1895	Richard Cross	Farmer	Reads & Writes	Jerusalem
1895	S. N. Gilliland	Farmer	Reads & Writes	Jerusalem
1895	Charley Jamison	Farmer	Reads & Writes	Jerusalem
1895	E. A. Rayford	Farmer	Reads & Writes	Jerusalem
1895	M. W. Sudduth	Farmer	Reads & Writes	Jerusalem
1895	T. R. Ross	Farmer	Reads & Writes	Jerusalem
1895	Tom Thompson	Farmer	Understands	Jerusalem
1895	John L. Wheeler Jr.	Farmer	Reads & Writes	Jerusalem
1895	Charles Wilson	Farmer	Reads & Writes	Jerusalem
1895	Hugh Wilson	Farmer	Reads & Writes	Jerusalem
1895	Thomas J. Wilson	Farmer	Reads & Writes	Jerusalem
1895	Cicero Adams	Farmer	Reads & Writes	Kosciusko
1895	Wade Ashford	Farmer	Reads & Writes	Kosciusko
1895	George W. Beauchamp	Teacher	Reads & Writes	Kosciusko
1895	Will Dickens	Farmer	Reads & Writes	Kosciusko
1895	A. D. Fondren	Farmer	Reads & Writes	Kosciusko
1895	Henry Jackson	Farmer	Reads & Writes	Kosciusko
1895	H. C. Lewis	Farmer	Reads & Writes	Kosciusko
1895	Silas S. Lynch	Teacher	Reads & Writes	Kosciusko
1895	Isaac Presley	Farmer	Reads & Writes	Kosciusko
1895	Nelson Presley	Farmer	Reads & Writes	Kosciusko
1895	P. R. Sanders	Farmer	Reads & Writes	Kosciusko
1895	William A. Singleton	Teacher	Reads & Writes	Kosciusko
1895	L. W. Wall	Blacksmith	Reads & Writes	Kosciusko

Year	Name	Occupation	Literacy	Precinct
1895	Green W. Winters	Farmer	Reads & Writes	Kosciusko
1895	William A. Carr	Farmer	Reads & Writes	Liberty Chapel
1895	E. J. Kimbrough	Farmer	Reads & Writes	Liberty Chapel
1895	A. J. Winters	Farmer	Understands	Liberty Chapel
1895	Joseph H. Bain	Blacksmith	Reads & Writes	McCool
1895	King Alston	Farmer	Reads & Writes	McCool
1895	Richard Bailey	Farmer	Reads & Writes	McCool
1895	Elbert Dobbs	Farmer	Reads & Writes	McCool
1895	W. T. Garrett	Farmer	Reads & Writes	McCool
1895	J. M. Knox	Farmer	Reads & Writes	McCool
1895	H. M. Miller	Farmer	Reads & Writes	McCool
1895	Charlie Rhodes	Farmer	Reads & Writes	McCool
1895	Louis Seward	Farmer	Reads & Writes	McCool
1895	William Smith	Farmer	Reads & Writes	McCool
1895	Simon Turnbo	Farmer	Reads & Writes	McCool
1895	Peter Williams	Farmer	Reads & Writes	McCool
1895	H. J. Winters	Farmer	Reads & Writes	McCool
1895	Lou Winters	Farmer	Reads & Writes	McCool
1895	Lincoln McMillan	Farmer	Reads & Writes	Newport
1895	G. L. Roby	Farmer	Reads & Writes	Newport
1895	Jesse Skinner	Farmer	Reads & Writes	Newport
1895	R. S. Riley	Farmer	Reads & Writes	Newport
1895	William Riley	Farmer	Understands	Newport
1895	A. J. Ferguson	Farmer	Reads & Writes	Peeler's Mill
1895	L. W. Ferguson	Farmer	Reads & Writes	Peeler's Mill
1895	J. L. Rimmer	Farmer	Reads & Writes	Providence
1895	George Burt	Farmer	Understands	Rochester
1895	Anthony Thompson	Farmer	Reads & Writes	Rochester
1895	W. A. Adams	Farmer	Reads & Writes	Rocky Point
1895	S. P. Bell	Farmer	Reads & Writes	Rocky Point
1895	W. S. Campbell	Farmer	Reads & Writes	Rocky Point
1895	A. J. Cottrell	Farmer	Reads & Writes	Rocky Point
1895	H. C. Harrison	Farmer	Reads & Writes	Rocky Point
1895	George Hill	Farmer	Reads & Writes	Rocky Point
1895	W. M. Jones	Teacher	Reads & Writes	Rocky Point

Year	Name	Occupation	Literacy	Precinct
1895	Frank Kimes	Farmer	Reads & Writes	Rocky Point
1895	William Love	Farmer	Reads & Writes	Rocky Point
1895	J. C. Lowery	Farmer	Reads & Writes	Rocky Point
1895	Perry Mallet	Farmer	Reads & Writes	Rocky Point
1895	G. W. Murff	Farmer	Reads & Writes	Rocky Point
1895	J. M. Murff	Farmer	Reads & Writes	Rocky Point
1895	Wiley Olive	Farmer	Reads & Writes	Rocky Point
1895	Isom Rodger	Farmer	Reads & Writes	Rocky Point
1895	J. C. Shanks	Farmer	Reads & Writes	Rocky Point
1895	John Short	Farmer	Understands	Rocky Point
1895	William Short	Farmer	Reads & Writes	Rocky Point
1895	William Thornton	Farmer	Reads & Writes	Rocky Point
1895	Buster Ware	Farmer	Reads & Writes	Rocky Point
1895	T. E. Wigley	Farmer	Reads & Writes	Rocky Point
1895	T. S. Wigley	Farmer	Reads & Writes	Rocky Point
1895	M. W. Williams	Farmer	Reads & Writes	Rocky Point
1895	Joe Allen	Farmer	Reads & Writes	Sallis
1895	G. B. Brown	Farmer	Reads & Writes	Sallis
1895	William Brown	Farmer	Reads & Writes	Sallis
1895	James Culpepper	Farmer	Reads & Writes	Sallis
1895	David Eubanks	Farmer	Reads & Writes	Sallis
1895	William M. Mallet	Farmer	Reads & Writes	Sallis
1895	Charles McDonald	Farmer	Reads & Writes	Sallis
1895	Milledge Roby	Farmer	Reads & Writes	Sallis
1895	B. R. Siggers	Farmer	Reads & Writes	Sallis
1895	James Campbell	Farmer	Reads & Writes	Shrock
1895	L. Campbell	Farmer	Reads & Writes	Shrock
1895	Robert Campbell	Farmer	Reads & Writes	Shrock
1895	Eddy Campbell	Farmer	Reads & Writes	Shrock
1895	Charlie Carson	Farmer	Reads & Writes	Shrock
1895	Robert Carson	Farmer	Reads & Writes	Shrock
1895	William Lee	Farmer	Reads & Writes	Shrock
1895	Ike Lusk	Farmer	Reads & Writes	Shrock
1895	Henry Ousley	Farmer	Understands	Shrock
1895	Nixon Ousley	Farmer	Reads & Writes	Shrock

Year	Name	Occupation	Literacy	Precinct
1895	William Rockett	Farmer	Reads & Writes	Shrock
1895	Greene Thompson	Farmer	Reads & Writes	Shrock
1895	Lee Smith	Farmer	Reads & Writes	Thompson School House
1895	Joe Winters	Farmer	Reads & Writes	Thompson School House
1896	Bill Clark	Farmer	Reads & Writes	Ayers
1896	C. H. Hathorn	Farmer	Reads Only	Ayers
1896	Thomas Holton	Farmer	Reads & Writes	Ayers
1896	Anthony Kern	Farmer	Understands	Ayers
1896	Isom Kern	Farmer	Understands	Ayers
1896	Abraham Miller	Farmer	Reads & Writes	Ayers
1896	Calvin Winters	Farmer	Understands	Ayers
1896	J. H. Turnbo	Section Hand	Reads & Writes	Ethel
1896	Wilson Booker	Laborer	Understands	Jerusalem
1896	L. F. Cross	Laborer	Reads & Writes	Jerusalem
1896	Daniel N. Gladney	Farmer	Understands	Jerusalem
1896	Jim Presley	Farmer	Reads Only	Jerusalem
1896	Alexander W. Wilks	Farmer	Reads & Writes	Jerusalem
1896	H. W. Williams	Laborer	Reads & Writes	Jerusalem
1896	J. W. Winnick	Laborer	Reads & Writes	Jerusalem
1896	George Adams	Farmer	Reads & Writes	Kosciusko
1896	Alexander Ashford	Laborer	Reads & Writes	Kosciusko
1896	Jerry Ashford	Laborer	Reads & Writes	Kosciusko
1896	Elbert Bell	Laborer	Reads & Writes	Kosciusko
1896	York Bennett	Pressman	Reads & Writes	Kosciusko
1896	James Bias	Farmer	Reads & Writes	Kosciusko
1896	Robert Bell	Farmer	Reads & Writes	Kosciusko
1896	J. H. Brown	Printer	Reads & Writes	Kosciusko
1896	Charles Bullock	Farmer	Reads & Writes	Kosciusko
1896	Alexander Burt	Farmer	Reads & Writes	Kosciusko
1896	Louis Burt	Farmer	Reads & Writes	Kosciusko
1896	T. C. Carter	Laborer	Reads & Writes	Kosciusko
1896	Henry Clark	Laborer	Understands	Kosciusko

Year	Name	Occupation	Literacy	Precinct
1896	George Crawford	Laborer	Understands	Kosciusko
1896	Dan Davis	Laborer	Reads & Writes	Kosciusko
1896	Moses Dickens	Farmer	Reads Only	Kosciusko
1896	J. H. Edwards	Blacksmith	Reads & Writes	Kosciusko
1896	Frank Evans	Farmer	Reads Only	Kosciusko
1896	Benton Flannigan	Laborer	Reads & Writes	Kosciusko
1896	Dennis Fondren	Carpenter	Reads & Writes	Kosciusko
1896	Thomas J. Griffin	Teacher	Reads & Writes	Kosciusko
1896	Charlie Hemphill	Porter	Reads & Writes	Kosciusko
1896	Adolphus Journey	Laborer	Reads & Writes	Kosciusko
1896	Austin Kilpatrick	Farmer	Understands	Kosciusko
1896	Charley A. Lovelady	Laborer	Reads & Writes	Kosciusko
1896	Ernest Mallett	Laborer	Reads & Writes	Kosciusko
1896	J. R. Mallett	Barber	Reads & Writes	Kosciusko
1896	W. M. Mallett	Farmer	Reads & Writes	Kosciusko
1896	Amos McAdory	Laborer	Reads & Writes	Kosciusko
1896	Grant McLemore	Laborer	Reads & Writes	Kosciusko
1896	C. L. Mitchell	Merchant	Reads & Writes	Kosciusko
1896	Arthur Newell	Laborer	Reads & Writes	Kosciusko
1896	Jeremiah J. Olive	Minister	Reads & Writes	Kosciusko
1896	John Owens	Laborer	Reads & Writes	Kosciusko
1896	Ned Owens	Laborer	Reads & Writes	Kosciusko
1896	Henry Raiford	Laborer	Reads & Writes	Kosciusko
1896	A. Ruff	Carpenter	Reads & Writes	Kosciusko
1896	Edmond Sanders	Farmer	Reads & Writes	Kosciusko
1896	J. W. Smith	Carpenter	Reads & Writes	Kosciusko
1896	Sam Snow	Laborer	Reads & Writes	Kosciusko
1896	G. T. Thomas	Minister	Reads & Writes	Kosciusko
1896	Coleman Watson	Laborer	Reads & Writes	Kosciusko
1896	Limas Watson	Laborer	Reads & Writes	Kosciusko
1896	H. Westbrooks	Minister	Reads & Writes	Kosciusko
1896	W. M. Wigley	Teacher	Reads & Writes	Kosciusko
1896	M. H. Wilkins	Minister	Reads & Writes	Kosciusko
1896	Will Williams	Laborer	Reads & Writes	Kosciusko
1896	A. W. Wright	Minister	Reads & Writes	Kosciusko

Year	Name	Occupation	Literacy	Precinct
1896	Price Hughes	Farmer	Reads & Writes	Liberty Chapel
1896	P. S. Adams	Farmer	Reads & Writes	McCool
1896	Alex Alston	Farmer	Reads & Writes	McCool
1896	A. G. Greenlee	Farmer	Reads & Writes	McCool
1896	A. M. Kimbrough	Farmer	Reads & Writes	McCool
1896	Willie Simpson	Farmer	Reads & Writes	McCool
1896	E. R. Smith	Laborer	Reads & Writes	McCool
1896	G. W. Smith	Farmer	Reads & Writes	McCool
1896	Henry Smith	Farmer	Reads & Writes	McCool
1896	S. A. Veazey	Farmer	Reads & Writes	McCool
1896	George Campbell	Farmer	Reads & Writes	Newport
1896	W. S. Sisson	Laborer	Reads & Writes	Peeler's Mill
1896	Wiley Hanna	Laborer	Reads & Writes	Providence
1896	George Murff	Farmer	Reads & Writes	Rocky Point
1896	R. B. Murff	Farmer	Reads & Writes	Rocky Point
1896	L. T. Brown	Laborer	Reads & Writes	Sallis
1896	Nelson Brown	Farmer	Reads & Writes	Sallis
1896	Andrew D. Byas	Farmer	Reads & Writes	Sallis
1896	J. C. Clark	Farmer	Reads & Writes	Sallis
1896	W. H. Roby	Farmer	Reads & Writes	Sallis
1896	Henry Ross	Farmer	Reads & Writes	Sallis
1896	Edmond Story	Farmer	Reads & Writes	Sallis
1896	Ely Hamblin	Farmer	Reads & Writes	Shrock
1896	Warren Russell	Farmer	Understands	Shrock
1896	J. H. Alston	Farmer	Reads & Writes	Thompson School House
1896	Robert Alston	Farmer	Reads & Writes	Thompson School House
1896	J. W. Smith	Farmer	Reads & Writes	Thompson School House
1897	J. W. Ellington	Farmer	Reads & Writes	Jerusalem
1897	Alex Gilliland	Farmer	Reads & Writes	Jerusalem
1897	Adam Morton	Laborer	Reads Only	Kosciusko

Year	Name	Occupation	Literacy	Precinct
1897	Gennie Newell	Laborer	Reads & Writes	Kosciusko
1897	Verge Rimmer	Farmer	Reads & Writes	Providence
1897	Rafe Jones	Farmer	Understands	Zilpha
1898	Albert J. McMichael	Farmer	Reads & Writes	Ayers
1898	A. R. Williamson	Farmer	Reads & Writes	Ayers
1898	Green Hill	Farmer	Reads & Writes	Jerusalem
1898	A. B. Miller	Farmer	Reads & Writes	Jerusalem
1898	Will Poole	Farmer	Reads & Writes	Jerusalem
1898	Tom Allen	Laborer	Reads & Writes	Kosciusko
1898	Lee Ashford	Printer	Reads & Writes	Kosciusko
1898	James Brooks	Laborer	Reads & Writes	Kosciusko
1898	Hilliard Kimbrough	Farmer	Reads & Writes	Kosciusko
1898	R. B. Rimmer	Laborer	Reads & Writes	Kosciusko
1898	W. M. Roberts	Minister	Reads & Writes	Kosciusko
1898	C. C. Rollins	Messenger	Reads & Writes	Kosciusko
1898	Eddie Sanders	Farmer	Reads & Writes	Kosciusko
1898	J. A. Simpson	Barber	Reads & Writes	Kosciusko
1898	C. O. H. Thomas	Minister	Reads & Writes	Kosciusko
1898	C. L. Walls	Minister	Reads & Writes	Kosciusko
1898	Charley Weeks	Laborer	Reads & Writes	Kosciusko
1898	Thomas B. Wheeler	Teacher	Reads & Writes	Kosciusko
1898	John Grant	Farmer	Reads & Writes	Newport
1898	John W. Adams	Farmer	Reads & Writes	Rocky Point
1898	Daniel Hays	Farmer	Reads Only	Rocky Point
1898	W. P. Lowery	Farmer	Reads & Writes	Rocky Point
1898	Delmore McAdory	Farmer	Understands	Rocky Point
1899	Henry Hathorn	Farmer	Reads Only	Ayers
1899	Nelson Landingham	Farmer	Understands	Ayers
1899	Willie Reeves	Farmer	Reads & Writes	Ayers
1899	Hilliard Spivey	Farmer	Reads & Writes	Ayers
1899	Elam Meek	Farmer	Reads & Writes	Jerusalem
1899	Harrison Segur	Farmer	Understands	Jerusalem
1899	Dave Thompson	Farmer	Reads & Writes	Jerusalem
1899	Louis Winnick	Farmer	Understands	Jerusalem
1899	John W. Bayne	Farmer	Reads & Writes	Kosciusko

Year	Name	Occupation	Literacy	Precinct
1899	Lewis Estes	Farmer	Reads & Writes	Kosciusko
1899	W. H. Harmon	Farmer	Reads & Writes	Kosciusko
1899	E. C. Hazley	Farmer	Reads & Writes	Kosciusko
1899	Frank McMillon	Farmer	Reads & Writes	Kosciusko
1899	Humphrey W. Micou	Farmer	Reads & Writes	Kosciusko
1899	Albert Murphy	Farmer	Reads Only	Kosciusko
1899	William W. Phillips	Teacher	Reads & Writes	Kosciusko
1899	Hugh Simmons	Farmer	Reads & Writes	Kosciusko
1899	Isaac Warren	Farmer	Reads & Writes	Kosciusko
1899	Marshall Weatherly	Farmer	Reads & Writes	Kosciusko
1899	John White	Farmer	Reads & Writes	Kosciusko
1899	Andrew G. Greenlee	Farmer	Reads & Writes	Liberty Chapel
1899	Monroe Hallum	Farmer	Reads Only	Liberty Chapel
1899	Crumby Kimbrough	Farmer	Reads Only	Liberty Chapel
1899	Henry Riley	Farmer	Reads & Writes	Liberty Chapel
1899	Lee Carter	Farmer	Reads & Writes	McCool
1899	David Docher	Carpenter	Reads & Writes	McCool
1899	Hillyard Gibbs	Farmer	Reads & Writes	McCool
1899	Horris Hemphill	Farmer	Reads & Writes	McCool
1899	Levi. Herring	Farmer	Reads & Writes	McCool
1899	E. B. Hughes	Farmer	Reads & Writes	McCool
1899	Jeff Hughes	Farmer	Reads & Writes	McCool
1899	S. McMillan	Teacher	Reads & Writes	McCool
1899	Durant Nunn	Farmer	Reads Only	McCool
1899	Alex Palm	Farmer	Reads & Writes	McCool
1899	Albert Townsend	Farmer	Reads & Writes	McCool
1899	Ben Townsend	Farmer	Reads & Writes	McCool
1899	Henry Young	Farmer	Reads & Writes	McCool
1899	Henry Clay	Farmer	Reads & Writes	Newport
1899	Daniel James	Farmer	Reads & Writes	Newport
1899	N. H. Nichols	Farmer	N/A	Newport
1899	Willie Nichols	Farmer	Reads & Writes	Newport
1899	J. D. Riley	Farmer	Reads & Writes	Newport
1899	John Atterberry	Farmer	Reads & Writes	Peeler's Mill
1899	Daniel B. Gaston	Farmer	Reads & Writes	Peeler's Mill

Year	Name	Occupation	Literacy	Precinct
1899	John Gaston	Farmer	Reads & Writes	Peeler's Mill
1899	J. M. Hearn	Farmer	Reads & Writes	Peeler's Mill
1899	Nelson Hunt	Farmer	Reads & Writes	Peeler's Mill
1899	Nelson Hunt Jr.	Farmer	Understands	Peeler's Mill
1899	George Prewitt Jr.	Farmer	Reads & Writes	Peeler's Mill
1899	George Prewitt Sr.	Farmer	Understands	Peeler's Mill
1899	Emmitt Seward	Farmer	Reads & Writes	Peeler's Mill
1899	J. R. Townsend	Farmer	Reads & Writes	Peeler's Mill
1899	John Veazey	Farmer	Reads & Writes	Peeler's Mill
1899	G. Winters	Farmer	Reads & Writes	Peeler's Mill
1899	William Carter	Farmer	Reads & Writes	Providence
1899	Jim Black	Farmer	Reads Only	Rochester
1899	Ned Hull	Farmer	Reads Only	Rochester
1899	J. A. Jones Jr.	Farmer	Reads & Writes	Rochester
1899	Willis Lee	Farmer	Reads & Writes	Rochester
1899	Henry Murphy	Farmer	Reads & Writes	Rochester
1899	Simon Veazey	Farmer	Reads & Writes	Rochester
1899	Zack Black	Farmer	Understands	Rocky Point
1899	Gordon Cone	Farmer	Reads & Writes	Rocky Point
1899	Wes Greer	Farmer	Reads & Writes	Rocky Point
1899	Albert Guess	Farmer	Reads & Writes	Rocky Point
1899	J. S. Hunter	Farmer	Reads & Writes	Rocky Point
1899	Jerry Jones	Farmer	Reads Only	Rocky Point
1899	J. M. Kennedy	Farmer	Reads & Writes	Rocky Point
1899	Frank Lispcomb	Farmer	Understands	Rocky Point
1899	J. S. Lispcomb	Farmer	Reads & Writes	Rocky Point
1899	Mose Love	Farmer	Reads Only	Rocky Point
1899	Duke McAfee	Farmer	Understands	Rocky Point
1899	M. McAfee	Farmer	Reads & Writes	Rocky Point
1899	Garfield Murff	Farmer	Reads & Writes	Rocky Point
1899	John Murff	Farmer	Reads Only	Rocky Point
1899	Eugene Palmer	Farmer	Reads & Writes	Rocky Point
1899	Monroe Palmer	Farmer	Read & Writes	Rocky Point
1899	Jerry Harmon	Farmer	Reads & Writes	Sallis
1899	Landen Campbell	Farmer	Understands	Shrock

Year	Name	Occupation	Literacy	Precinct
1899	A. D. Gerrin	Minister	Reads & Writes	Shrock
1899	P. G. McAtee	Farmer	Reads & Writes	Shrock
1899	Moses Phillips	Farmer	Reads & Writes	Shrock
1900	Allen Peeler	Farmer	Reads & Writes	Jerusalem
1900	Pleasant S. Bowie	Minister	Reads & Writes	Kosciusko
1900	William L. Hamblin	Minister	Reads & Writes	Kosciusko
1900	Columbus Phillips	Teacher	Reads & Writes	Kosciusko
1901	Richard Jenkins	Farmer	Reads & Writes	Kosciusko
1901	Charley Clark	Farmer	Reads & Writes	Sallis
1901	Wesley Williams	Farmer	Read Only	Sallis
1902	James A. Carr	Farmer	Reads & Writes	Liberty Chapel
1902	L. A. Carr	Farmer	Reads & Writes	Liberty Chapel
1902	Noah Cook	Farmer	Reads & Writes	Rocky Point
1902	Ben Cotton	Farmer	Reads & Writes	Rocky Point
1902	Will Carson	Farmer	Reads & Writes	Shrock
1902	A. A. Smith	Farmer	Reads & Writes	Thompson School House
1903	Wesley Dodd	Farmer	Reads & Writes	Ayers
1903	R. R. Rimmer	Teacher	Reads & Writes	Kosciusko
1903	D. P. Supples	Teacher	Reads & Writes	Kosciusko
1903	John D. Zuber	Minister	Reads & Writes	Kosciusko
1903	W. H. Harmon	Farmer	Reads & Writes	Rocky Point
1903	Milton Kennedy	Farmer	Reads & Writes	Rocky Point
1903	Tom Murff	Farmer	Read Only	Rocky Point
1903	H. V. Zollicoffer	Farmer	Reads & Writes	Rocky Point
1903	L. B. Browning	Farmer	Reads & Writes	Sallis
1903	J. W. Ellis	Farmer	Reads & Writes	Sallis
1903	A. J. Journey	Farmer	Reads & Writes	Sallis
1903	W. D. Peteet	Farmer	Reads & Writes	Sallis
1903	William Peteet	Farmer	Reads & Writes	Sallis
1903	Charlie Thompson	Farmer	Read Only	Thompson School House
1904	Dave Beamon	Farmer	Reads & Writes	Jerusalem
1904	Charley Clark	Farmer	Reads & Writes	Jerusalem

Year	Name	Occupation	Literacy	Precinct
1904	L. W. Ferguson	Farmer	Reads & Writes	Kosciusko
1904	Arthur Winters	Farmer	Reads & Writes	McCool
1907	W. B. Seward	Farmer	Reads & Writes	Sallis
1907	Singleton McWillie	Farmer	Reads & Writes	Shrock
1908	Oscar Nash	Farmer	Reads & Writes	Jerusalem
1908	John Edwards	Farmer	Reads & Writes	McCool
1908	Nathan Winters	Farmer	Reads & Writes	McCool
1909	Frank Carr Jr.	Teacher	Reads & Writes	Liberty Chapel
1909	Robert Carr	Teacher	Reads & Writes	Liberty Chapel
1911	Garrison Bridges	Farmer	Reads & Writes	Liberty Chapel
1912	Emmitt H. Cotton	Farmer	Reads & Writes	Jerusalem
1912	Charlie Bullock	Farmer	Reads & Writes	Kosciusko
1912	Ed Bullock	Farmer	Reads & Writes	Kosciusko
1912	Jim Funches	Farmer	Reads & Writes	Kosciusko
1912	Arthur Hazley	Farmer	Reads & Writes	Kosciusko
1912	George Hazley	Farmer	Reads & Writes	Kosciusko
1912	Lee B. Turner	Teacher	Reads & Writes	Kosciusko
1912	Richard Dobbs	Farmer	Reads & Writes	Newport
1914	Zanney McMichael	Farmer	Reads & Writes	Ayers
1915	Otha T. Greenlee	Farmer	Reads & Writes	Liberty Chapel

APPENDIX B

1. **Mary Alice Alston:** (1861–1937); parents, Vina Alston; education, Jackson College; church affiliation, First Missionary Baptist; organizations, Women General Baptist Missionary Society, Aged Women and Orphan's Home, Union District Society, and Women's State Convention.

2. **D. M. P. Hazley:** (1862–1947); parents, Frances Rice; spouse, Georgia Simpson and Minnie Lovelady; professional positions, minister of Buffalo United Methodist, Wesley United Methodist, and Mount Vernon; political leadership, Republican National Convention delegate; church affiliation; Buffalo United Methodist; organizations, Knights of Honor of the World.

3. **Thomas Porter Harris:** (1867–1951); parents, William Porter Harris and Mariah; education, Union Academy, Fisk University; degrees earned, bachelor of arts; teaching positions, Rust College; administrative positions, president of Ministerial Institute and College, principal of Union Academy, president of Central Mississippi College, and principal of Attala County Training School; professional positions, assistant cashier of Columbus Penny Savings Bank and district manager of Mississippi Life Insurance Company.

4. **Silas S. Lynch:** (1868–1949); parents, Pickens Lynch and Aisley; spouse; Winnie Snow and Daisy Wicks; education, Jackson College and Morehouse College; teaching positions, Jackson College, Bogue Chitto Normal Industrial College, and Central Mississippi College; administrative positions; Dean and President of Central Mississippi College; organizations, Mississippi Association of Teachers, Luxis Club, Colored Congress; church affiliation, Christian Liberty Missionary Baptist.

5. **William Wendell Phillips:** (1872–1932); parents, Moses Phillips Sr. and Annis Lacy; spouse, Sarah C. Wells; education, Tougaloo Southern Christian College, Rust College, and Hampton Institute; degrees earned, bachelor of arts; professional positions, principal of Sam Young/Attala County Training School; church affiliation; First Missionary Baptist; political leadership, Republican National Convention delegate; organizations,

Mississippi Association of Teachers, W. M. Stringer Grand Lodge, and National Negro Business League.

6. **William Porter Ashford:** (1874–1968); parents, George Ashford and Elizabeth Crittenden; spouse; Leona Brown and Elizabeth Funches; profession, meat peddler, dairy farmer, and co-director of Ashford & Turner Funeral Home.

7. **Lee Boston Turner:** (1877–1961); parents, Lewis Turner and Anna Brown; spouse, Dovie Quinn, Emma Senior Greenlee, and Louria Stingley; education, Central Mississippi College, Commercial Business College, and Chicago University; teaching positions, Bogue Chitto Normal Industrial College and Central Mississippi College; administrative positions, dean of Central Mississippi College and principal of Attala County Training School; professional positions; Universal Life Insurance Company; church affiliation, Christian Liberty Missionary Baptist; organizations, Choctaw County Republican Executive Committee, Mt. Olive Baptist Association, National Laymen's Movement, and Colored Red Cross

8. **Howard Huffman:** (1883–1935); parents, Charlotte Thompson; spouse, Carrie Brooks; professional positions, owner of Huffman Café, Press Shop, and Barber Shop; organizations, M. W. Stringer Grand Lodge; church affiliation, Wesley United Methodist

9. **Emmit Hezekiah Cotton:** (1884–1960); parents, Quitman Cotton and Harriet Gilliland; spouse, Kittie Daniel; education, Central Mississippi College, Rust College, Jackson College, Campbell College, and Tuskegee Institute.

10. **Calvin Perkins:** (1890–1959); spouse, Geneva Byas; education, Natchez College, Lane College, Campbell College, Daniel College, Coleman College, Arkansas Baptist College, Ideal Bible College, Mississippi Baptist Seminary, Indiana University, and Illinois University; degrees earned, doctor of philosophy, doctor of law, doctor of divinity, doctor of theology, master of theology, master of science, bachelor of divinity, bachelor of science, and bachelor of arts; administrative positions; president of Greenville Industrial College, president of Natchez College, supervisor of East Carroll Parish Training School, and president of Central Mississippi College; church affiliations, King David Baptist Church, St. Paul Baptist Church, 23rd Street Baptist Church, and Southside Calvary Church; organizations, National Baptist Convention.

11. **Mary Bradford (McLemore) Evans:** (1905–1998); parents, Howard McLemore and Virginia Hazley; spouse, Willie Clyde Evans; education, Marble Rock, Mary Holmes Seminary, Tougaloo Southern Christian College, and Jackson State University; degrees earned, bachelor of science in elementary education; teaching career, 1938–1974; teaching positions; Bunker Hill, Marble Rock, Buffalo Rosenwald, and Northside Elementary; church affiliations; Buffalo United Methodist Church, Marble Rock Missionary Baptist Church, and First Missionary Baptist; political engagement, poll worker; organizations, Socialite Club.

12. **James Edgar Williams:** (1907–1991); parents, Weldon Williams and Rosa Windham; spouse, Lucille Greenlee; education, Alcorn State A&M; professional positions, founder of Central Mississippi Training School, president of Negro Brotherhood-Christian Liberty chapter, president of Mississippi Association of Negro County Extension Workers, Chairmen of Special Projects Committee for the Circle of 100 Black Men; church affiliation, Christian Liberty Missionary Baptist; organizations, National Association for the Advancement of Colored People, Attala County Improvement Club, and Boy Scouts of America.

13. **Jessie Mae (Wright) Harper:** (1908–2014); parents, James Wright and Amanda Griggs; spouse, Reverend Benjamin Frank Harper; education, Clark College, Rust College, Tougaloo Southern Christian College, Jackson State University, and Mississippi State

University; degrees earned, bachelor of arts in English; teaching career, 1939–1975; teaching positions, Union High School, Sims High School, Choctaw County Training School, Monroe County High School, Rock Hill High School, Murphy High School, Tipton Street High School, and Kosciusko High School; church affiliations; Wesley United Methodist.

14. **Eva Bernice (McLemore) Phillips-Turner:** (1910–1985); parents, Howard McLemore and Virginia Hazley; education, Mary Holmes Seminary; professional positions, Carroll County Jeanes Agent.

15. **Clarence Miller Cooper:** (1910–1986); parents, William Cooper and Volina Miller; spouse, Verneda Greenlee; education, Alcorn A&M College Prep High School, Alcorn A&M College, and Tuskegee Institute; degrees earned, bachelor's degree and MED degree; teaching career, 1935–1974; administrative positions; principal of Northside Elementary; professional positions, Jackson & Renfroe Insurance Agency; church affiliation, First Missionary Baptist; organizations, Phi Beta Sigma.

16. **Mannie Whitt Stingley:** (1911–1979); parents, Thomas Stingley and Maggie Guyton; spouse, Dorotha Jenkins; education, Alcorn A&M, Tuskegee Institute, and Tougaloo Southern Christian College; degrees earned, master of science; teaching positions, Buffalo Rosenwald; administrative positions, principal of Little Hill School; professional positions, assistant director of Winters & Stingley Funeral Home; organizations, executive director of Attala County Improvement Club and Lone Star Masonic Lodge 51; church affiliation, Christian Liberty Missionary Baptist Church.

17. **Isaac Paul Presley Jr.:** (1912–1976); parents, Isaac Paul Presley Sr. and Lula Thompson; spouse, Ever Lee Huffman; education, Rust College, Wiley College, and University of Barritz (France); degrees earned, bachelor of arts in business administration; occupation, gas-station owner and livestock farm; professional positions, founder of Negro Brotherhood of Kosciusko, assistant director of Central Mississippi Inc., and chairman of the board of the National Business League-Kosciusko chapter; church affiliation, Wesley United Methodist; organizations, Omega Psi Phi.

18. **Iley (McLemore) Shelby:** (1912–1977); parents, Grandison McLemore and Della Munson; spouse, Jasper Shelby; education, Mary Holmes Seminary, Rust College, Tougaloo Southern Christian College, Jackson State University, Mississippi State University, and Kentucky State University; degrees earned, bachelor of science in elementary education; teaching positions, Greenlee; church affiliations, Buffalo United Methodist Church, First Missionary Baptist Church.

19. **Viola (Bain) Garland-Wragg:** (1913–1989); parents, John Wesley Bain and Lillian Tallulah Virginia Adams; spouse, Daniel Lee Garland and Hiram Wragg Sr.; education, Rust College, Northwestern University; degrees earned, master's in education; teaching career, 1931–1975; teaching positions, Buffalo Rosenwald; administrative positions, Attala County Jeanes Agent, principal at Long Creek Elementary; church affiliations, Buffalo United Methodist; organizations, Heroines of Jericho, National Retired Teachers Association, and Jolly Glee Club.

20. **Mary C. (Terry) Walker:** (1917–1961); parents, William Terry and Alcola Phillips; spouse, Leslie Walker; education, teaching positions, Tipton Street School; administrative positions, head of mathematics department at Tipton Street School; organizations, New March of Dimes and board of directors of Phillips Community Credit Union.

21. **Ella Louise (Holsey) Smith:** (1918–1985); parents, Joseph Samuel Holsey and Elma Bell; spouse, Homer George Smith; education, Attala County Training School and Rust College; degrees earned, bachelor of science in elementary education; teaching career,

1936–1975; teaching positions, South Union Elementary, Buffalo Rosenwald, Tipton Street High School, and Kosciusko Junior High; administrative positions, principal of Buffalo Rosenwald; church affiliations, First Missionary Baptist Church; organizations, National Council of Negro Women.

22. **Ever Lee (Huffman) Presley:** (1919–2007); parents, Howard Huffman and Carrie Brooks; spouse, Isaac Paul Presley Jr.; education, Attala County Training School, Rust College, Tougaloo Southern Christian College, Jackson State University, and Mississippi State University; degrees earned, bachelor of arts in education; teaching positions, Tipton Street High School; church affiliations; Wesley United Methodist; organizations, National Council of Negro Women, National Association for the Advancement of Colored People, Mississippi and Attala Retired Teachers Association, and Claude Martin Presley Ladies Auxiliary VFW Post 5051.

23. **Genevieve (Allen) Newell:** (1919–2012); parents, Aaron Allen and Mary Jane Eichelberger; spouse, James Newell; education, Jackson State University, Butler University, and Mississippi State University; degrees earned, bachelor of science and master's degree in education; teaching career, 1942–1981; teaching positions, Greenlee Elementary; church affiliations, First Missionary Baptist Church; organizations, Mississippi Retired Teachers, Attala County Advisory Council, National Council of Negro Women, and Eastern Star.

24. **Velma Christine (Carr) Pullum:** (1924–1997); parents, Frank Anderson Carr Jr. and Willie B. Micou; spouse, Clarence Frederick Pullum; education, Tougaloo Southern Christian University; teaching career, 1947–1981; teaching positions, Buffalo Rosenwald, Tipton Street School, Pearl-McLaurin and Ethel High School; organizations, Claude Martin Presley Ladies Auxiliary VFW Post 5051; church affiliation, Buffalo United Methodist Church.

25. **Gladys (Shumaker) Langdon:** (1931–2015); parents, Daniel Shumaker and Annie Dickens; spouse, Douglas Langdon; education, Jackson State University, Indiana University, Mississippi State University, and Mississippi University for Women; degrees earned, bachelor of science in elementary education and master of science; teaching career, 1952–1985; teaching positions, W. A. Higgins Junior and Senior High, Northside Elementary, and Tipton Street School; church affiliation, Christian Liberty Missionary Baptist Church.

NOTES

INTRODUCTION

1. W. E. B. Du Bois, *The Souls of Black Folk: Essay and Sketches* (Amherst: University of Massachusetts Press, 2018), 132.

2. Dennis J. Mitchell, *A New History of Mississippi* (Jackson: University Press of Mississippi, 2014), 8.

3. Ronald N. Satz, "The Mississippi Choctaw: From the Removal Treaty to the Federal Agency," in *After Removal: The Choctaw in Mississippi*, edited by Samuel J. Wells and Tubby Roseanna (Jackson: University Press of Mississippi, 1986), 3–4.

4. Tara Barrett, Attala County 1850 Slave Schedule Transcription, 1999. Dale Sallis Fleming. (2006). *The War Between the States 1861–1865.*

5. Carter G. Woodson, *The Rural Negro* (New York: Russell & Russell, 1969), 112.

6. Hortense Powdermaker, *After Freedom: A Cultural Study in the Deep South* (New York: Atheneum, 1968), xiv.

7. Vernon Lane Wharton, *The Negro in Mississippi 1865–1890* (New York: Harper and Row, 1965), 63, 208, 220, 232.

8. Albert D. Kirwan, *Revolt of the Rednecks: Mississippi Politics, 1876–1925* (New York: Harper & Row, 1951), vii.

9. Stephen Cresswell. *Rednecks, Redeemers, and Race: Mississippi After Reconstruction, 1877–1917* (Jackson: University Press of Mississippi for the Mississippi Historical Society, 2006), 9.

10. William C. Harris, *The Day of the Carpetbagger: Republican Reconstruction in Mississippi* (Baton Rouge: Louisiana State University Press, 1979), 70, 130.

11. Michael Perman, *Road to Redemption: Southern Politics, 1869–1879* (Chapel Hill: University of North Carolina Press, 1984), 23–25.

12. Christopher M. Span, *From Cotton Field to Schoolhouse: African American Education in Mississippi, 1862–1975* (Chapel Hill: University of North Carolina Press, 2009), 11–12. Justin Behrend, *Reconstructing Democracy. Grassroots Black Politics in the Deep South after the Civil War* (Athens: University of Georgia Press, 2015), 7–9.

13. C. L. R. James, *The Black Jacobins: Toussaint L'Ouverture and the San Domingo Revolution*, 2nd ed. (New York: Vintage, 1989), 81–83, 96, 101; Herbert Aptheker, *American Negro Slave Revolts: Nat Turner, Denmark Vesey, Gabriel, and Others*, 2nd ed. (New York: International Publishers, 1983), 82–87. Also see *In Hope of Liberty: Culture, Community, and Protest among Northern Free Blacks, 1700–1860* and *Black Abolitionist, All Bound Up Together: The Woman's Question in African American Public Culture, 1830–1900* for a historiographical framework explaining the role that free blacks played during the abolitionist movement that helped to shape and create post–Civil War policies.

14. Justin Behrend, "Facts and Memories: John R. Lynch and the Revising of Reconstruction History in the Era of Jim Crow," *Journal of African American History* 97, no. 4 (2012): 429–30.

15. Behrend, 443.

16. Eric Foner, *Reconstruction: America's Unfinished Revolution 1863–1877* (New York: HarperCollins, 1989), xxv.

17. Foner, *Reconstruction*, xxiii.

18. Michael Perman, *Road to Redemption: Southern Politics, 1869–1879* (Chapel Hill: University of North Carolina Press, 1984), xii, 23–25, 31.

19. Leon Litwack, *Been in the Storm So Long: The Aftermath of Slavery* (New York: Vintage Books, 1979), 296, 309, 316, 399, 406–7, 414–15, 502, 507, 543, 546.

20. *In the Words of Frederick Douglass: Quotations from Liberty's Champion*, edited by John R. McKivigan and Heather L. Kaufman (Ithaca: Cornell University Press, 2012), 138.

21. Timothy S. Huebner, *Liberty and Union: The Civil War Era and American Constitutionalism* (Lawrence: University Press of Kansas, 2016), 57–58.

22. Black Power is commonly associated with Stokely Carmichael's Black-power vision centered on political control in areas where African Americans were the racial majority and power allocation in areas where they were the minority. Stokely Carmichael and Ekwueme Michael Thelwell, *Ready for Revolution: The Life and Struggles of Stokely Carmichael {Kwame Ture}* (New York: Scribner, 2003), 510. Walter Rodney concluded that the Reconstruction era was the only time in America's history that African Americans achieved the type of Black power that Carmichael spoke of. Rodney explained that in African American–majority areas, they used their newfound voting freedom to start the process of building institutions that reflected their own needs and not so much those of the white minority. Walter Rodney, *The Groundings with my Brothers* (Bogle-L'Ouverture Publications, Chicago: 1969), 20. Lerone Bennett Jr. echoed this correlation between power and political office in *Black Power U.S.A.: The Human Side of Reconstruction 1867–1876*, stating, "The assassins—highly placed aristocrats and their poor white allies—huddled in dimly lit rooms in Clinton, Mississippi, and decided that Charles Caldwell had to die. He had to die because he was black, because he was powerful, and because the black power he personified stood between the assassins and absolute control of the state." Lerone Bennett Jr., *Black Power U.S.A.: The Human Side of Reconstruction, 1867–1976* (Chicago: Johnson, 1967), 327. While providing some nuance to what constituted black power, Stephen Hahn also equated black power to African Americans holding political office. Stephen Hahn, *A Nation Under Our Feet: Black Political Struggles in the Rural South from Slavery to the Great Migration* (Cambridge: Belknap Press of the Harvard University Press, 2003), 353.

23. Roger L. Ransom and Richard Sutch, *One Kind of Freedom: The Economic Consequences of Emancipation* (Cambridge: Cambridge University Press, 1977), 39.

24. Chokwe Lumumba, "Repression and Black Liberation," in *Black Scholar* 5, no. 2 (1973): 36.

25. Elizabeth Fox-Genovese and Eugene D. Genovese, *Slavery in White and Black: Class and Race in the Southern Slaveholders' New World Order* (Cambridge: Cambridge University Press, 2008), 2–3.

26. Ibid., 4–5, 9.

27. Charles C. Bolton, *Poor Whites of the Antebellum South: Central North Carolina and Northeast Mississippi* (Durham: Duke University Press, 1994), 43.

28. Rayford Logan, *The Negro in American Life and Thought: The Nadir 1877–1901* (New York: Dial Press, 1954), 11.

29. Leon F. Litwack, *How Free Is Free? The Long Death of Jim Crow* (Cambridge: Harvard University Press, 2009), 5.

30. Johnathan M. Bryant, *How Curious a Land: Conflict and Change in Greene County, Georgia, 1850–1885* (Chapel Hill: University of North Carolina Press, 1996), 16.

31. John Blassingame, *The Slave Community: Plantation Life in the Antebellum South,* (New York, Oxford University Press, 1977), 78.

32. G. P. Hamilton, *Beacon Lights of the Race* (Memphis: P. H. Clarke, 1911), 423.

33. Thomas L. Webber, *Deep Like the Rivers. Education in the Slave Quarter Community 1831–1865* (New York: W. W. Norton, 1978), 91–93.

34. Herbert Gutman dismissed Blassingame by asserting that to understand Black action best required examining the white master. Herbert Gutman, *The Black Family in Slavery and Freedom, 1750–1925* (New York: Vintage Press, 1976), xxi, 261. Gutman's centering white behavior to explain Black activity positioned the colonizer above and before the colonized. The slave owner promoted docility and dependency, not action and autonomy.

35. Norman L. Crockett, *The Black Towns* (Lawrence: Regents Press of Kansas, 1979), 51, 59, 65–75.

36. Elizabeth Rauh Bethel, *Promiseland: A Century of Life in a Negro Community* (Philadelphia: Temple University Press, 1981), 5.

37. Mark Shultz, *The Rural Face of White Supremacy Beyond Jim Crow* (Chicago: University of Illinois Press, 2007), 8.

38. Schultz, 11.

39. Derrick Bell, *Faces at the Bottom of the Well: The Permanence of Racism* (New York: Basic Books, 1992), 40.

40. John Dittmer, *Local People: The Struggle for Civil Rights in Mississippi* (Urbana: University of Illinois Press, 1994), 89.

41. John H. Bracey Jr., Ralph Watkins Lecture, SUNY Oneonta, February 19, 2020.

42. Isaac Crawford and Patrick H. Thompson, *Multum in Parvo*, 2nd ed. (Jackson: Consumers Printing, 1912), 54.

43. Eugene Genovese, *In Red and Black: Marxian Explorations in Southern and Afro-American History* (Knoxville: University of Tennessee Press, 1984), 107–8.

CHAPTER 1. A NEW DAWN: EMBARKING ON THE LIBERATION JOURNEY

1. Thomas L. Webber, *Deep Like the Rivers. Education in the Slave Quarter Community 1831–1865* (New York: W. W. Norton, 1978), 91.

2. Bradley G. Bond, *Political Culture in the Nineteenth-Century South: Mississippi 1830–1900* (Baton Rouge: Louisiana State University Press, 1995), 13.

3. Diary of Jason Niles, 168, https://docsouth.unc.edu/imls/niles/niles.html.

4. W. J. Cash, *The Mind of the South* (New York: Vintage Books, 1941), 40.

5. W. E. B. Du Bois, *Black Reconstruction in America: Toward a History of the Part Which Black Folk Played in the Attempt to Reconstruct Democracy in America, 1860–1880* (New York: Harcourt, 1935), 399.

6. *Weekly Mississippian*, July 4, 1851.

7. *Southern Press*, September 5, 1850.

8. *Weekly Vicksburg Whig*, March 14, 1860.

9. Timothy B. Smith, *The Mississippi Secession Convention: Delegates and Deliberations in Politics and War, 1861–1865* (Jackson: University Press of Mississippi), 10, 220.

10. Diary of Jason Niles, 53, 66, https://docsouth.unc.edu/imls/niles/niles.html.

11. *Mississippi, U.S., Wills and Probate Records, 1780–1982*, Ancestry.com.

12. Mississippi Narratives Prepared by the Federal Writer's Project of the Works Progress Administration for the State of Mississippi, transcribed by Ann Allen Geoghegan, http://msgw.org/slaves/roby-edd-xslave.htm.

13. Ibid.

14. Powell, 318; Mississippi Narratives Prepared by the Federal Writer's Project of the Works Progress Administration for the State of Mississippi.

15. Diary of Jason Niles, 103–4, https://docsouth.unc.edu/imls/niles/niles.html

16. Ibid., 157.

17. Susie V. Powell, *Works Progress Administration for Mississippi: Source Material for Mississippi Attala County*, vol. IV, part one, 317–18.

18. Diary of Jason Niles, 55, 114.

19. Powell, 319.

20. Maude Kelley Jamison Waggoner, *The Jamisons*, 1947, 30.

21. Heather Andrea Williams, *Self-Taught: African American Education in Slavery and Freedom* (Chapel Hill: University of North Carolina Press, 2005), 7.

22. W. E. B. Du Bois, *The Negro Church: Report of a Social Study Made Under the Direction of Atlanta University by the Eighth Atlanta Conference* (Atlanta: Atlanta University Press, 1903), 22. South Carolina legislature passed the following law: "It shall not be lawful for any number of slaves, free Negroes, mulattoes, or mestizoes [sic], even in company with white persons, to meet together and assemble for the purpose of mental instruction or religious worship, either before the rise of the sun or after the going down of the same. And all magistrates, sheriffs, militia officers, etc., etc., are hereby vested with power, etc., for dispersing such assemblies" (W. E. B. Du Bois, *The Negro Church*, 22). This law, as in Virginia, was modified to limit assembly after 9:00 p.m. Alfred Holt Stone, *The Early Slave Laws of Mississippi: Being Some Brief Observations Thereon in a Paper Read before the Mississippi Historical Society at a Meeting Held in the City of Natchez, April 20th–21st, 1899*, 137. The Mississippi law does not indicate religious instruction, rather focuses on assembly for educational purposes. Chapter 33, Article 51, of the revised Mississippi code of 1856–1857 elaborated on slave assembly, stating,

> All meetings or assemblies of slaves, or free negroes or mulattoes mixing and asso-ciating with such slaves, above the number of five, including such free negroes and mulattoes, at any place of public resort, or at any meeting-house or houses in the night, or at any school for teaching them reading or writing, either in the day time or night, under whatsoever pretext, shall be deemed an unlawful assembly, and any justice of the peace of the county, or mayor or chief magistrate of any incorporated town, wherein such assemblage shall be held, either from his own knowledge, or

on the information of others, may issue his warrant, directed to the proper officer, authorizing him to enter the house where such unlawful assemblage or meeting may be, for the purpose of apprehending the offenders, and dispersing the assemblage; and all slaves offending herein, shall be tried in the manner hereinafter provided for the trial of slaves, and on conviction, shall be punished by not more than thirty-nine lashes on the bare back. Provided, that nothing herein contained shall be construed to prevent any master or employer of slaves from giving them permission in writing to go to any place whatever, for the purpose of religious worship, provided such worship be conducted by a regularly ordained or licensed white minister, or attended by at least two discreet and respectable white persons, appointed for that purpose by some regular church or religious society. (*Revised Code of the Statute Laws of the State of Mississippi*, 247).

By 1833, slaves began organizing independent churches. In Natchez, the Rose Hill Baptist Church served as the first recognized and established Negro church during Mississippi's slave era. Baptist ministers who came from South Carolina to the Natchez country in the late eighteenth century established the Baptist church in the Mississippi Territory. During the early years of the nineteenth century, churches arose in Woodville (1800) and New Providence (1805), in what became Wilkinson and Amite Counties. On the eve of Mississippi receiving statehood in 1820, seventeen churches existed, and by 1836, the number increased to 117 churches. A free black man named Marshall held the deed to the church. Although Mississippi had no licensed Negro minister, a slave named Randle Pollard became the church's minister. The origins of Mt. Helm Baptist Church in Jackson, Mississippi, date back to 1835 when Reverend Holloway donated the slave-built Baptist church to the white Baptists. Negro worship took place in the church's basement. George Holloman, a Negro preacher from church, was the "first colored preacher" of the basement church, including members John Shelton, Isaac Berry, Andrew Dawson, Lucinda McMillan, and Nancy Austin. Patrick Henry Thompson, *The History of Negro Baptist in Mississippi* (Jackson: R. W. Bailey, 1898), 18, 21, 24, 27, 31–32.

23. Attala County Churches and Cemeteries. Two churches in neighboring counties organized before the Civil War, Wilkens Chapel (1851) and Mount Pisgah Baptist Church (1856).

24. Susie V. Powell, *Works Progress Administration for Mississippi: Source Material for Mississippi Attala County*, vol. IV part one, 317.

25. Powell, 319.

26. Powell, 319.

27. *Mississippi. Probate Court (Attala County)*; Probate Place: *Attala, Mississippi*. Notes: *Wills and Accounts, Vol A, 1858–1872*, Ancestry.com. *Mississippi, Wills and Probate Records, 1780–1982* [database online]. Provo, UT, U.S.A.: Ancestry.com Operations, Inc., 2015. Original data: Mississippi County, District and Probate Courts, 227.

28. Powell, 319. The amount Tom kept for himself is not known.

29. "Mississippi, Confederate Veterans and Widows Pension Applications, 1900–1974."

30. Ibid.

31. Jason Niles Diary, 170–71, https://docsouth.unc.edu/imls/niles/niles.html.

32. Ibid., 172. Slaves in Attala County likely heard of this liberating black army, even though the regiment never reached them.

33. Edward C. Coleman Jr., "The Period of Reconstruction in Attala County," in *Reconstruction in Northern Mississippi Counties*. Archives and Special Collections, J. D. Williams Library, University of Mississippi, 1910, 3.

34. Ibid., 2.

35. Ibid., 9.

36. Diary of Jason Niles, 199, https://docsouth.unc.edu/imls/niles/niles.html.

37. Edward C. Coleman Jr., "The Period of Reconstruction in Attala County," in *Reconstruction in Northern Mississippi Counties*. Archives and Special Collections, J. D. Williams Library, University of Mississippi, 1910, 5.

38. Ronald L. F. Davis, *Good and Faithful Labor: From Slavery to Sharecropping in the Natchez District 1860–1890* (Westport: Greenwood Press, 1982), 4, 184.

39. Eugene Genovese, *Roll, Jordan, Roll: The World the Slaves Made* (New York: Vintage Books, 1976), 3, 5–6.

40. Ira Berlin, *Many Thousands Gone: The First Two Centuries of Slavery in North America* (Cambridge: Belknap Press of Harvard University Press, 1998), 34.

41. Ronald L. F. Davis, *Good and Faithful Labor: From Slavery to Sharecropping in the Natchez District 1860–1890* (Westport: Greenwood Press, 1982), 7.

42. C. Vann Woodward, *Origins of the New South 1877–1913* (Baton Rouge: Louisiana State University Press, 1951), 208. William C. Harris, *Presidential Reconstruction in Mississippi* (Baton Rouge: Louisiana State University Press, 1967), 27.

43. Ira Berlin, Steven F. Miller, Leslie S. Rowland, "Afro-American Families in the Transition from Slavery to Freedom," in *Radical History Review* 42, October1988: 113.

44. United States Freedmen's Bureau Labor Contracts, Indenture and Apprenticeship Records, 1865–1872.

45. Ibid.

46. *Daily Clarion*, August 5, 1864.

47. Loren Schweninger, *Black Property Owners in the South, 1790–1915* (Urbana and Chicago: University of Illinois Press, 1990), 11.

48. Schweninger, 14.

49. Susie V. Powell, *Works Progress Administration for Mississippi: Source Material for Mississippi Attala County*, vol. IV, part one, 317.

50. Eric Foner, *Reconstruction: America's Unfinished Revolution 1863–1877* (New York: HarperCollins, 1989), 105.

51. Early Attala Residents, http://attala-county-history-genealogy.org/benayers.html.

52. Eric Foner, *Reconstruction*, 121.

53. Edwin A. Miles, "The Mississippi Slave Insurrection Scare of 1835," *Journal of Negro History* 42(1); January 1957, 50–51, 55. There are doubts about whether the events were based on credible evidence as confessions resulted from violent interrogation of both slaves and suspected whites. In the aftermath of Nat Turner's insurrection, the Mississippi insurrection scare fueled the white imagination and fear concerns. The counties involved, Madison, Hinds, and Warren, were counties where whites were the minority. The county's population makeup may have contributed to the deadly response inflicted on the alleged perpetrators.

54. Nell Irvin Painter, *Exodusters: Black Migration to Kansas after Reconstruction* (New York: W. W. Norton, 1976), x.

55. Diary of Jason Niles, vol. 18, 92.

56. Diary of Jason Niles, 187, https://docsouth.unc.edu/imls/niles/niles.html.

57. Walter Rodney, *The Groundings with my Brothers* (London: Bogle L'Ouverture, 1969), 22.

58. William C. Harris, *Presidential Reconstruction in Mississippi* (Baton Rouge: Louisiana State University Press, 1967), 122; Dennis J. Mitchell, *A New History of Mississippi* (Jackson:

University Press of Mississippi, 2014), 169. The Black Codes stated, "No freedman, free Negro, or mulatto, not in the military service of the United States Government, and not licensed to do so by the board of police of his or her county, shall keep or carry firearms of any kind" W. E. B. Du Bois, *Black Reconstruction in America: Toward a History of the Part Which Black Folk Played in the Attempt to Reconstruct Democracy in America, 1860–1880* (New York: Harcourt, 1935), 172.

59. John Hope Franklin and Evelyn Brooks Higginbotham, *From Slavery to Freedom: A History of African Americans*, 9th ed. (New York: McGraw-Hill, 2011), 239.

60. William C. Harris, *Presidential Reconstruction in Mississippi* (Baton Rouge: Louisiana State University Press, 1967), 107.

61. James Wilford Garner, *Reconstruction in Mississippi* (New York: MacMillan, 1902), 94–96; Vernon Lane Wharton, *The Negro in Mississippi 1865–1890* (New York: Harper Torchbooks, 1965), 134–35.

62. No information exists on Sam Winters, the murdered African American.

63. *Daily Clarion*, September 25, 1866.

64. Ibid.

65. Ibid. Judge Campbell sentenced Winters to one year in the Attala County jail in addition to legal fees.

66. Garner, 117; Joseph A. Ranney, *A Legal History of Mississippi: Race, Class, and the Struggle for Opportunity* (Jackson: University Press of Mississippi, 2019), 86.

67. Wharton, 136.

68. *Daily Clarion*, December 22, 1866.

69. Barrington Moore Jr., *Social Origins of Dictatorship and Democracy: Lord and Peasant in the Making of the Modern World* (Boston: Beacon Press, 1993), 119, 121–22.

70. C. Vann Woodward, *Origins of the New South 1877–1913* (Baton Rouge: Louisiana State University Press, 1951), 208.

71. Pete Daniel, *Breaking the Land: The Transformation of Cotton, Tobacco, and Rice Cultures since 1880* (Chicago: University of Illinois Press, 1985), 4.

72. W. J. Cash, *The Mind of the South* (New York: Vintage Books, 1941), 40.

73. Edward C. Coleman Jr., "The Period of Reconstruction in Attala County," in *Reconstruction in Northern Mississippi Counties*. Archives and Special Collections, J. D. Williams Library, University of Mississippi, 1910, 5.

74. Ibid., 6. Census records indicate birthplace as Virginia and Maine.

75. *Weekly Clarion*, March 18, 1869.

76. "Mississippi Freedmen's Bureau Field Office Records, 1865–1872."

77. Ibid.

78. Ibid. In Holmes County, Louisa filed a complaint against Mr. Perkins after he "severely beat her," resulting in Louisa refusing to fulfill her contract. The agent awarded Louisa three months' wages and the return of her possessions, while the bureau official reminded Mr. Perkins of slavery's abolishment, and the assault was a crime.

79. Richard Paul Fuke, "Planters, Apprenticeship, and Forced Labor: The Black Family under Pressure in Post Emancipation Maryland," *Agricultural History* 62, no. 4 (1988): 63. Mississippi law allowed for

all freedmen, free Negroes and mulattoes, under the age of eighteen, within their respective counties, beats, or districts, who are orphans, or whose parent or parents have not the means, or who refuse to provide for and support said minors, and thereupon it shall be the duty of said probate court to order the clerk of said court to apprentice said minors to some competent and suitable person on such terms as the court may direct, having a particular care to the interest of said minors; Provided, that the former owner of said minors shall have the preference when, in the opinion of the court, he or she shall be a suitable person for that purpose.

W. E. B. Du Bois, *Black Reconstruction in America: Toward a History of the Part Which Black Folk Played in the Attempt to Reconstruct Democracy in America, 1860–1880* (New York: Harcourt, 1935), 175–76.

80. Attala County Final Account Book D.

81. Dylan C. Pennington, *The Claims of Kinfolk: African American Property and Community in the Nineteenth-Century South* (Chapel Hill: University of North Carolina Press, 2003), 166–68. In Neshoba County, John Stribling apprenticed Mariah Stribling's children, Josephine, Mary, and Thomas, to Joseph Stribling and Thomas McCullough. On October 21, 1867, Mariah filed a complaint with the Philadelphia sub-assistant commissioner to regain custody. Officials ordered John Stribling to return Mariah's children on the grounds of illegal apprenticeship. *United States, Freedmen's Bureau Labor Contracts, Indenture and Apprenticeship Records, 1865–1872.*

82. George M. Frederickson, *Black Liberation: A Comparative History of Black Ideologies in the United States and South Africa* (New York: Oxford University Press, 1995), 58. James H. Cone, *A Black Theology of Liberation* (Philadelphia: J. B. Lippincott, 1970), 23. Cone's work adds depth to Genovese's analysis of slave religion centered on the white and black preacher. The white preacher was the master's key weapon to control slave religion. The black preacher was a dynamic individual who held the most significant appreciation in the slave community (which extended into the post–Civil War era). Slaves wanted to hear the gospel preached by a black preacher in some capacity. Whites understood the black preacher's significance and potential to disrupt the power currency within the master-slave relationship; however, whites could not prevent slaves from hearing the gospel from the African perspective altogether (*Roll Jordan Roll: The World the Slaves Made*, 202–4, 258–61). Black church establishment started a statewide organizing effort to build unity amongst the race while institutionalizing a call for freedom and upward mobility. At the First Antioch Association, the association resolved the following:

> Resolved further, That as we are a down-trodden and oppressed race, but through the providence of God we have obtained our freedom, and as such as we will pray the Lord to sustain us and this nation in the right, and make it an asylum for the poor and oppressed of every land; and further, that we, as an association, will ever pray for the success of that great party known as the Republican Party, that gave us our freedom, and we will discountenance any and all parties that are opposed to us having equal rights before the law; and furthermore, we recommend to all the churches that compose this association, and sister and neighboring churches, to adopt these resolutions; and furthermore, we will dis-countenance any and all persons that will go with any party that is opposed to our rights either by preaching or speaking. (History of Negro Baptists, 44)

83. History: First Missionary Baptist Church.

84. Patrick Henry Thompson, *The History of Negro Baptist in Mississippi* (Jackson: R. W. Bailey, 1898), 568–69.

85. *Sedalia Democrat*, July 21, 1895, and *St. Joseph News-Press*, June 7, 1907.

86. Hanes Walton Jr. discussed Black Republicans displaying greater political cohesion and effectiveness at the national level. Democratic backlash and a Republican Party faction that did not want to pursue the fight for African American rights diminished their viability at the state level. Hanes Walton Jr., *Black Republicans: The Politics of the Black and Tans* (Metuchen: Scarecrow Press, 1975), 20–21, 24. Harris interpreted Black Republicans as both benefactors of white Republican advocacy and active political agents who came to have legitimate power in shaping Mississippi's state policies. Harris discussed that African Americans benefited from Governor Adelbert Ames's forward-thinking views on suffrage, social equality, and economic fairness. Harris also acknowledged Ames's understanding that African Americans played a vital role in controlling the agenda that affected their race. William C. Harris, *The Day of the Carpetbagger*, 70, 130, 137–38. Michael Perman solidified both Walton Jr. and Harris's analysis of the relationship between the Republican Party and Black Republicans. He detailed the response of Black Republicans to a Republican Party that wanted to play both sides of the political coin. The party wanted white respect to gain legitimacy and a party identity as a party of all and not just African Americans; therefore, it wanted Black support but not to the point that it disillusioned whites. Michael Perman, *Road to Redemption: Southern Politics, 1869–1879* (Chapel Hill: University of North Carolina Press, 1984), 23–25.

87. Hanes Walton Jr., *Black Republicans: The Politics of the Black and Tans* (Metuchen: Scarecrow Press, 1975), 4–5. 8. The Dred Scott decision of 1857 played an essential role in the shifting attitudes that African Americans held towards Republicans. The pathway to ending slavery was to dispose of the Democratic Party's control. African Americans understood that no one party would come to suit their needs entirely and that allying with the Republican Party was better than having no party affiliation. The Republican Party offered the most promise for interparty progression and influence on issues important to the African American community. Support for Republicans was not uniform within the African American community; several men believed that the Republican platform did not go far enough on the issue of slavery and that Lincoln's views on colonization and emancipation were modest at best (pp. 15, 18).

88. William C. Harris, *The Day of the Carpetbagger*, 1, 96–97. Harris noted that African Americans in Leake County had great enthusiasm for becoming registered voters. Harris included examples of African American political participation outside of majority-Black counties. Leake County had 442 African American registered voters. *Weekly Democrat*, October 7, 1867.

89. Edward C. Coleman Jr., "The Period of Reconstruction in Attala County," in *Reconstruction in Northern Mississippi Counties*. Archives and Special Collections, J. D. Williams Library, University of Mississippi, 1910, 3.

90. William C. Harris, *The Day of the Carpetbagger*, 108–9.

91. *Daily Clarion*, May 8, 1867.

92. Edward C. Coleman Jr., "The Period of Reconstruction in Attala County," in *Reconstruction in Northern Mississippi Counties*. Archives and Special Collections, J. D. Williams Library, University of Mississippi, 1910, 7.

93. *Vicksburg Daily Herald*, May 5, 1867; *Weekly Democrat*, October 7, 1867; *Natchez Democrat*, November 30, 1867.

94. Stephen Hahn, *A Nation Under Our Feet: Black Political Struggles in the Rural South from Slavery to the Great Migration* (Cambridge: Belknap Press of the Harvard University Press, 2003), 164–65.

95. Edward C. Coleman Jr., "The Period of Reconstruction in Attala County," in *Reconstruction in Northern Mississippi Counties*. Archives and Special Collections, J. D. Williams Library, University of Mississippi, 1910, 9.

96. William C. Harris, *The Day of the Carpetbagger*, 115.

97. Michael Perman, *Road to Redemption: Southern Politics, 1869–1879* (Chapel Hill: University of North Carolina Press, 1984), 36–37.

98. William C. Harris, *The Day of the Carpetbagger*, 96–97.

99. *New York Times*, July 22, 1868. There are discrepancies between the reported number and actual number. The reported defeat margin is 7,629.

100. William C. Harris, *The Day of the Carpetbagger*, 195.

101. Mississippi Freedmen's Bureau Field Office Records, 1865–1872. The sub-assistant agent in Durant heard the case. Parrish relocated to Poplar Creek in Montgomery County.

102. William C. Harris, *The Day of the Carpetbagger*, 227.

103. *Weekly Clarion*, July 15, 1869.

104. Ibid.

105. Stephen Hahn, *A Nation Under Our Feet: Black Political Struggles in the Rural South from Slavery to the Great Migration* (Cambridge: Belknap Press of the Harvard University Press, 2003), 229.

106. Ibid., 226–29.

107. *Star-Herald*, July 28, 1905.

108. William C. Harris, *The Day of the Carpetbagger*, 175–76.

109. *Weekly Clarion*, August 19, 1869.

110. *Weekly Clarion*, August 5, 1869, and August 19, 1869. Thomas spoke to the African American attendees; however, his words also drew applause from white attendees.

111. William C. Harris, *The Day of the Carpetbagger*, 237–38.

112. Harris, 239.

113. *Weekly Clarion*, September 16, 1869. Universal suffrage passed as a resolution at a convention held on June 23, 1869. *Weekly Clarion*, July 1, 1869.

114. *Tri-Weekly Clarion*, October 5, 1869.

115. The 1870 state legislature included Black Republicans: W. Stringer, Charles Caldwell, Robert Gleed (senators), H. P. Jacobs, Ambrose Henderson, Matthew T. Newsome, E. Handy, Marion Campbell, Henry Mayson, Cicero Mitchell, J. A. Moore, George Charles, James J. Spelman, Eli Buchanan, Isham Stewart, Peter Barrow, John Morgan, and William H. Foote (representatives). *Tri-Weekly Clarion*, December 4, 1869.

CHAPTER 2. PICK YO' OWN DAMN COTTON:
BUILDING THE FOUNDATIONS OF ZION

1. William C. Harris, *The Day of the Carpetbagger*, 268.

2. Allen C. Gueizo, *Reconstruction: A Concise History* (New York: Oxford University Press, 2018), 13–14. See Edward Magdol's "Local Black Leaders in the South, 1867–75: An Essay toward the Reconstruction of Reconstruction History."

3. Stephen Cresswell, *Rednecks, Redeemers, and Race: Mississippi After Reconstruction, 1877–1917* (Jackson: University Press of Mississippi for the Mississippi Historical Society, 2006), 9.

4. W. E. B. Du Bois, *Black Reconstruction in America: Toward a History of the Part Which Black Folk Played in the Attempt to Reconstruct Democracy in America, 1860–1880* (New York: Harcourt, 1935), 204; Stokely Carmichael, *Stokely Speaks: From Black Power to Pan-Africanism* (Chicago, Lawrence Hill Books, 2007), 35–36.

5. Dylan C. Pennington, *The Claims of Kinfolk: African American Property and Community in the Nineteenth-Century South* (Chapel Hill: University of North Carolina Press, 2003), 6–7, 12, 185. Pennington's analysis does not explain how landownership, tactics, and community development changed over time.

6. Ibid., 131.

7. Claude F. Oubre, *Forty Acres and a Mule: The Freedmen's Bureau and Black Land Ownership* (Baton Rouge: Louisiana State University Press, 1978), 20.

8. Ibid., 26.

9. O. Nigel Bolland, *The Meaning of Freedom: Economics, Politics, and Culture after Slavery* (Pittsburg: University of Pittsburg Press, 1992), 128. Bolland refers to Caribbean emancipation; however, the same concept can be applied to the United States as Attala County land surplus correlated with economic misfortunes led to a buyers' market.

10. Alexander Crummell, *Civilization and Black Progress: Selected Writings of Alexander Crummell on the South* (Charlottesville: University of Virginia Press, 1995), 92–93.

11. Claude F. Oubre, *Forty Acres and a Mule: The Freedmen's Bureau and Black Land Ownership* (Baton Rouge: Louisiana State University Press, 1978), 94–95, 97.

12. William C. Harris, *Presidential Reconstruction in Mississippi* (Baton Rouge: Louisiana State University Press, 1967), 219.

13. Attala County Chancery Court Deed Book F, page 671–72.

14. Maude Kelley Jamison Waggoner, *The Jamisons*, 30.

15. Waggoner, 5.

16. Attala County Land Deeds, Book Q, page 476. The transaction occurred on June 2, 1877.

17. Charlie Rabb Ashford Sr., *Some of the Ancestors and Descendants of James and George Ashford Jr. of Fairfield County, South Carolina* (Starkville, 1956), 14, 17, 21, 72.

18. Eileen Nail, *Winston County Mississippi Slave Index*, 39. Sarah was Bartholomew's wife. The Confederate Army exempted James from service, provided he produce "food and cotton" for the army, given his large slave inventory. Charlie Rabb Ashford Sr., *Some of the Ancestors and Descendants of James and George Ashford Jr. of Fairfield County, South Carolina*, 22.

19. William L. Jenkins, *Mississippi United Methodist Churches: Two Hundred Years of Heritage and Hope* (Tennessee: Providence House, 1998), 27–28; Buffalo Community Folk Reunion booklet, 2001.

20. Attala County Chancery Court Land Deeds, Book L, page 467.

21. Attala County Chancery Court Land Deeds, Book R, page 630.

22. Attala County Chancery Court Land Deeds, Book U, page 503.

23. On December 21, 1898, John Wesley Bain paid three-hundred and fifty dollars at a public auction for twenty acres in the Blackjack neighborhood after his grandfather-in-law defaulted on a loan. John kept bidders from potentially disrupting their neighborhood and the broader community.

24. Douglas R. Egerton, *The Wars of Reconstruction: The Brief, Violent History of America's Most Progressive Era* (New York: Bloomsbury Press, 2014), 137, 149.

25. Horace Mann Bond, *Education of the Negro in the American Social Order* (New York: Octagon Books, 1970), 35.

26. *Daily Clarion*, May 2, 1867.

27. Christopher M. Span, *From Cotton Field to Schoolhouse: African American Education in Mississippi, 1862–187*. (Chapel Hill: University of North Carolina Press, 2009), 10.

28. Vernon Lane Wharton, *The Negro in Mississippi 1865–1890* (New York: Harper and Row Publishers, 1965), 244; Christopher M. Span, *From Cotton Field to Schoolhouse: African American Education in Mississippi, 1862–1875* (Chapel Hill: University of North Carolina Press, 2009), 11.

29. William C. Harris, *The Day of the Carpetbagger*, 149–51

30. Fairclough, Adams, *A Class of Their Own: Black Teachers in the Segregated South* (Cambridge: Belknap Press of Harvard University Press, 2007), 67.

31. Edward C. Coleman Jr., "The Period of Reconstruction in Attala County," in *Reconstruction in Northern Mississippi Counties*. Archives and Special Collections, J. D. Williams Library, University of Mississippi, 1910, 6

32. James D. Anderson, *The Education of Blacks in the South, 1860–1935* (Chapel Hill: University of North Carolina Press, 1988), 19.

33. Christopher M. Span, *From Cotton Field to School House: African American Education in Mississippi 1862–1975* (Chapel Hill: University of North Carolina Press, 2009), 9. Span assessed that African American interest in school development began as early as 1862. Although the earliest school of record was Sam Young, the earliest school establishment in Attala County dates to the early years of Reconstruction, as indicated by Edward C. Coleman's description in his work *Reconstruction in Attala County*. Coleman described a northern teacher who taught freedmen soon after slavery.

34. William E. Montgomery, *Under Their Own Vine and Fig Tree: The African-American Church in the South 1865–1900* (Baton Rouge: Louisiana State University Press, 1993), 148.

35. Patrick Henry Thompson, *The History of Negro Baptist in Mississippi* (Jackson: R. W. Bailey, 1898), 62.

36. William C. Harris, *The Day of the Carpetbagger*, 329.

37. 1870 United States Federal Census.

38. Sam Young's letter, March 23, 1871.

39. Christopher M. Span, *From Cotton Field to School House: African American Education in Mississippi 1862–1975* (Chapel Hill: University of North Carolina Press, 2009), 9.

40. *Star-Herald*, May 13, 1976.

41. See Vernon Lane Wharton, *The Negro in Mississippi 1865–1890*, 246. Attala schools noting mixed racial attendance included Line School House, Berea, Shiloh, Rocky Point, Sallis, Smyrna, and Shrock, located in the northeastern and northwestern regions.

42. Wharton, 246.

43. Early Attala Residents, "Jason Niles," http://attala-county-history-genealogy.org/jason_niles.html. *Weekly Clarion*, December 29, 1870.

44. Edward C. Coleman Jr., "The Period of Reconstruction in Attala County," in *Reconstruction in Northern Mississippi Counties*. Archives and Special Collections, J. D. Williams Library, University of Mississippi, 1910, 9.

45. William C. Harris, *The Day of the Carpetbagger*, 265–66, 433.

46. "*Weekly Clarion*, May 4, 1871.

47. George M. Fredrickson, *The Black Image in the White Mind: The Debate on Afro-American Character and Destiny, 1817–1914* (New York: Harper Torchbooks, 1971), 64.

48. *Lexington Advertiser*, June 3, 1870; *Weekly Mississippi Pilot*, June 18, 1870; *Memphis Daily Appeal*, June 22, 1870. Frank and Elijah were the sons of Elijah Wood Sr. of Holmes County. In 1887, Elijah Sr.'s son John William Wood was sentenced to life for murder.

49. C. Vann Woodward, *Origins of the New South 1877–1913* (Baton Rouge: Louisiana State University Press, 1951), 236–37.

50. *Weekly Clarion*, October 26, 1871.

51. *Weekly Clarion*, May 26, 1870.

52. Ibid.

53. William C. Harris, *The Day of the Carpetbagger*, 439.

54. *Weekly Clarion*, April 13, 1871, and May 18, 1871.

55. *Weekly Clarion*, October 26, 1871.

56. "Mississippi Freedmen's Bureau Field Office Records, 1865–1872."

57. Edward C. Coleman Jr., "The Period of Reconstruction in Attala County," in *Reconstruction in Northern Mississippi Counties*. Archives and Special Collections, J. D. Williams Library, University of Mississippi, 1910, 12–13.

58. Coleman, 13–14.

59. Allen W. Trelease, *White Terror: The Ku Klux Klan Conspiracy and Southern Reconstruction* (New York: Harper Torchbooks, 1971), 287–88.

60. Trelease, 290.

61. Edward C. Coleman Jr., "The Period of Reconstruction in Attala County," in *Reconstruction in Northern Mississippi Counties*. Archives and Special Collections, J. D. Williams Library, University of Mississippi, 1910, 15–16.

62. *Semi-Weekly Clarion*, December 26, 1871.

63. Edward C. Coleman Jr., "The Period of Reconstruction in Attala County," in *Reconstruction in Northern Mississippi Counties*. Archives and Special Collections, J. D. Williams Library, University of Mississippi, 1910, 15.

64. Vernon Lane Wharton, *The Negro in Mississippi 1865–1890* (New York: Harper and Row, 1965), 245.

65. *Testimony Taken by the Joint Selection Committee to Inquire into the Condition of Affairs in the Late Insurrectionary States, Mississippi Volume I* (Washington, Government Printing Office, 1872), 492–94

66. Eric Foner, *Reconstruction: America's Unfinished Revolution 1863–1877* (New York: HarperCollins, 1989), 278.

67. *Weekly Clarion*, August 10, 1871.

68. *Weekly Clarion*, October 26, 1871.

69. *Semi-Weekly Clarion*, November 14, 1871.

70. *Weekly Clarion*, October 2, 1871. Only a third of registered voters voted. J. C. Lucas won election to Niles' seat.

71. *American Citizen*, March 16, 1872; *Natchez Democrat*, April 4, 1872; *Weekly Clarion*, April 11, 1872.

72. *Weekly Clarion*, August 15, 1872.

73. Andrew L. Slap, *The Doom of Reconstruction: The Liberal Republicans in the Civil War Era* (New York: Fordham University Press, 2006), xii–xiii.

74. Slap, xiv.

75. Justin Behrend, *Reconstruction Democracy: Grassroots Democracy in the Deep South after the Civil War* (Athens: University of Georgia Press, 2015), 120–21.

76. Michael Perman, *The Road to Redemption: Southern Politics, 1869–1879* (Chapel Hill: University of North Carolina Press, 1985), 39–40.

77. Perman, 54–55.

78. *Semi-Weekly Clarion*, November 12, 1872.

79. *American Citizen,* September 21, 1872. The latter part of the newspaper article references the need for whites to vote for Greeley in the presidential election; therefore, the article possibly served as propaganda to rally the white Democratic vote.

80. *Weekly Clarion,* November 13, 1873. In 1874, Governor Adelbert Ames acknowledged that blacks influenced and controlled state legislation as James Hill became secretary of state and T. W. Cardozo served as the superintendent of education. Once they seized power, Black Republicans revisited past defeated legislation to get it signed into law, affecting other states, including Arkansas, Louisiana, and Florida. Michael Perman, *The Road to Redemption: Southern Politics, 1869–1879* (Chapel Hill: University of North Carolina Press, 1985), 138–39.

81. *Vicksburg Herald,* September 15, 1874.

82. Michael Perman, *Road to Redemption: Southern Politics, 1869–1879* (Chapel Hill: University of North Carolina Press, 1984), 258.

83. Justin Behrend, *Reconstruction Democracy: Grassroots Democracy in the Deep South after the Civil War* (Athens: University of Georgia Press, 2015), 210.

84. *Weekly Mississippi Pilot,* August 21, 1875.

85. *Canton Mail,* May 8, 1875.

86. *Daily Clarion,* October 13, 1875.

87. *Weekly Clarion,* November 3, 1875; *Macon Beacon,* November 20, 1875. According to the *Memphis Daily Appeal,* November 10, 1875, the following counties had Democratic majorities: Alcorn, Amite, Attala, Calhoun, Carroll, Chickasaw, Claiborne, Clarke, Colfax, Copiah, Desoto, Franklin, Greene, Grenada, Hancock, Harrison, Hinds, Holmes, Itawamba, Jackson, Jasper, Jones, Kemper, Lafayette, Lauderdale, Lee, Lincoln, Lowndes, Marion, Marshall, Monroe, Montgomery, Newton, Panola, Pike, Pontotoc, Prentiss, Rankin, Scott, Tallahatchie, Tishomingo, Warren, Washington, Winston, and Yazoo. Republican-majority counties were Adams, Issaquena, Madison, Noxubee, Oktibbeha, and Wilkinson.

88. Rayford W. Logan, *The Negro in American Life and Thought: The Nadir 1877–1901* (New York: Dial Press Inc., 1954), 7.

89. *Yazoo Herald,* June 13, 1879.

90. *Jackson Daily Times,* November 8, 1877.

91. Edward C. Coleman Jr., "The Period of Reconstruction in Attala County," in *Reconstruction in Northern Mississippi Counties.* Archives and Special Collections, J. D. Williams Library, University of Mississippi, 1910, 7.

92. James D. Anderson, *The Education of Blacks in the South, 1860–1935* (Chapel Hill: University of North Carolina Press, 1988), 25, 27.

93. Vernon Lane Wharton, *The Negro in Mississippi 1865–1890* (New York: Harper and Row, 1965), 244.

94. Christopher M. Span, *From Cotton Field to Schoolhouse: African American Education in Mississippi, 1862–1875* (Chapel Hill: University of North Carolina Press, 2009), 11.

95. Jay S. Stowell, *Methodist Adventures in Negro Education* (New York: Methodist Book Concern, 1922), xxi.

96. Report of the Commissioner of Education for the Year 1880 (Washington, DC, 1880), 179.

97. Christopher M. Span, *From Cotton Field to Schoolhouse: African American Education in Mississippi, 1862–1875* (Chapel Hill: University of North Carolina Press, 2009), 120.

98. Aimé Césaire, *Discourse On Colonialism* (New York: Monthly Review Press), 31.

CHAPTER 3. TAKING FLIGHT: MOVING TOWARDS A LIBERATED ZION

1. *Weekly Clarion*, April 21, 1880.

2. George Frederickson, *The Black Image in the White Mind: The Debate on Afro-American Character and Destiny, 1817–1914* (New York: Harper Torchbooks, 1971), 185.

3. *Columbus Index*, July 16, 1875; Michael Ayers, *The Promise of a New South: Life After Reconstruction* (New York: Oxford University Press, 1992), 136. Ayers, like Woodward, indicated that the color line was a southern white invention. An interpretation of their account would be to look at Jim Crow as a process that evolved into a sophisticated tool to control African American social, economic, and political activity void of African American stimuli. See George Frederickson's *The Black Image in the White Mind: The Debate on African American Character and Destiny, 1817–1914* and Joel Williamson's *The Crucible of Race: Black-White Relations in the American South Since Emancipation* for further explanation of the vision southern whites created about African American containment and control. For a discussion on homogeneity and how middle-class whites envisioned the New South, see Bradley Bond's *Political Culture in the Nineteenth Century South, 1830–1890*.

4. C. Vann Woodward, *Origins of the New South 1877–1913* (Baton Rouge: Louisiana State University Press, 1951), 236.

5. W. E. B. Du Bois, *Black Reconstruction in America: Toward a History of the Part Which Black Folk Played in the Attempt to Reconstruct Democracy in America, 1860–1880* (New York: Harcourt, 1935), 399.

6. Michael Ayers, *The Promise of a New South: Life After Reconstruction* (New York: Oxford University Press, 1992), 136. Woodward's analysis of the African American reaction to "Jim Crowism" in *The Strange Career of Jim Crow* indicated that as early as 1867, African Americans protested laws that segregated the races. The rejection of segregation was in response to the passage of the Reconstruction Act (p. 27).

7. Leon Litwack, *Been in the Storm So Long: The Aftermath of Slavery* (New York: Vintage Books, 1979), 252, 256.

8. Charles Johnson contended that infractions against racial etiquette were less likely to occur in southern rural areas because the region's society and culture were not conducive to change. Johnson countered his argument as he explained room existed within segregation for "personal intimacy" as long as both parties understood, accepted, and maintained required social distances. Charles S. Johnson, *Patterns of Negro Segregation* (New York: Harper, 1943), 118. The South is diverse, and racial relationships vary from area to area. Johnson referred to situations where a white person was in the power position and an African American person in an inferior position (traveling servant, mammy). Johnson did not examine African Americans as equal or elevated players.

9. United States Federal Census, 1900, Attala County, MS; United States Federal Slave Schedule, 1850, Attala County, MS; United States Federal Census 1850, Attala County.

10. The death records of James, Alexander, Franklin, and Elizabeth all indicate that Alfred was their father. The consistency of the records indicated that a long relationship between Alfred and Ceele existed. Although Alfred was their father, the children all had the Johnson last name as the Johnson family still owned Ceele during this period.

11. The census listed Alfred as Alfred Johnson, not Alfred Carr. Using Neil McMillen's 1876 historical reference point, in which interracial marriage became illegal, Alfred and Ceele's marriage did not conform to segregation law.

12. United States Federal Slave Schedules 1840, 1850, and 1860.

13. Attala County State Census Returns, 1818–1880, 138. Following her relationship with George Evans, Jeanette used his surname. The 1880 census listed Mary, Mattie, Eliza, and James as Evans.

14. Ann Breedlove compiled Guyton Family Research.

15. Attala County Chancery Court Docket 852, Attala County Chancery Court Docket, 852 1/2.

16. "Indeed, the greater portion of the colored women, in the days of slavery, had no greater aspiration than that of becoming the finely dressed mistress of some white man" (Paula Giddings. *When and Where I Enter: The Impact of Black Women on Race and Sex in America*, 61). William Wells Brown's statement underscores the African American women's ability to recognize that her benefit from the relationship was fleeting at most; however, the children had the most to gain. Whiteness cannot be seen as a benefit because whiteness did not extend to the mistress. The privileges that whiteness carried for certain men could crossover to the children of their relationship.

17. Vivian M. May, "Writing the Self into Being: Anna Julia Cooper's Textual Politics," *African American Review* 43, no. 1 (2009): 23. Gwyn Campbell and Elizabeth Elbourne, *Sex, Power, and Slavery* (Athens: Ohio University Press, 2014), 14, 57, 65. Deborah Gray White. *Ar'n't I a Woman?: Female Slaves in the Plantation South* (New York: W. W. Norton, 1999), 29–30. White speaks of freedom through manumission; however, this concept applied to the post-slavery era as the power white men held did not lessen. It therefore remained a source of upward advancement. Campbell, Elbourne, and White fostered a conversation suggesting that African American women caught onto the concept that their bodies held power.

18. Gwyn Campbell and Elizabeth Elbourne, *Sex, Power, and Slavery* (Athens: Ohio University Press, 2014), 63. African American women were not necessarily seeking a legal union with white men, as marriage provided little to no security. An August 17, 1885, article in the Washington Post titled "Mixed Marriages in the South: Less Intermixture of the White and Black Races Than Before the War" stated, "In Mississippi it is still a crime for the two races to intermarry, but the crime is seldom punished. This week, for the first time in many years, a white man has been sent to the penitentiary for marrying a negress." Paula Giddings wrote of African American women wanting to be the wives of their white lovers (*When and Where I Enter: The Impact of Black Women on Race and Sex in America*, 73). Her perspective demonstrates that African American women approached their relationships with white men differently and held different expectations. Campbell and Elbourne stated, "Sexuality is as much an intellectual exercise as a physical one, and the mind is as important as the body." Gwyn Campbell and Elizabeth Elbourne, *Sex, Power, and Slavery* (Athens: Ohio University Press, 2014), 70. Campbell and Elbourne are alluding to how African American women utilized their sexuality to gain mental power over white men, who sought physical, sexual domination. White men believed they held full power; however, African American women created a pathway for their children to navigate society using their white father's position. This analysis does not negate the fact that rape existed in the post-emancipation South. Hannah Rosen articulated that rape was underreported and occurred frequently following the Civil War (*Terror in the Heart of Freedom: Citizenship, Sexual Violence, and the Meaning of Race in the Post Emancipation South*, 202).

19. James Baldwin, *The Fire Next Time* (New York: Dial Press, 1963), 110.

20. Headstone, Sallis Cemetery, Sallis, MS.

21. The 1850 and 1860 Mississippi Federal Census indicated that Bettie was living with Judith Malone during these periods.

22. Sam Young's letter dated March 23, 1871.

23. Sam Young's letter dated March 23, 1871.

24. Thavolia Glymph, *Out of the House of Bondage: The Transformation of the Plantation Household* (Cambridge: Cambridge University Press, 2008), 4.

25. "United States Freedmen's Bureau, Records of the Assistant Commissioner, 1865–1872."

26. Stephanie Shaw, *What a Woman Ought to Be and Do: Black Professional Women Workers During the Jim Crow Era* (Chicago: University of Chicago Press, 1996), 14.

27. Eugene W. Hilgard, *Report on the Cotton Production of the State of Mississippi with a Discussion of the General Agricultural Features of the State*, 205. There is a 748-cotton bale discrepancy between Hilgard's report and the Attala County State Census return.

28. Series 100, State Census Returns, 1818–1880, http://www.mdah.ms.gov/arrec/digital_archives/series/100/detail/46141

29. Pete Daniel, *Breaking the Land: The Transformation of Cotton, Tobacco, and Rice Cultures since 1880* (Chicago: University of Illinois Press, 1985), 4; Harold Woodman. *King Cotton and His Retainers: Financing and Marketing the Cotton Crop of the South, 1800–1925* (Lexington: University of Kentucky Press, 1968), 313.

30. Woodman, 335.

31. Harold Woodman, *King Cotton and His Retainers: Financing and Marketing the Cotton Crop of the South, 1800–1925* (Lexington: University of Kentucky Press, 1968), 334.

32. Eugene W. Hilgard, *Report on the Cotton Production of the State of Mississippi with a Discussion of The General Agricultural Features of the State*, 205.

33. *Grenada Sentinel*, May 19, 1883.

34. *Memphis Daily Appeal*, April 30, 1882, and *Weekly Clarion*, June 21, 1882.

35. Amie Cesaire discussed in *Discourse on Colonialism* that Africa was the origin of agricultural development. Although slavery dictated how African Americans practiced agriculture, the post-emancipation period provided African Americans the opportunity to reclaim a significant part of their African heritage. Ransom and Sutch alluded to farming as an occupation that African Americans sought to escape rather than embrace. Their discussion plays into stereotyping farming as either typical or inferior. Roger L. Ransom and Richard Sutch, *One Kind of Freedom: The Economic Consequences of Emancipation* (Cambridge: Cambridge University Press, 1977), 31–35.

36. Elizabeth Rauh Bethel, *Promiseland: A Century of Life in a Negro Community* (Philadelphia: Temple University Press, 1981), 27.

37. Ibid., 28. Bethel highlighted African American farmers as possessing the freedom to choose how to diversify their labor. Some understood the necessity to use their land and labor to propel themselves beyond the status quo.

38. According to the 1880 county census returns, occupations and number practicing those occupations were as follows: railroad employees (7), jeweler (2), peddler (1), barber (1), publisher (1), teacher (45), surveyor (1), druggist (7), physician (42), confectioner (2), servant (10), milliner (1), porter (4), cook (47), butcher (3), washerwoman (25), nurse (10), printer (1), hotel/boarding housekeeper (4), machinist (5), carpenter (15), brick mason (2), painter (1) shoemaker (8), and mechanic (8). These numbers are misleading because the record listed most women's occupations as farmhands and housekeepers, which may not indicate working outside the home. Certain occupations listed in the federal census, such as blacksmith, do not appear in the county records.

39. Bradley G. Bond, *Political Culture in the Nineteenth-Century South: Mississippi 1830–1900* (Baton Rouge: Louisiana State University Press, 1995), 155.

40. Diary of Jason Niles, volume 17, 211.

41. Ibid.

42. See Arthur L. Tolson's "Historical and Modern Trends in Black Capitalism" in *The Black Scholar* 6 (7), 8–14. Loren Schweninger looked at occupational shifts toward draymen, porters, and servants as capital-earning ventures; however, he limits African Americans to domestic service only, without regard to the black entrepreneurial spirit. Loren Schweninger, *Black Property Owners in the South, 1790–1915* (Urbana and Chicago: University of Illinois Press, 1990), 149.

43. *Star-Herald*, December 10, 1896. Seaborn resettled in Mound Bayou, where he operated a jewelry shop.

44. Susie V. Powell, *Works Progress Administration for Mississippi: Source Material for Mississippi Attala County* vol. IV, 315; *The Clarion*, October 13, 1886.]

45. Ted Ownby, *American Dreams in Mississippi: Consumers, Poverty, and Culture, 1830–1998* (Chapel Hill: University of North Carolina Press, 1999), 74.

46. Ibid., 72.

47. *Mississippi Farmer*, December 9, 1898.

48. *Kosciusko Star*, July 13, 1894.

49. Kosciusko Historical Society, *Kosciusko-Attala History* (1984), 60.

50. *Kosciusko Star*, April 19, 1895.

51. Wesley United Methodist Church history.

52. Nell Irvin Painter, *Exodusters: Black Migration to Kansas after Reconstruction* (New York: W. W. Norton, 1976), 4.

53. *Weekly Clarion*, January 15, 1879; *Pascagoula Democrat-Star*, January 17, 1879.

54. *Weekly Clarion*, April 21, 1880. The paper did not specify where the individuals originated; therefore, whether they were all Attala residents is undeterminable. Few Attala residents left and remained in Kansas; however, those who migrated included Asa Simpson and his family.

55. *Star-Herald*, April 11, 1957.

56. Wesley United Methodist Church history.

57. Patrick Henry Thompson, *The History of Negro Baptist in Mississippi*, 666. Whether Sam and Amy are Harrison's parents remains unclear. Harrison's father was born in Virginia, and the 1860 census listed him as Samuel Young, born in 1821, living in Carroll County.

58. Thompson, *Negro Baptists*, 632.

59. Ibid., 566–67, 666.

60. Ibid., 427.

61. Patrick Henry Thompson, *The History of Negro Baptist in Mississippi*, 419.

62. Thompson, 522.

63. Patrick Henry Thompson, *The History of Negro Baptist in Mississippi*, 541.

64. Bettye Collier-Thomas, *Jesus, Jobs, and Justice: African American Women and Religion* (Philadelphia: Temple University Press, 2014), 77–78.

65. Patrick Henry Thompson, *The History of Negro Baptist in Mississippi*, 527.

66. Thompson, 527–28.

67. Bettye Collier-Thomas, 77.

68. James D. Anderson, *The Education of Blacks in the South, 1860–1935* (Chapel Hill: University of North Carolina Press, 1988), 25, 27.

69. Report of the Commissioner of Education for the Year 1880 (Washington, DC: 1880), 179.

70. *The Clarion*, August 19, 1885.

71. "Mississippi Enumeration of Educable Children, 1850–1892; 1908–1957." The state census returns indicated that Attala County developed a dual school system, one system serving the city of Kosciusko and the other the county. The Kosciusko school system was a separate school system within Attala County.

72. *The Clarion*, August 19, 1885.

73. Bradley Bond, *Political Culture in the Nineteenth-Century South Mississippi 1830–1890* (Baton Rouge: Louisiana State University Press, 1995), 218–21.

74. Horace Mann Bond, *Education of the Negro in the American Social Order* (New York: Octagon Books, 1970), 92.

75. Bradley Bond, *Political Culture in the Nineteenth-Century South Mississippi 1830–1890* (Baton Rouge: Louisiana State University Press, 1995), 222–25. Horace Mann Bond, *Education of the Negro in the American Social Order* (New York: Octagon Books, 1970), 94. Bradley Bond omitted Horace Bond's analysis from his analysis, thus overlooking the early foundation of separate but equal in primary and secondary education.

76. Bond, *Political Culture in the Nineteenth-Century South Mississippi 1830–1890*, 222.

77. Patrick Henry Thompson, *The History of Negro Baptist in Mississippi*, 563–64.

78. G. P. Hamilton, *Beacon Lights of the Race* (Memphis: P. H. Clarke, 1911), 426–27.

79. *Who's Who in Colored America: A Biographical Dictionary of Notable Persons of African Descent in America 1928–1929 (Second Edition)*, 60.

80. Powell, 314. *Nashville Globe*, April 5, 1907.

81. *Memphis Daily Appeal*, May 21, 1879.

82. Melissa Milewski, *Litigating across the Color Line: Civil Cases between Black and White Southerners* (New York: Oxford University Press, 2018), 4. Assuming that African Americans had involuntary participation in criminal court lacks historical inquiry and renders them as nonparticipants in shaping local and state politics through their judicial participation.

83. Charles Johnson explained that lower-class whites, believing upper-class blacks had contempt for them, sought respect from this group. Charles Spurgeon Johnson, *Patterns of Negro Segregation* (New York: Harper, 1943), 118.

84. Judge Jason Niles Diary, vol. 22, 104.

85. *New York Times*, January 17, 1887; Judge Jason Niles Diary, vol. 22, 104. Jordan Teague's wife's identity did not appear in the newspaper or Niles's diary. The 1880 federal census identified her as Dora Teague.

86. Judge Jason Niles Diary, vol. 22, 105, 107.

87. Judge Jason Niles Diary, vol. 32, 93–94,

88. *Magnolia Gazette*, November 5, 1880.

89. *New York Times*, June 24, 1887.

90. *Daily Commercial Herald*, May 24, 1889.

91. *The Mississippian*, July 11, 1888.

92. *Yazoo City Herald*, January 27, 1888.

93. *Grenada Sentinel*, November 16, 1889.

CHAPTER 4. UNITED WE STAND:
ORGANIZING IN THE DECADE OF WHITE SUPREMACY

1. African Mississippian citizenship conflicted with white Mississippian's post–Civil War political agenda. Bradley Bond explained, "After 1848, with their political culture purged of divisive issues, white Mississippians refocused their energies on fostering cultural

homogeneity, at the heart of which lay efforts to define black residents—free and enslaved—and undeserving whites as a submissive underclass" (Bond, 82). Citizenship carried two different meanings to two different groups, inherited vs. permitted.

2. Shawn Leigh Alexander, *An Army of Lions: The Civil Rights Struggle Before the NAACP* (Philadelphia: University of Pennsylvania Press, 2012), 3–5, 7. Alexander writes of the Afro-American League as one that would be the defender of black freedom. However, the league itself missed African Americans already challenging and shaping the society in which they lived. The idea of an organization accounting for an entire people is troubling because it sends the message that African Americans need centralization to guide them. Alexander puts too much emphasis on the league's importance to the conditions of the black community. It is difficult to gauge the outlook of an entire community of people based on a few observations since these individuals cannot ascertain what is occurring in others' everyday lives or changes over time.

3. Woodward, *Origins of the New South*, 218; Wharton. *The Negro in Mississippi 1865–1890*, 202–3; Walton, *Black Republicans*, 15; Beatty, *Revolution Gone Backward*, 47.

4. Ibid., 99, 122, 127.

5. Rayford W. Logan, *The Negro in American Life and Thought: The Nadir 1877–1901* (New York: Dial Press Inc., 1954), 56

6. Logan, 53. African Americans began leaving the party during the 1880s due to the Republican Party's shift to protecting big business and not civil rights. Woodward, *Origins of the New South*, 218.

7. *Clarion-Ledger*, November 14, 1889.

8. *Weekly Clarion*, November 25, 1880.

9. Alexander, 65.

10. See C. Vann Woodward's *Origin of the New South, 1877–1914*; Rayford Logan's *The Negro in American Life and Thought: The Nadir 1877–1901*; and Paul Lewison's *Race, Class, & Party: A History of Negro Suffrage and White Politics in the South*.

11. Dennis J. Mitchell, *A New History of Mississippi* (Jackson: University Press of Mississippi, 2014), 217.

12. Mississippi State Constitution of 1890. In 1875, voting qualifications required the individual to be twenty-one years of age, a resident of the state for six months and of the county for one month, and possessing mental capability (not being an idiot or untaxed Indian) and no felonies. Literacy and poll-tax additions spoke to assumptions regarding the African American electorate, including African Americans not possessing disposable income for poll taxes or not having acquired enough, if any, education to meet literacy requirements. Residency requirements and criminal history were equally important restrictions, although not as historically discussed. The convict-leasing era guaranteed that many African American men and women could not establish permanent residence, and the likelihood of possessing a criminal record increased. For this discussion, we will not examine the latter two.

13. Albert D. Kirwan, *Revolt of the Redneck: Mississippi Politics 1876–1925* (New York, Harper Torchbooks, 1951), 69.

14. *Daily Clarion-Ledger*, September 16, 1890.

15. Charles W. Chesnutt, "The Disenfranchisement of the Negro," in *The Negro Problem: Booker T. Washington, W. E. B. Du Bois, and Others*, 24–26.

16. Patrick H. Thompson, *The History of Negro Baptist in Mississippi* (Jackson: R.W. Bailey, 1898), 271.

17. Thompson, 264–65, 267, 275–76.

18. Patrick H. Thompson, *The History of Negro Baptist in Mississippi* (Jackson: R. W. Bailey, 1898), 567–68. The Simon family was a Jewish immigrant family from Germany who lived in Kosciusko since the 1850s.

19. Thompson, 532, 534–35.

20. Thompson, 158.

21. *Oklahoma Safeguard*, March 9, 1905.

22. History of the Mt. Hope District Women's Convention, 1, 5.

23. Bettye Collier-Thomas, *Jesus, Jobs, and Justice: African American Women and Religion* (Philadelphia: Temple University Press, 2014), 122.

24. Jay S. Stowell, *Methodist Adventures in Negro Education* (New York: Methodist Book Concern, 1922), 129.

25. Writings of Lavonia Avery Holly, the story told to her by Charles' son, Martin Luther McMichael.

26. Ibid. The story of Laurel Hills told by Gregory A. Jones.

27. Mississippi during this period had several incidents of mob violence and lynching. George Stevenson lynched for "attempted outrage" against a white woman. Will McGregory of Lafayette County lynched for "attempting to outrage a Mrs. Cooper. In January 1891, an African American whose last name was Burnside was lynched and shot multiple times for allegedly robbing William Fox of $50 worth of cotton." In July 1891, Sam Gillespie of DeSoto County lynched after attempting to help another African American accused of larceny. Gillespie was no stranger to altercations with whites as he was involved in a fight with a white man six months earlier. *Los Angeles Herald*, June 3, 1890; *DeSoto Times*, December 11, 1890; and *Macon Beacon*, January 17, 1891. The NAACP identified the individual's surname as Sharp (*Thirty Years of Lynching in the United States*, 75). However, Sharp was Burnside's white accomplice. *Globe-Republican*, January 7, 1891; *Fort Worth Gazette*, July 15, 1891.

28. *Arizona Republican*, November 28, 1891.

29. *Grenada Sentinel*, December 5, 1891. No records exist indicating whether D. L. Smythe Jr. faced any criminal sanctions for the incident. By 1900, he worked as a physician in Leake County, boarding in the home of an African American couple, Peter and Venus Williams.

30. *Hinds County Gazette*, August 28, 1891.

31. Neil R. McMillen, *Dark Journey: Black Mississippians in the Age of Jim Crow* (Urbana: University of Illinois Press, 1990), 44; Michael Perman. *Pursuit of Unity: A Political History of the American South* (Chapel Hill: University Press of North Carolina Press, 2009), 186; Paul Lewinson, *Race, Class, and Party: A History of Negro Suffrage and White Politics in the South* (New York: Universal Library, 1965), 107–8. Lewinson focused on states that adopted state constitutions in the mid-1890s and discussed their impact after 1900. He did not discuss Mississippi, which was the first to adopt such measures.

32. The numbers do not include the missing Sallis precinct book.

33. Christopher Hager, *Word By Word: Emancipation and the Act of Writing* (Cambridge: Harvard University Press, 2013), 31.

34. Ben E. Bailey, *Kermit W. Holly Sr.: The Unsung Hero* (Jackson: Mrs. Lavonia Holly, 1996), 25. Miller and Melissa lived in Leake County prior to moving to the Center Community in Attala.

35. This number exceeds six hundred; however, the Sallis precinct book was not available for analysis. Sallis has a sizeable Black population. These figures precede the 1892

reregistration. The 303 figure includes deceased individuals but does not include those not located in the 1900 census, but a death status could not be applied.

36. "History." www.jsums.edu/ourhistory

37. Susie V. Powell, *Works Progress Administration for Mississippi: Source Material for Mississippi Attala County* vol. IV, part 1, 308.

38. Isaac Crawford and Patrick Henry Thompson, *Multum in Parvo*, 2nd ed. (Jackson: Consumers Printing, 1912), 116.

39. Patrick Henry Thompson, *The History of Negro Baptist in Mississippi* (Jackson: R. W. Bailey, 1898), 316, 568.

40. Julius E. Thompson, *The Black Press in Mississippi, 1865–1985* (Gainesville: University Press of Florida, 1993), xi. Thompson provided a historical outline of the Mississippi Press; however, his analysis of the press during this time mainly established a foundation for a more in-depth analysis of the state's twentieth-century press.

41. *Daily Clarion-Ledger*, June 7, 1894; *Daily Commercial Herald*, June 8, 1894. Other African American newspapers included the *Vidette, Zion Harp, Negro World*, and *Advocate. Daily Commercial Herald*, November 14, 1896.

42. *St. Louis Globe-Democrat*, June 9, 1894.

43. *Kosciusko Star*, August 2, 1895.

44. *Weekly Clarion-Ledger*, November 28, 1895.

45. Albert D. Kirwan, *Revolt of the Rednecks: Mississippi Politics, 1876–1925* (New York: Harper & Row, 1951), 139.

46. *Daily Commercial Herald*, December 22, 1895.

47. *Daily Clarion-Ledger*, January 25, 1898; *Star-Herald*, May 13, 1976; *Kosciusko Star*, April 12, 1895; *Mississippi Farmer*, June 10, 1897.

48. *Kosciusko Star*, August 2, 1895.

49. *Kosciusko Star*, March 8, 1895

50. *Kosciusko Star*, November 8, 1895

51. *Weekly Clarion-Ledger*, November 7, 1895.

52. Bess Beatty, *A Revolution Gone Backward: The Black Response to National Politics, 1876–1896* (New York: Praeger, 1987), 161. *Kosciusko Star-Herald*, November 6, 1896. Mississippi overwhelmingly supported Democratic candidate William Jennings Bryan, who garnered sixty-three thousand votes. Republican candidate William McKinley garnered 4,601. These numbers indicate how disenfranchisement affected the African American vote, given that the majority of African Americans voted Republican. Voting records from Attala County's poll books reported 467 registered African Americans. One hundred and fifty-five African Americans voted in the 1896 election, a 33 percent voter turnout. There were 145 Republican voters compared to 961 Democratic and 392 Populist voters. There is no clear evidence that indicates party affiliation; however, given that the African American majority supported the national Republican ticket, the 145 Republican voters in Attala County included a significant African American presence. The Republican vote did not affect the Electoral College; however, their vote allowed McKinley to win the popular vote. The African American vote continued to play a role in national politics. A federal Republican presence ensured that the African American political agenda remained relevant. Had African Americans surrendered their vote entirely, they would have risked Democratic rule at all government levels, which would have further threatened their constitutional rights.

53. Bess Beatty, *A Revolution Gone Backward: The Black Response to National Politics, 1876–1896* (New York: Praeger, 1987), 162.

54. *Democrat-Star*, December 11, 1896.

55. *Kosciusko Farmer*, November 5, 1896. The critical acclaim mirrored universal white praise for Washington's speech. James E. Everette was a lawyer, former senator, and postmaster in Yazoo County, Mississippi.

56. *Daily Clarion-Ledger*, October 9, 1896.

57. Washington's speech both challenged disenfranchisement policies and appealed to the fragile white mentality. Mainstream white society ordained Washington as "leader of the black race." The proclamation allowed African Americans to have a political voice on the national stage. Washington's speech had a widespread impact. Other political figures, both known and obscure, used Washington as a template to organize and rally African American political support. Failure of the African American League and National Negro Council was not representative of African American organizational efforts. Washington's Atlanta address presented a new alternative for organizing that was politically subversive. Upon closer reading, Washington's address alluded to ways to defeat disenfranchisement. The constitution granted unabridged voting rights; therefore, African Americans did not have to fight for a constitutional right. However, federal law did not prevent states from creating voting requirements (except for race or previous condition of servitude). Washington focused on enfranchisement. He urged African Americans to acquire the needed enfranchisement components. Education provided literacy, which allowed passage of the literacy test. Land fulfilled property-value requirements—wealth (presumably the byproduct of education and land obtainment) allowed for poll-tax payment. Washington made a concerted effort to diminish white fear regarding social equality and miscegenation, calling for a segregated society to protect both races' interests.

58. Kwame Ture and Charles V. Hamilton, *Black Power: The Politics of Liberation in America* (New York: Vintage, 1992), 5.

59. *Mississippi Farmer*, November 5, 1896; *Mississippi Farmer*, November 19, 1896.

60. *Daily Clarion-Ledger*, December 17, 1896. On August 25, 1898, Chairman R. A. Simmons and Secretary L. S. Nelson called the party to meet in Kosciusko to discuss party business. *Mississippi Farmer*, August 19, 1898.

61. *Mississippi Farmer*, September 16, 1897.

62. *Daily Clarion-Ledger*, April 13, 1896.

63. Horace Mann Bond, *Education of the Negro in the American Social Order* (New York: Octagon Books, 1970), 98.

64. *Kosciusko Star*, May 3, 1895.

65. *Mississippi Farmer*, July 7, 1899.

66. Charles C. Bolton, *The Hardest Deal of All: The Battle Over School Integration in Mississippi, 1870–1980* (Jackson: University Press of Mississippi, 2005), 27.

67. G. P. Hamilton, *Beacon Lights of the Race* (Memphis: P. H. Clarke, 1901), 423, 425.

68. Patrick Henry Thompson and Isaac Crawford, *Multum in Parvo*, 2nd ed. (Natchez: Consumers Printing Company, 1912), 249–50. Susie V. Powell, *Works Progress Administration for Mississippi: Source Material for Mississippi Attala County*, vol. IV, 311–12.

69. *Star Ledger*, June 16, 1899.

70. *Mississippi Farmer*, May 13, 1897; *Star Ledger*, June 10, 1898. Albert Poston (1895–1897) and Thomas B. Wheeler (1898–1900) served as principals, and Roxie Carter served as the assistant.

71. *Mississippi Farmer*, September 9, 1898. Colored teachers associations came into existence in the prior decade. The Clay County Teachers' Association was formed on August

8, 1885 (*Vicksburg Herald*, August 20, 1885). Matilda Winters (Oprah Winfrey's great-great-aunt) also attended this institute.

72. Patrick Henry Thompson, *The History of Negro Baptist in Mississippi* (Jackson: R. W. Bailey, 1898), 555–56.

73. *Mississippi Farmer*, May 20, 1897.

74. Thompson, *History of Negro Baptist*, 322.

75. Michael Ayers, *The Promise of a New South: Life After Reconstruction* (New York: Oxford University Press, 1992), 132.

76. *Kosciusko Star*, September 13, 1895. Census records provide Rousselot's first name, which newspapers give only as A. Rousselot.

77. *Star Ledger*, February 18, 1898; "Louisiana, New Orleans Passenger Lists, 1820–1945."

78. *Kosciusko Star*, October 11, 1895.

79. *Star Ledger*, December 9, 1898.

80. Doty's son, Claude, became a doctor. Dr. Jackson was a fixture in the Black community as a trusted individual and medical provider.

81. *Canton Times*, October 7, 1898.

82. Ibid.

Chapter 5. There Shall Be Blood: The Price of Liberation

1. W. E. B. Du Bois, *The Souls of Black Folk: Essay and Sketches* (Amherst: University of Massachusetts Press, 2018), 13.

2. *New York Times*, May 6, 1900, 2.

3. Bradley G. Bond wrote

Behind statements of revulsions at African-American liberty lay a long-standing fear: if blacks, purportedly incapable of assuming a place in the social order, gained equal access to markets and to civil and political liberty, the social order itself was doomed. . . . But white Mississippians feared too a revolution against the social order sponsored by those engaged in drudgery, including yeoman whites suddenly indistinguishable from ex-slaves by their poverty. African-American political independence, an illogical and dangerous fallacy under the assumptions of white southerners, not only promised to destroy the social ethic but threatened the laws of nature. In the postbellum period whites' concepts of liberty and virtue still depended upon the presence of an underclass without full access to the market or the electoral process.

Political Culture in the Nineteenth-Century South: Mississippi 1830–1900 (Baton Rouge: Louisiana State University Press, 1995), 154.

4. *Kosciusko Herald*, May 7, 1900.

5. *New York Times*, May 9, 1900.

6. *Kosciusko Herald*, May 7, 1900.

7. *Kosciusko Herald*, May 11, 1900. The same issue published a piece from the *Winona Democrat* that stated the following regarding Black census takers.

It is reliably understood that negros have been appointed by President McKinly [sic] to take the census in Montgomery County, the recomendations [sic] for white census supervisors having been completely ignored. This is a direct insult upon the intelligence and manhood of our citizenship to which our people cannot afford to submit, and we doubt not that when the negro thus appointed proceeds to discharge this hazardous undertaking over the white citizens and in direct opposition to their wishes, it will prove a more difficult job than they anticipated and not without its unpleasant features to the aforesaid coon. Our people are patient and long-suffering in many things, but some times patience ceases to be a virtue, and there is a limit to all things. The negro has no better friend than the white citizens so long as he remains in his place, but when he oversteps the bounds he must suffer the consequences. This is a white man's country, has ever been and will always be so long as intelligence predominates, and we will never tolerate even the merest suggestion of negro rule, and woe betide the coon so incautious as to try to pose a socal [sic] equal of the Anglo Saxon race. No one better knows this than the negro; he knows it from observation; some know it from personal experience. He also knows that the white people of the South bitterly condemn this damnable action of McKinley in this suggestion of negro domination, then if they will persist, with their eyes open to the facts, in insisting upon discharging the duties of the office to which they have been appointed solely for the purpose of further insulting the intelligence and manhood of the South, they display a spirit of bullyism of which no worthy, honest, humble negro is ever found guilty, and it would, therefore, be no matter of surprise nor regret should the indignant white citizens rise and assert their superiority by instituting a means of forever ridding themselves of their obnoxious presence. The negro must and shall be made to remain in his place.

8. Bradley Bond, *Political Culture in the Nineteenth-Century South Mississippi 1830–1890* (Baton Rouge: Louisiana State University Press, 1995), 291.

9. "*Daily Morning Journal and Courier*. May 14, 1900,

10. *Kosciusko Herald*, May 18, 1900.

11. Lerone Bennett Jr., *The Shaping of Black America: The Struggles and Triumphs of African Americans, 1619 to the 1990s* (New York: Penguin, 1993), 209.

12. Ibid., 210. The political arena was shared by both Blacks and whites, whereas education and land ownership were the most segregated spheres. Although whites used violence in these areas, education and land ownership were less stable. Politics was one area in which whites had a clear advantage and could use their power to control African American activity.

13. *St. Louis Republic*, May 23, 1900.

14. *Pascagoula Democrat-Star*, May 25, 1900.

15. *Daily Morning Journal and Courier*, May 14, 1900; and *Rock Island Argus*, June 15, 1900.

16. *The Proceedings of the State of Mississippi: Journal of The Constitutional Convention*, 191.

17. Albert D. Kirwan, *Revolt of the Rednecks: Mississippi Politics, 1876–1925* (New York: Harper & Row, 1951), 138–40. *Star-Herald* and *Star Ledger*, November 9, 1900. Available polls books indicated that sixty-six African Americans voted.

18. *Star Ledger*, July 6, 1900; *Kosciusko Herald*, October 19, 1900; *Star Ledger*, November 9, 1900. Available polls books indicated that sixty-six African Americans voted.

19. *Star Ledger*, February 23, 1900.

20. *Kosciusko Herald*, March 23, 1900.

21. Neil R. McMille, *Dark Journey: Black Mississippians in the Age of Jim Crow* (Urbana: University of Illinois Press, 1990), 55.

22. *Oklahoma Safeguard*, April 13, 1905.

23. *Kosciusko Herald*, October 20, 1905.

24. Kosciusko Historical Society, *Kosciusko-Attala History*, 84.

25. *The Appeal*, July 26, 1902; *Kosciusko Herald*, September 16, 1904.

26. *Kosciusko Farmer*, May 27, 1898.

27. Dennis J. Mitchell, *A New History of Mississippi* (Jackson: University Press of Mississippi, 2014), 213.

28. Jim Gaston's parentage is unknown. Monroe Hallum was the son of Queen Hallum. Jim and Monroe were relatives through the Gaston family. Jim and Monroe lived in the Liberty Chapel Community near the Ethel and McCool townships.

29. The margins of the Liberty Chapel poll book specified Monroe Hallum's death. It was not uncommon to note the death of a registered voter; however, to specify the death's cause was unique to Monroe Hallum.

30. *Kosciusko Herald*, July 25, 1902.

31. *New York Times*, September 14, 1902. The *Kosciusko Herald* reported, likely reflecting upon the case, that two African American men, Ernest and Green Adams, provided the testimony that led to arrests and indictments. *Kosciusko Herald*, September 16, 1904.

32. *Grenada Sentinel*, January 24, 1903.

33. *Woodville Republican*, January 31, 1903. The statement made in the Woodville Republican needs further clarification. The paper seems to distinguish lynching as a special form of murder. The court tried Cicero Bain in 1887 for murdering Jordan Teague. Newspapers did not label the act a lynching. Samuel Winters was indicted and convicted for murdering Sam Winters. This incident did not receive the lynching label. Lynching appeared to be one's death at the hands of a mob, not an individual or small group.

34. *Kosciusko Herald*, September 16, 1904.

35. See Gwin Terrell Turner, "The Administration of Gov. Andrew Houston Longino," 1954.

36. Circuit Court of Attala County, Minute Book J, 522

37. Ibid., 540. The judge's illness continued to postpone the start of the trial as of March 16, 1903.

38. Ibid., 546–47. No further records, including court transcripts, are available to provide an in-depth look into what happened on the day of the lynching. Ben Wilks was the only African American present during these proceedings in the role of the janitor.

39. *Kosciusko Herald*, September 16, 1904.

40. David M. Oshinsky, *"Worse Than Slavery": Parchman Farm and the Ordeal of Jim Crow Justice* (New York: Free Press, 1997), 87.

41. Ibid., 90.

42. Ibid., 91.

43. *Times-Promoter*, March 4, 1904,

44. Stephen Cresswell, *Rednecks, Redeemers, and Race: Mississippi After Reconstruction, 1877-1917* (Jackson: University Press of Mississippi for the Mississippi Historical Society, 2006), 197, 199.

45. Thompson, *The Black Press in Mississippi*, 13–14.

46. *Brandon News*, March 10, 1904.

47. *Columbus Weekly Dispatch*, September 1, 1904.

48. *Water Valley Progress*, September 24, 1904.

49. *Columbus Dispatch*, November 13, 1898.

50. *Star-Herald*, December 1, 1905. Lucius Love's headstone provided the death date that newspapers did not indicate.

51. *New-York Tribune*, December 2, 1905.

52. *Lexington Advertiser*, December 14, 1905.

53. *Star Ledger*, December 29, 1905.

54. *Kosciusko Herald*, August 26, 1904.

55. Leon Litwack, *Trouble in Mind: Black Southerners in the Age of Jim Crow* (New York: Random House, 1998), 327.

56. Ibid., 328.

57. Akinyele Omowale Umoja, *We Will Shoot Back: Armed Resistance in the Mississippi Freedom Movement* (New York: NYU Press, 2013), 21.

58. Michael C. Dawson, *Blacks in and out of the Left* (Cambridge: Harvard University Press, 2013), 31; Walter Rodney, *The Groundings with my Brothers* (Bogle L'Ouverture Publications, 1969), 22.

59. Simon Wendt, *The Spirit and the Shotgun: Armed Resistance and the Struggle for Civil Rights* (Gainesville: University Press of Florida, 2007), 12.

60. *Oklahoma Safeguard*, March 16, 1905.

61. "To Oswald Garrison Villard," August 1903, 273. Louis R. Harlan and Raymond W. Smock, eds, *Booker T. Washington Papers Volume 7: 1903–4* (University of Illinois Press, 1977).

62. Albert D. Kirwan, *Revolt of the Rednecks: Mississippi Politics, 1876–1925* (New York: Harper & Row, 1951), 145.

63. Ibid., 162.

64. Ibid., 165.

65. *Oklahoma Safeguard*, February 2, 1905.

66. *Oklahoma Safeguard*, April 19, 1906.

67. History of Central Mississippi College.

68. *Oklahoma Safeguard*, May 25, 1905.

69. *Oklahoma Safeguard*, May 18, 1905; the August 9, 1906, issue stated the final cost was $6,000.

70. *Oklahoma Safeguard*, December 7, 1905.

71. *Oklahoma Safeguard*, July 27, 1905.

72. Dr. Lee E. Williams Sr., *Mt. Helm Baptist Church 1935–1988: The Parade of Pastors 1864–1988*, 19.

73. *Port Gibson Reveille*, July 6, 1905.

74. Williams Sr., *Mt. Helm Baptist Church 1935–1988*, 20.

75. Patrick H. Thompson and Isaac W. Crawford, *Multum in Parvo*, 2nd ed. (Jackson: Consumers Printing, 1912), 300.

76. The Booker T. Washington papers do not indicate any correspondence between Washington and Thompson.

77. See Frank Andre Guridy, *Forging Diaspora: Afro-Cubans and African Americans in a World of Empire and Jim Crow* for a discussion of how Afro-Cubans used Tuskegee to advance Afro-Cuban upward mobility.

78. Crawford and Thompson, *Multum in Parvo*, 300.

79. Ibid.

80. *Oklahoma Safeguard*, April 19, 1906.

81. *Oklahoma Safeguard*, August 3, 1905.

82. *Oklahoma Safeguard*, February 2, 1905.

83. *Oklahoma Safeguard*, May 3, 1906. The college created jobs within the Black community. Central Mississippi College imitated its counterpart's hiring practices. Bogue Chitto Industrial College and Ministerial Industrial College placed teaching advertisements. Bogue Chitto specifically asked for mechanical, musical, and photography teachers. Ministerial, run by Attala County native John D. Zuber, sought a mechanical and musical teacher in addition to kindergarten and preparatory teachers.

84. Patrick Henry Thompson, *The History of Negro Baptist in Mississippi* (Jackson: R. W. Bailey, 1898), 652.

85. Williams Sr., *Mt. Helm Baptist Church 1935–1988*, 20

86. *Oklahoma Safeguard*, May 17, 1906

87. *Oklahoma Safeguard*, September 6, 1906.

88. *Oklahoma Safeguard*, September 13, 1906.

89. *Pittsburg Courier*, July 18, 1964.

90. *Boston Globe*, May 27, 1979; *Portsmouth Herald*, February 10, 1923; *Boston Globe*, August 27, 1928.

91. Ancestry.com. *Alabama, U.S., Marriages, Deaths, Wills, Court, and Other Records, 1784–1920*

92. Dr. Thomas Luther Zuber. *Journal of the National Medical Association* 48 no. 5 (1956), 373.

93. *Alton Evening Telegraph*, June 10, 1921; *Urbana Daily Courier*, March 29, 1924.

94. Louis Ray, "Revisiting Charles H. Thompson's Proposals for Educating Gifted African American Students, 1933–1961," *Journal of Negro Education* 81, no. 3 (2012): 191.

95. Ibid., 190–92.

96. *Aberdeen Weekly*, April 10, 1908.

97. William Harris, *The Day of the Carpetbagger*, 56.

98. *Aberdeen Weekly*, April 10, 1908.

99. *Aberdeen Weekly*, October 8, 1909. Judge Henry Clay Niles served as the presiding judge during Hazley and Phillips' tenure on the grand jury.

100. *Kosciusko Herald*, September 25, 1908.

101. *Kosciusko Herald*, October 2, 1908.

102. *Kosciusko Herald*, October 15, 1909.

103. Charles Johnson, *Patterns of Negro Segregation*, 269.

104. W. E. B. Du Bois, *The Souls of Black Folk: Essay and Sketches* (Amherst: University of Massachusetts Press, 2018), 87

105. W. E. B. Du Bois, "The Atlanta Conferences," *Voice of the Negro* 1, no. 3 (March 1904): 87.

Chapter 6. Unfinished Business: Liberation and Jim Crow

1. "South Objects to Negro Enumerators" in the *Hartford Courant*, July 5, 1909.

2. Leon Litwack, *Trouble in Mind: Black Southerners in the Age of Jim Crow* (New York: Random House, 1998), 365–66.

3. *Jackson Daily News*, March 28, 1912; *Natchez Democrat*, June 14, 1912.

4. 1910 Attala County census data.

5. This figure comes from the 1910 census record. The number of landowners and those within their households constitute this figure. This figure does not include kinship ties, which increase the number significantly.

6. Attala County Chancery Court Docket, 2358.

7. In Stokely Carmichael's speech "Power and Racism," he emphasized the importance of landownership. He discussed how African Americans who own land hold power over themself and the ability to self-govern. Stokley Carmichael, *Stokley Speaks: From Black Power to Pan-Africanism* (Chicago: Lawrence Hill Books, 2007), 19.

8. Leo McGee and Robert Boone, "Black Rural Land Decline in the South," *Black Scholar* 8, no. 7 (May 1977), 11. John C. Willis stated in his book *Forgotten Times: The Yazoo-Mississippi Delta after the Civil War* relating to the Mississippi Delta, "Former slaves were able to work their way up the 'agricultural ladder' toward property ownership. By 1900 two-thirds of the region's farm owners were black, not white. No other part of the South saw comparable black dominance of landowning" (2). Willis's analysis indicated that it took whites decades to transform the Mississippi Delta into the region that historians choose to emphasize. The twentieth-century Mississippi Delta does play into Barrington Moore Jr.'s discussion of how black labor was the plantation society's foundation.

9. Stephen Cresswell, *Rednecks, Redeemers, and Race: Mississippi After Reconstruction, 1877–1917* (Jackson: University Press of Mississippi for the Mississippi Historical Society, 2006), 220.

10. *Neshoba Democrat*, March 24, 1910.

11. "Educator Dies at Mississippi Home," *Chicago Defender* (National Edition), October 19, 1940.

12. Numbers averaged based on dollar values provided by the Department of the Interior Bureau of Education. *Negro Education: A Study of the Private and Higher Schools for Colored People in the United States*, vol. II, 334.

13. Leon Litwack, *Trouble in Mind: Black Southerners in the Age of Jim Crow* (New York: Random House, 1998), 107.

14. *Oklahoma Safeguard*, April 26, 1906.

15. Adam Fairclough, *A Class of Their Own: Black Teachers in the Segregated South* (Cambridge: Belknap Press of Harvard University Press, 2007), 173.

16. Fairclough, *A Class of Their Own*, 142, 174.

17. *Star-Herald*, December 31, 1953.

18. *Oklahoma Safeguard*, February 15, 1906; May 17, 1906.

19. *Oklahoma Safeguard*, March 9, 1905. Volina published a piece titled, "Dedicated to the Memory of E. A. Johnson, Author of Negro History, Raleigh, N.C.," in the *Oklahoma Safeguard*, April 13, 1905.

20. History of Sam Young Public School. Susie V. Powell, *Works Progress Administration for Mississippi: Source Material for Mississippi Attala County*, vol. IV, 310.

21. Adam Fairclough, *A Class of Their Own: Black Teachers in the Segregated South* (Cambridge: Belknap Press of Harvard University Press, 2007), 172.

22. Ibid., 242–43.

23. In *Black Bourgeoisie: The Rise of a New Middle Class in the United States*, Franklin stated that "Negro higher education has become devoted chiefly to the task of educating the black bourgeois" (76). Frazier missed the true mark of African American education. Black teachers returned to rural or semi-rural areas and continued to spread their college

education to the masses. Their role as the bourgeois's foundation stemmed from their status and importance rather than their economic output.

24. Patrick H. Thompson and Isaac W. Crawford, *Multum in Parvo*, 2nd ed. (Jackson: Consumers Printing, 1912), 8–9.

25. Attala County Chancery Court Docket, 2940.

26. Tiyi M. Morris, *Womanpower Unlimited and the Black Freedom Struggle in Mississippi* (Athens: University of Georgia Press, 2015), 3–5. Women like Bettie Johnson were not rare as washerwomen likely possessed a freedom mentality given their importance to their community and the white community. Johnson was a prototype for what became Garveyites in the United Negro Improvement Association, the membership of which was made up of washerwomen; Adam Ewing, "Garvey or Garveyism?" *Transition*, no. 105 (2011): 141.

27. *Jackson Daily News*, April 19, 1915.

28. Gerald David Jaynes, *Branches Without Roots: Genesis of the Black Working Class in the American South, 1862–1882* (New York: Oxford University Press, 1986), 63.

29. Tera W. Hunter, *To 'Joy My Freedom: Southern Black Women's Lives and Labor After the Civil War* (Cambridge: Harvard University Press, 1997), 26.

30. Thavolia Glymph. *Out of the House of Bondage: The Transformation of the Plantation Household* (Cambridge: Cambridge University Press, 2008), 4.

31. On June 18, 1866, Black women in Jackson, Mississippi, organized their wage labor and formed the "first known collective action of free Black working women in American history" and "the first labor organization of Black workers in Mississippi." Paula Giddings, *When and Where I Enter: The Impact of Black Women on Race and Sex in America* (New York: Quill William Morrow, 1984), 63. Carter G. Woodson stated, "These hard-working, successful washerwomen paid for the maintenance of their families' homes." Pero Gaglo Dagbovie, "Black Women, Carter G. Woodson, and the Association for the Study of Negro Life and History, 1915–1950," *Journal of African American History* 88, no. 1 (2003): 24.

32. Thavolia Glymph, *Out of the House of Bondage: The Transformation of the Plantation Household* (Cambridge: Cambridge University Press, 2008), 150–51, 155.

33. Diary of Jason Niles, volume 10, 135.

34. *Oklahoma Safeguard*, April 13, 1905.

35. Pero Gaglo Dagbovie, "Black Women, CarterG. Woodson, and the Association for the Study of Negro Life and History, 1915–1950," 24. See Bettye Collier-Thomas, *Jesus, Jobs, and Justice: African American Women and Religion*, 86.

36. *Kosciusko Courier*, March 21, 1913; Mississippi State Board of Health, Certificate of Death, 3957. Lee's death record recorded his death as March 24, 1913; however, this story appeared in the March 21 issue of the *Kosciusko Courier*.

37. *Kosciusko Courier*, March 21, 1913.

38. *Kosciusko Courier*, May 23, 1913.

39. *Star Ledger*, November 7, 1913.

40. *Winston County Journal*, October 10, 1913.

41. *Kosciusko Herald*, March 26, 1915.

42. Dr. Lee E. Williams Sr., *Mt. Helm Baptist Church 1935–1988: The Parade of Pastors 1864–1988*, 21.

43. *Kosciusko Herald*, November 24, 1916.

44. *Kosciusko Herald*, June 16, 1916. The issue republished the October 1915 pardon request.

45. *Jackson Daily News*, July 18, 1916.

46. David M. Oshinsky, *"Worse Than Slavery": Parchman Farm and the Ordeal of Jim Crow Justice* (New York: Free Press, 1997), 182.

47. *Newton Record*, March 4, 1920.

48. *Kosciusko Herald*, April 20, 1917.

49. *Kosciusko Herald*, April 27, 1917.

50. *Kosciusko Herald*, October 12, 1917.

51. *Star Ledger*, February 15, 1918.

52. *Kosciusko Herald*, March 1, 1918. On October 30, 1918, Lee B. Turner, Columbus Moody, William P. Ashford, Silas Lynch, S. L. Brown, George Hall, Pink Bullock, Dovie Turner, Mary Phillips, Cora Raiford, and Daisy Burt formed a committee for the United War Work Drive. *Star Ledger*, November 1, 1918.

EPILOGUE

1. Katherine Carr Esters, *Jay Bird Creek and My Recollections: A Memoir* (Kosciusko, 2005), 40.

2. Ibid., 25.

3. Ibid., 27.

4. Jeanes Agents resulted from Booker T. Washington's association with northern philanthropist Anna T. Jeanes, who established a $1 million fund to better Black education. Jeanes supervising teachers oversaw the implementation of the Hampton-Tuskegee education model in the rural county schools. In some cases, Jeanes supervising teachers served as superintendents. They worked with white county superintendents to report African American county schools' conditions. Louis R. Harlan, Raymond W. Smock, and Geraldine McTigue, eds. "From Anna T. Jeanes" in *Booker T. Washington Papers Volume 8: 1904–6* (Chicago: University of Illinois Press, 1979), 202–3.

5. *Star-Herald*, July 25, 1957.

6. The earliest record of Volina's involvement with the Chicago Defender began in the 1920s. Whether Volina wrote before 1920 is unknown.

7. *Weekly Review*, November 4, 1944.

8. Presley's World War II draft card provided his occupation.

9. *Star-Herald*, February 1, 1951, and August 9, 1951.

10. *Star-Herald*, May 24, 1956.

11. Stokely Carmichael, "Berkley Speech" in *Stokely Speaks: From Black Power to Pan-Africanism* (Chicago: Lawrence Hill, 2007), 46.

12. Carmichael stated in "Toward Black Liberation" that "Negroes are defined by two forces: their blackness and their powerlessness. There have been, traditionally, two communities in America: the white community, which controlled and defined the forms that all institutions within the society would take, and the Negro community, which has been excluded from participation in the power decisions that shaped the society and has traditionally been dependent upon and subservient to the white community" (*Stokely Speaks*, 35–36). Stokely surmised that liberation escaped Blacks if they depended on institutions controlled by whites. African Americans in the nineteenth and early twentieth centuries controlled institutions, including churches, schools, businesses, and public spaces. The control afforded them the room to maneuver and create avenues for upward progression. In the same speech, "Toward Black Liberation," Stokely stated, "The fact is

that what must be abolished is not the black community but the dependent colonial status that has been inflicted upon it. The racial and cultural personality of the black community must be preserved and the community must win its freedom while preserving its cultural integrity. This is the essential difference between integration as it is currently practiced and the concept of Black Power" (39).

13. Walton Jr., Hanes, "Public Policy Reponses to the Million Man March," *Black Scholar* 25, no. 4 (1995): 17–18.

14. Kwame Ture and Charles V. Hamilton, *Black Power: The Politics of Liberation in America* (New York: Vintage, 1992), 34–35.

15. *Ready for Revolution: The Life and Struggles of Stokely Carmichael {Kwame Ture}* (New York: Scribner, 2003), 5.

BIBLIOGRAPHY

Books and Articles

Alexander, Shawn Leigh. *An Army of Lions: The Civil Rights Struggle before the NAACP.* Philadelphia: University of Pennsylvania Press, 2012.

Anderson, James D. *The Education of Blacks in the South, 1860–1935.* Chapel Hill: University of North Carolina Press, 1988.

Aptheker, Herbert. *American Negro Slave Revolts: Nat Turner, Denmark Vesey, Gabriel, and Others.* 2nd ed. New York: International Publishers, 1983.

Ashford, Charlie Rabb, Sr. *Some of the Ancestors and Descendants of James and George Ashford Jr. of Fairfield County, South Carolina.* Starkville, 1956.

Ayers, Michael. *The Promise of a New South: Life after Reconstruction.* New York: Oxford University Press, 1992.

Baldwin, James. *The Fire Next Time.* New York: Dial Press, 1963.

Beatty, Bess. *A Revolution Gone Backward: The Black Response to National Politics, 1876–1896.* New York: Praeger, 1987.

Behrend, Justin. "Facts and Memories: John R. Lynch and the Revising of Reconstruction History in the Era of Jim Crow." *Journal of African American History* 97, no. 4 (2012): 427–48.

Behrend, Justin. *Reconstruction Democracy: Grassroots Democracy in the Deep South after the Civil War.* Athens: University of Georgia Press, 2015.

Bell, Derrick. *Faces at the Bottom of the Well: The Permanence of Racism.* New York: Basic Books, 1992.

Bennett, Lerone, Jr. *Black Power U.S.A.: The Human Side of Reconstruction, 1867–1877.* Chicago: Johnson Publishing Company, Inc., 1967.

Berlin, Ira. *Many Thousands Gone: The First Two Centuries of Slavery in North America.* Cambridge: Belknap Press of Harvard University Press, 1998.

Berlin, Ira, Steven F. Miller, and Leslie S. Rowland. "Afro-American Families in the Transition from Slavery to Freedom." *Radical History Review* 1, October 1988 (42): 89–121.

Bethel, Elizabeth Rauh. *Promiseland: A Century of Life in a Negro Community*. Philadelphia: Temple University Press, 1981.

Blassingame, John. *The Slave Community: Plantation Life in the Antebellum South*. New York, Oxford University Press, 1977.

Bolland, O. Nigel. *The Meaning of Freedom: Economics, Politics, and Culture after Slavery*. Edited by Frank McGlynn and Seymour Drescher. Pittsburg: University of Pittsburg Press, 1992.

Bolton, Charles C. *The Hardest Deal of All: The Battle over School Integration in Mississippi, 1870–1980*. Jackson: University Press of Mississippi, 2005.

Bolton, Charles C. *Poor Whites of the Antebellum South: Central North Carolina and Northeast Mississippi*. Durham: Duke University Press, 1994.

Bond, Bradley. *Political Culture in the Nineteenth-Century South: Mississippi 1830–1900*. Baton Rouge: Louisiana State University Press, 1995.

Bond, Horace Mann. *Education of the Negro in the American Social Order*. New York: Octagon Books, 1970.

Bryant, Jonathan M. *How Curious a Land: Conflict and Change in Greene County, Georgia, 1850–1885*. Chapel Hill: University of North Carolina Press, 1996.

Campbell, Gwyn, and Elizabeth Elbourne. *Sex, Power, and Slavery*. Athens: Ohio University Press, 2014.

Carmichael, Stokely. *Stokely Speaks: From Black Power to Pan-Africanism*. Chicago: Lawrence Hill Books, 2007.

Carmichael, Stokely, and Ekwueme Michael Thelwell. *Ready for Revolution: The Life and Struggles of Stokely Carmichael {Kwame Ture}*. New York: Scribner, 2003.

Cash, W. J. *The Mind of the South*. New York: Vintage Books, 1941.

Collier-Thomas, Bettye. *Jesus, Jobs, and Justice: African American Women and Religion*. Philadelphia: Temple University Press, 2014.

Cone, James H. *A Black Theology of Liberation*. Philadelphia: J. B. Lippincott, 1970.

Cresswell, Stephen. *Rednecks, Redeemers, and Race: Mississippi After Reconstruction, 1877–1917*. Jackson: University Press of Mississippi for the Mississippi Historical Society, 2006.

Crockett, Norman L. *The Black Towns*. Lawrence: Regents Press of Kansas, 1979.

Crummell, Alexander. *Civilization and Black Progress: Selected Writings of Alexander Crummell on the South*. Edited by J. R. Oldfield. Charlottesville: University of Virginia Press, 1995.

Dagbovie, Pero Gaglo. "Black Women, Carter G. Woodson, and the Association for the Study of Negro Life and History, 1915–1950." *Journal of African American History* 88, no. 1 (2003): 21–41.

Daniel, Pete. *Breaking the Land: The Transformation of Cotton, Tobacco, and Rice Cultures Since 1880*. Urbana and Chicago: University of Illinois Press, 1985.

Davis, Ronald L. F. *Good and Faithful Labor: From Slavery to Sharecropping in the Natchez District 1860–1890*. Westport: Greenwood Press, 1982.

Dawson, Michael C. *Blacks in and out of the Left*. Cambridge: Harvard University Press, 2013.

Dittmer, John. *Local People: The Struggle for Civil Rights in Mississippi*. Urbana: University of Illinois Press, 1994.

Du Bois, W. E. B. *Black Reconstruction in America: Toward a History of the Part Which Black Folk Played in the Attempt to Reconstruct Democracy in America, 1860–1880*. New York: Harcourt, 1935.

Du Bois, W. E. B. *The Negro Church: Report of a Social Study Made Under the Direction of Atlanta University.by the Eighth Atlanta Conference.* Atlanta: Atlanta University Press, 1903.

Du Bois. W. E. B. *The Souls of Black Folk: Essays and Sketches.* Amherst: University of Massachusetts Press, 2018.

Ewing, Adam. "Garvey or Garveyism?" *Transition: An International Review* 105 (2011): 130–45.

Fairclough, Adam. *A Class of Their Own: Black Teachers in the Segregated South.* Cambridge: Belknap Press of Harvard University Press, 2007.

Foner, Eric. *Reconstruction: America's Unfinished Revolution 1863–1877.* New York: HarperCollins, 1989.

Franklin, John Hope, and Evelyn Brooks Higginbotham. *From Slavery to Freedom: A History of African Americans, Ninth Edition.* New York: McGraw-Hill, 2011.

Frederickson, George M. *The Black Image in the White Mind: The Debate on Afro-American Character and Destiny, 1817–1914.* New York: Harper Torchbooks, 1971.

Frederickson, George M. *Black Liberation: A Comparative History of Black Ideologies in the United States and South Africa.* New York: Oxford University Press, 1995.

Fuke, Richard Paul. "Planters, Apprenticeship, and Forced Labor: The Black Family under Pressure in Post Emancipation Maryland." *Agricultural History* 62, no. 4 (1988):57–74.

Garner, James Wilford. *Reconstruction in Mississippi.* New York: MacMillan, 1902.

Genovese, Eugene, and Elizabeth-Fox Genovese. *Slavery in White and Black: Class and Race in the Southern Slaveholders' New World Order.* Cambridge: Cambridge University Press, 2008.

Giddings, Paula. *When and Where I Enter: The Impact of Black Women on Race and Sex in America.* New York: Quill William Morrow, 1984.

Glymph, Thavolia. *Out of the House of Bondage: The Transformation of the Plantation Household.* Cambridge: Cambridge University Press, 2008.

Gueizo, Allen C. *Reconstruction: A Concise History.* New York: Oxford University Press, 2018.

Gutman, Herbert. *The Black Family in Slavery and Freedom, 1750–1925.* New York: Vintage Press, 1976.

Hager, Christopher. *Word By Word: Emancipation and the Act of Writing.* Cambridge: Harvard University Press, 2013.

Hahn, Stephen. *A Nation Under Our Feet: Black Political Struggles in the Rural South from Slavery to the Great Migration.* Cambridge: Belknap Press of Harvard University Press, 2003.

Hamilton, G. P. *Beacon Lights of the Race.* Memphis: P. H. Clarke, 1911.

Harris, William C. *The Day of the Carpetbagger: Republican Reconstruction in Mississippi.* Baton Rouge: Louisiana State University Press, 1979.

Harris, William C. *Presidential Reconstruction in Mississippi.* Baton Rouge: Louisiana State University Press, 1967.

Huebner, Timothy S. *Liberty and Union: The Civil War Era and American Constitutionalism.* Lawrence: University Press of Kansas, 2016.

James, C. L. R. *The Black Jacobins: Toussaint L'Ouverture and the San Domingo Revolution.* 2nd ed. New York: Vintage, 1989.

Jaynes, Gerald David. *Branches without Roots: Genesis of the Black Working Class in the American South, 1862–1882.* New York: Oxford University Press, 1986.

Johnson, Charles Spurgeon. *Patterns of Negro Segregation.* New York: Harper & Brothers, 1943.

Lewinson, Paul. *Race, Class, & Party: A History of Negro Suffrage and White Politics in the South*. New York: Universal Library, 1965.

Litwack, Leon. *Been in the Storm so Long: The Aftermath of Slavery*. New York: Vintage Books, 1979.

Litwack, Leon. *How Free Is Free? The Long Death of Jim Crow*. Cambridge: Harvard University Press, 2009.

Litwack, Leon. *Trouble in Mind: Black Southerners in the Age of Jim Crow*. New York: Random House, 1998.

Logan, Rayford W. *The Negro in American Life and Thought: The Nadir 1877–1901*. New York: Dial Press, 1954.

Lumumba, Chokwe. "Repression and Black Liberation." *Black Scholar* 5, no. 2 (1973): 34–42.

May, Vivian M. "Writing the Self into Being: Anna Julia Cooper's Textual Politics." *African American Review* 43, no. 1 (2009): 17–34.

McGee, Leo, and Robert Boone. "Black Rural Land Decline in the South." *Black Scholar* 8 no. 7 (May 1977): 8–11.

McKivigan, John R., and Heather L. Kaufman, eds. *In the Words of Frederick Douglass: Quotations from Liberty's Champion*. Ithaca: Cornell University Press, 2012.

McMillen, Neil R. *Dark Journey: Black Mississippians in the Age of Jim Crow*. Urbana: University of Illinois Press, 1990.

Milewski, Melissa. *Litigating across the Color Line: Civil Cases between Black and White Southerners*. New York: Oxford University Press, 2018.

Mitchell, David J. *A New History of Mississippi*. Jackson: University Press of Mississippi, 2014.

Montgomery, William E. *Under Their Own Vine and Fig Tree: The African-American Church in the South 1865–1900*. Baton Rouge: Louisiana State University Press, 1993.

Moore Jr., Barrington. *Social Origins of Dictatorship and Democracy: Lord and Peasant in the Making of the Modern World*. Boston: Beacon Press, 1993.

Oubre, Claude F. *Forty Acres and a Mule: The Freedmen's Bureau and Black Land Ownership*. Baton Rouge: Louisiana State University Press, 1978.

Ownby, Ted. *American Dreams in Mississippi: Consumers, Poverty and Culture, 1830–1998*. Chapel Hill: University of North Carolina Press, 1999.

Painter, Nell Irvin. *Exodusters: Black Migration to Kansas after Reconstruction*. New York: W. W. Norton, 1976.

Pennington, Dylan C. *The Claims of Kinfolk: African American Property and Community in the Nineteenth-Century South*. Chapel Hill: University of North Carolina Press, 2003.

Perman, Michael. *Road to Redemption: Southern Politics, 1869–1879*. Chapel Hill: University of North Carolina Press, 1984.

Powdermaker, Hortense. *After Freedom: A Cultural Study in the Deep South*. New York: Atheneum, 1968.

Ranney, Joseph A. *A Legal History of Mississippi: Race, Class, and the Struggle for Opportunity*. Jackson: University Press of Mississippi, 2019.

Ransom, Roger L., and Richard Sutch. *One Kind of Freedom: The Economic Consequences of Emancipation*. 2nd ed. New York: Cambridge University Press, 2001.

Ray, Louis. "Revisiting Charles H. Thompson's Proposals for Educating Gifted African American Students, 1933–1961." *Journal of Negro Education* 81, no. 3 (2012): 190–99.

Rodney, Walter. *The Groundings with My Brothers*. Chicago: Bogle-L'Ouverture Publications, 1969.

Satz, Ronald N. "The Mississippi Choctaw: From the Removal Treaty to the Federal
    Agency." In *After Removal: The Choctaw in Mississippi*, edited by Samuel J. Wells and
    Tubby Roseanna. Jackson: University Press of Mississippi, 1986.

Schweninger. Loren. *Black Property Owners in the South, 1790–1915*. Urbana and Chicago:
    University of Illinois Press, 1990.

Shaw, Stephanie. *What a Woman Ought to Be and Do: Black Professional Women Workers
    during the Jim Crow Era*. Chicago: University of Chicago Press, 1996.

Slap, Andrew L. *The Doom of Reconstruction: The Liberal Republicans in the Civil War Era*.
    New York: Fordham University Press, 2006.

Smith, Timothy B. *The Mississippi Secession Convention: Delegates and Deliberations in
    Politics and War, 1861–1865*. Jackson: University Press of Mississippi, 2014.

Span, Christopher M. *From Cotton Field to Schoolhouse: African American Education in
    Mississippi, 1862–1875*. Chapel Hill: University of North Carolina Press, 2009.

Stone, Albert Holt. *The Early Slave Laws of Mississippi: Being Some Brief Observations
    Thereon in a Paper Read before the Mississippi Historical Society at a Meeting Held in the
    City of Natchez, April 20th–21st, 1899*.

Stowell, Jay S. *Methodist Adventures in Negro Education*. New York: Methodist Book
    Concern, 1922.

Thompson, Julius E. *The Black Press in Mississippi, 1865–1985*. Gainesville: University Press
    of Florida, 1993.

Thompson, Patrick Henry. *The History of Negro Baptist in Mississippi*. Jackson: R. W. Bailey,
    1898.

Trelease, Allen W. *White Terror: The Ku Klux Klan Conspiracy and Southern Reconstruction*.
    New York: Harper Torchbooks, 1971.

Ture, Kwame and Charles V. Hamilton. *Black Power: The Politics of Liberation in America*.
    New York: Vintage, 1992.

Umoja, Akinyele Omowale. *We Will Shoot Back: Armed Resistance in the Mississippi
    Freedom Movement*. New York: NYU Press, 2013.

Walton, Hanes, Jr. *Black Republicans: The Politics of the Black and Tans*. Metuchen:
    Scarecrow Press, 1975.

Walton, Hanes, Jr. "Public Policy Reponses to the Million Man March." *Black Scholar* 25, no. 4
    (1995): 17–22.

Webber, Thomas L. *Deep Like the Rivers: Education in the Slave Quarter Community 1831–
    1865*. New York: W. W. Norton, 1978.

Wendt, Simon. *The Spirit and the Shotgun: Armed Resistance and the Struggle for Civil
    Rights*. Gainesville: University Press of Florida, 2007.

Wharton, Vernon Lane. *The Negro in Mississippi 1865–1890*. New York: Harper Torchbooks,
    1965.

Woodman, Harold. *King Cotton and His Retainers: Financing and Marketing the Cotton
    Crop of the South, 1800–1925*. Lexington: University of Kentucky Press, 1968.

Woodson, Carter G. *The Rural Negro*. New York: Russell & Russell, 1969.

Woodward, C. Vann. *Origins of the New South 1877–1913*. Baton Rouge: Louisiana State
    University Press, 1951.

INDEX

ABOUT THE AUTHOR

Photo by Bertram Knight

Dr. Evan Howard Ashford was born in Florissant, Missouri, and raised in Kosciusko, Mississippi. He graduated as class valedictorian from Kosciusko High School in 2004, becoming the first African American to hold that honor. He earned his bachelor's degree in accounting and master's degree in public policy and administration from Mississippi State University in 2008 and 2010. In 2013, he earned a master's degree in history from Jackson State University, where he worked at the Mississippi Department of Archives and History. He earned a master's degree and a doctorate in Afro-American Studies from the University of Massachusetts Amherst in 2016 and 2018. Dr. Ashford currently works at the State University of New York College at Oneonta. He is assistant professor of African American history and department chair of the Africana and Latinx Studies Department. Dr. Ashford's research centers on late-nineteenth-century rural Black-liberation politics and its role in shaping twentieth-century southern Jim Crow society from a genealogical and local-history perspective. His published articles include "Freedom Courts: An Analysis of Black Women's Divorce in Attala County during Mississippi's Anti-Divorce Campaign, 1890–1940" in *USAbroad: Journal of American History and Politics* and "Medical Messiahs: African American Women in Mississippi Medicine, 1900–1940" in the *Journal of Health Science and Education*. He published two book reviews in the *Journal of African American History* and the *Journal of Southern History*. He created an exhibition titled, *Mammy to Michelle: The Journey of African American Women in the Rural South*. Dr. Ashford sits on the National Association of African American Studies' national board, serving as the editor of its *Journal of Science and Exploratory Studies*. SUNY Oneonta honored Dr. Ashford with the Richard Siegfried Junior Faculty Prize for Academic Excellence. He has received grants and fellowships from the LSU Libraries Special Collections, Southern Jewish Historical Society, the North Carolinian Society, W. E. B. Du Bois Library Fellowship, and the Medgar and Myrlie Evers Research Scholars.

Printed in the United States
by Baker & Taylor Publisher Services